Colloquial

Slovene

Colloquial Slovene: The Complete Course for Beginners has been carefully developed by an experienced teacher to provide a step-by-step course to Slovene as it is written and spoken today.

Combining a clear, practical and accessible style with a methodical and thorough treatment of the language, it equips learners with the essential skills needed to communicate confidently and effectively in Slovene in a broad range of situations. No prior knowledge of the language is required.

Colloquial Slovene is exceptional; each unit presents a wealth of grammatical points that are reinforced with a wide range of exercises for regular practice. A full answer key, a grammar summary, bilingual glossaries and English translations of dialogues can be found at the back as well as useful vocabulary lists throughout.

Key features include:

- A clear, user-friendly format designed to help learners progressively build up their speaking, listening, reading and writing skills
- Jargon-free, succinct and clearly structured explanations of grammar
- An extensive range of focused and dynamic supportive exercises
- Realistic and entertaining dialogues covering a broad variety of narrative situations
- Helpful cultural points explaining the customs and features of life in Slovenia.
- An overview of the sounds of Slovene

Balanced, comprehensive and rewarding, *Colloquial Slovene* is an indispensable resource both for independent learners and students taking courses in Slovene.

Audio material to accompany the course is available to download free in MP3 format from www.routledge.com/cw/colloquials. Recorded by native speakers, the audio material features the dialogues and texts from the book and will help develop your listening and pronunciation skills.

THE COLLOQUIAL SERIES
Series Adviser: Gary King

The following languages are available in the Colloquial series:

Afrikaans	German	Romanian
Albanian	Greek	Russian
Amharic	Gujarati	Scottish Gaelic
Arabic (Levantine)	Hebrew	Serbian
Arabic of Egypt	Hindi	Slovak
Arabic of the Gulf	Hungarian	Slovene
Basque	Icelandic	Somali
Bengali	Indonesian	Spanish
Breton	Irish	Spanish of Latin America
Bulgarian	Italian	Swahili
Burmese	Japanese	Swedish
Cambodian	Kazakh	Tamil
Cantonese	Korean	Thai
Catalan	Latvian	Tibetan
Chinese (Mandarin)	Lithuanian	Turkish
Croatian	Malay	Ukrainian
Czech	Mongolian	Urdu
Danish	Norwegian	Vietnamese
Dutch	Panjabi	Welsh
English	Persian	Yiddish
Estonian	Polish	Yoruba
Finnish	Portuguese	Zulu (forthcoming)
French	Portuguese of Brazil	

COLLOQUIAL 2s series: *The Next Step in Language Learning*

Chinese	German	Russian
Dutch	Italian	Spanish
French	Portuguese of Brazil	Spanish of Latin America

Colloquials are now supported by FREE AUDIO available online. All audio tracks referenced within the text are free to stream or download from www.routledge.com/cw/colloquials. If you experience any difficulties accessing the audio on the companion website, or still wish to purchase a CD, please contact our customer services team through www.routledge.com/info/contact.

Colloquial
Slovene

The Complete Course for Beginners

Marta Pirnat-Greenberg

Routledge
Taylor & Francis Group

LONDON AND NEW YORK

Second edition published 2012
by Routledge
2 Park Square, Milton Park, Abingdon, Oxon OX14 4RN

Simultaneously published in the USA and Canada
by Routledge
711 Third Avenue, New York, NY 10017

Routledge is an imprint of the Taylor & Francis Group, an informa business

First edition published by Routledge 1995

British Library Cataloguing in Publication Data
A catalogue record for this book is available from the British Library

Library of Congress Cataloging in Publication Data
Pirnat-Greenberg, Marta.
  Colloquial Slovene : the complete course for beginners / Marta Pirnat-Greenberg. — 2nd ed.
    p. cm. — (The colloquial series)
  Text in English and Slovene.
  Includes bibliographical references and index.
    1. Slovenian language—Textbooks for foreign speakers—English.
2. Slovenian language—Spoken Slovenian. 3. Slovenian language—Sound recordings for English speakers. 4. Slovenian language—Self-instruction. I. Title.
  PG1827.5.E5A38 2011
  491.8′4321—dc22

                                                                2010049693

ISBN 978-1-138-95015-3 (pbk)

Typeset in Avant Garde and Helvetica
by Graphicraft Limited, Hong Kong

Printed and bound in Great Britain by
TJ International Ltd, Padstow, Cornwall

Contents

Introduction

In the last couple of decades the position of the Slovene language in the world as well as the world in which it is used have changed dramatically. Slovene not only became the official language of a sovereign state, but also one of the official languages of the European Union. While the forces of globalization have on the one hand threatened the existence of languages with a small number of speakers, the freer flow of people, services, and ideas, on the other hand, has multiplied the number of English speakers engaging with Slovenia who have the need and interest to learn Slovene. Often self-study is their only option. The textbook before you attempts to fill this need by providing effective and up-to-date language-learning materials that also reflect the recent societal and cultural changes in Slovenia.

Basic facts about Slovenia and Slovenes

The Slovene (also called Slovenian) language is spoken by about 2.4 million speakers in the Republic of Slovenia and border areas in Austria, Italy, and Hungary as well as in the Slovene diaspora, with the largest concentrations in North America, Argentina, Australia, Germany, Switzerland, and Sweden. Slovenia is located on a fairly small (20,000 km^2) territory between the Eastern Alps, the Mediterranean, and the Pannonian plane, which is also the meeting point of the Romance, Germanic, Hungarian, and Slavic language families. Both of these factors contributed to the fact that despite its small size the country is extremely varied in terms of its landscape, climate, and culture. In a little more than an hour one can travel from its Alpine north, over the foothills of the Alps and the Dinaric Karst, to the Adriatic sea in its south-western corner.

Slavic speakers arrived in this region—originally settling a territory about three times the size of the present-day Slovenia—in the 6th–7th

centuries. They enjoyed a short period of independence in the beginning, but for most of their history, Slovenes lived within the framework
of other states, i.e., the Habsburg Empire, Austria-Hungary, the
Kingdom of Serbs, Croats, and Slovenes, and pre- and post-Second
World War Yugoslavia. In each of these arrangements the Slovene
language, under dominance of German or Serbo-Croatian, had limited
use and rights. Independent Slovenia, a parliamentary republic,
emerged in 1991 after the secession from communist Yugoslavia.
It joined NATO and the European Union in 2004 and was the first of
the former East European countries to join the euro zone in 2007. The
country successfully transitioned to a market economy, with manu-
facturing (pharmaceutical, auto, chemical) and service as its main
sectors. With its extraordinary natural beauty, well-preserved history
and tradition, and developed tourism, it is also an attractive vacation
destination. Its capital is Ljubljana (pop. 300,000); other major cities
are Maribor, Celje, Kranj, Koper, and Novo mesto.

In the absence of a state, Slovene language and literature played
the major role in building and maintaining the Slovene national iden-
tity. The publication of the first Slovene books in the sixteenth century
not only laid the foundation for the Slovene standard language, but
also planted the idea of commonality between speakers of various
Slovene dialects living in several historic regions of the Habsburg
Empire. It took until the early nineteenth century for the consolidation
and the beginning of modern standard Slovene, which was elevated
to the level of a language with a developed literature by the romantic
poet France Prešeren (1800–1849). The aspirations for unity, freedom,
and self-determination expressed in his poetry inspired Slovene
national movements for over a century. A stanza from one of his
poems was adopted as the national anthem of the newly independent Slovenia.

The Slovene language

Slovene is a south-Slavic language, most closely related to Croatian,
Serbian, Bosnian, and more remotely to Slovak (with which it is often
confused because of the similar name), Czech, and other Slavic languages. Like English, it is also an Indo-European language; therefore,
there is a certain amount of lexicon with common origin and some

degree of structural similarity. However, Slovene (as other Slavic languages) is a highly inflected language, which means that some words change form according to their function in the sentence—a concept not entirely unknown to English (think of 'she' vs. 'her' or 'work' vs. 'works'), but not present to the extent that it is in Slovene.

Relative to its number of speakers, Slovene is the most dialectally varied Slavic language with more than 40 dialects; the most disparate of them are hardly mutually intelligible. The standard language is based on the central Slovene dialects, but it is not exactly like any of them. Since it also differs from everyday spoken language used by educated speakers, natives learn it in school. It is used in writing, formal public speaking, in school, on stage, radio, and television. The gap between standard and everyday spoken language can be considerable, but it depends on the level of formality of speech. Educated speakers freely change codes, depending on the situation. This book will teach you the standard language, so that you can develop proficiency in reading and writing besides speaking and understanding. To help you negotiate the gap between the written and spoken variants, the dialogues introduce lexicon and sentence structures of contemporary spoken discourse with standard forms and pronunciation, but the author notes when these substantially differ from the spoken language.

Using the book

The course is intended for self-study and does not assume any previous knowledge of Slovene. It aims to develop communicative skills for a wide range of everyday personal and social needs. The themes of conversations, the ways in which their protagonists interact with each other, as well as the explicit cultural commentary should also introduce you to the Slovene culture and help you to engage with native speakers effectively and appropriately.

Each unit, sixteen in all, attempts to develop communicative skills for particular topics and situations. The dialogues serve as examples of appropriate discourse for targeted situations, but also as a vehicle for building your vocabulary and understanding of the ways the language works—its grammar, word-formation, and sentence-formation. The book aims to cover systematically all basic grammar necessary for everyday communicative competence; for more comprehensive grammar coverage further reading is suggested. The main thread of the book is the conversation between a middle-aged Slovene couple and their American guest (of Slovene origin) in various everyday situations in which a foreign guest would typically find him- or herself. The couple and the guest communicate on a semi-formal level, as at first they only have professional ties and develop a more personal relationship through the course of the book. Most units have one or two other dialogues: a conversation between college students (demonstrating non-formal discourse) and/or some type of transaction in a public setting (demonstrating entirely formal discourse).

Each dialogue is furnished with a list of new vocabulary and in the first eight units with an English translation. The vocabulary lists provide the meanings the words have in the given text, and glossaries at the end of the book the meanings in which the words appear in the textbook, though they do not replace a dictionary (some suggestions are given below). Each dialogue is followed by an explanation of new language points and expressions; all major points have one or more exercises for practice. When the dialogues cannot capture all the vocabulary and expressions essential to the main topic(s) of the unit, a thematic vocabulary list is included to help you with vocabulary building. At the end of most units there is a text for reading, if at all possible connected to the main topic and employing the material learned in the unit. The idea is to expose you to unadulterated Slovene texts, however short and basic they might be, right from the beginning. These texts, of course, grow in length and complexity—from a simple list, advert, or postcard, to a short anecdote, biography, or description of a landmark. They should all be accessible with the aid of vocabulary lists after you have worked through the material of each unit. The units are followed by a grammar summary, key to exercises, a two-way glossary, and an index. The audio portion of the course includes practice for pronunciation and recordings of all the conversations and texts for reading as well as some speaking exercises. It is essential for the development of your speaking and listening proficiency that you listen to the speakers carefully and practice pronunciation with the recording.

Many factors will determine how quickly you will progress through the book, but your previous experience with foreign languages, motivation, and the amount of work you put into the study will be the main ones. It is possible that initially some Slovene sounds and clusters will be hard to pronounce and the concept of your name appearing in several different forms might be daunting, but if you follow the gradual steps of this course with consistency and perseverance, you will overcome these potential difficulties. The final reward of your hard work—the ability to communicate in the language—not only has practical benefits, but will add another dimension to your experience of a country of exceptional beauty, its rich history and culture, and the creativity of its people.

Suggestions for further reference materials and reading

Greenberg, Marc L. 'Slovene.' *Encyclopedia of Language and Linguistics, 2ⁿᵈ Edition* [print and electronic editions], ed. by Keith Brown, vol. 11: 424–8. Oxford: Elsevier.

Greenberg, Marc L. 2008. *A Short Reference Grammar of Slovene* (= *LINCOM Studies in Slavic Linguistics* 30). Munich: Lincom.

Herrity, Peter. 2000. *Slovene: A Comprehensive Grammar*. London, New York: Routledge.

Plut-Pregelj, Leopoldina, Carole Rogel. 1996. *Historical Dictionary of Slovenia* (= *European Historical Dictionaries*, No. 13). Lanham, Md., and London: The Scarecrow Press.

Dictionaries

Grabnar, Katja. *Priročni angleško–slovenski & slovensko–angleški slovar = Concise English–Slovenian & Slovenian–English Dictionary*. 2010. Ljubljana: Državna založba Slovenije.

Grad, Anton, Henry Leeming. 1996. *Slovensko–angleški slovar = Slovene–English Dictionary*. Ljubljana: Državna založba Slovenije.

Zaranšek, Petra et al. *Mali angleško–slovenski & slovensko–angleški slovar = English–Slovenian & Slovenian–English Pocket Dictionary*. 2006. Ljubljana: Državna založba Slovenije.

Acknowledgments

I am most grateful to the people who have read the manuscript for this textbook at its different stages and contributed valuable comments with regard to the appropriateness and accuracy of the Slovene material as well as effectiveness of explanations and progression of the course. My sincere thanks go to Helga Glušič, Marc L. Greenberg, Lea Greenberg, Nicole Schmidt, Shay Wood, and editors and reviewers at Routledge. My travel to Slovenia to acquire some of the material for the textbook was partially made possible by the US Department of Education Grant, Title VI, administered by the Center for Russian, East European, and Eurasian Studies at the University of Kansas.

Abbreviations and symbols

Abbreviations:

A	accusative	imp.	imperative
abbr.	abbreviated	ipf.	imperfective
adj.	adjective	L	locative
adv.	adverb	lit.	literally
coll.	colloquial	m.	masculine
conj.	conjunction	N	nominative
D	dative	n.	neuter
direct.	directional	pf.	perfective
du.	dual	pl.	plural
Eng.	English	prep.	preposition
f.	feminine	sg.	singular
G	genitive	Sln.	Slovene
I	instrumental	V	vowel

Symbols:

1	first person
2	second person
3	third person
→	changes to; yields
+	added; takes

Pronunciation guide

Slovene alphabet (Audio 1:2)

Slovene uses an adapted version of the Roman alphabet with 25 letters. As you can see below, it differs from the English alphabet in that it includes letters **č**, **š**, **ž**, but excludes **q**, **w**, **x**, and **y** (although they are used in the spelling of foreign names or borrowings).

**A a B b C c Č č D d E e F f G g H h I i J j K k L l
M m N n O o P p R r S s Š š T t U u V v Z z Ž ž**

In Slovene each letter corresponds to a sound, i.e., there are no silent letters. The letter-sound correspondences are fairly straightforward, as outlined below.

Vowels and stress (Audio 1:3–6)

Slovene has eight vowels, all monophthongs, and five letters to represent them. Unstressed vowels are short, while stressed vowels are long unless in the only or word-final syllable, where they can be short or long. The letters representing more than one vowel are **e** and **o**. In long-stressed syllables, **o** and **e** can be open or closed (see description below and listen carefully to the recording). In short-stressed and non-stressed syllables, **o** can only be open, while **e** can be open or a neutral vowel (also called 'schwa'). You will have to learn the quality of the vowel with the word. All the dialogues, examples, and glossaries in this book help you with pronunciation by marking the close **e** and **o** with a dot under the letter and the schwa by underlining the **e**; if there is no mark under these letters, it means they are pronounced as open **e** or **o**, respectively. Pay special attention to the pronunciation of the closed **e** and **o**, since there are no similar sounds in English.

Letter	Pronounced approximately like Eng.	Sln. example*
A a	'a' in 'father'	**Sava**
E e	'e' in 'bet' (open **e**)	**teta** aunt
	no Eng. approximate; a sound between 'e' in 'bet' and 'ee' in 'seen' (close **e**)	**Reka**
	'o' in 'hammock' (schwa)	**pes** dog
I i	'ee' in 'seen'	**Mirna**
O o	'o' in 'cot' (open **o**)	**gora** mountain
	no Eng. approximate; a sound between 'o' in 'cot' and 'ou' in 'you' (close **ọ**)	**Sọra**
U u	'ou' in 'you'	**Mura**

* The capitalized words are names of Slovene rivers.

Most words in Slovene have at least one stressed syllable (more prominent). Any syllable in the word can carry the stress, i.e., the stress is not predictable and must be learned with the word. Stress is normally not marked, but in this book the stressed vowels are italicized to help you, together with recordings, with proper accentuation.

Vowel reduction

Dialects and also educated everyday speech of Central Slovenia tend to reduce unstressed vowels, particularly **i** and **u**, to schwa or drop them entirely in endings, which is the main factor that contributes to the aforementioned disparity between the standard and spoken language. Examples:

Sln. standard	Sln. spoken	Eng.
v Kamniku	**u Kamenk**	in Kamnik (town)
v Sọri	**u Sọr**	in the Sora river
pri Muri	**per Mur**	by the Mura river

Consonants (Audio 1:7–8)

Letter	Pronounced approx. like Eng.	Sln. example*
B b	'b'	banka
C c	'ts' in 'cats'	center
Č č	'ch' in 'cheese'	čokolada
D d	'd'	diploma
F f	'f'	festival
G g	'g' in 'green'	galerija
H h	'h' in 'house'	helikopter
J j	'y' in 'yellow'	januar
K k	'k'	karta
L l	'l' (1)	limona
M m	'm'	milijon
N n	'n'	november
P p	'p'	profesor
R r	'r' (rolled) (2)	radio
S s	's'	saksofon
Š š	'sh' in 'show'	študent
T t	't' (but dental)	tableta
V v	'v' (3)	vikend
Z z	'z' in 'zoo'	zebra
Ž ž	's' in 'leisure'	žirafa

1 At the end of the word or syllable and/or before a consonant (except **j**), l is usually pronounced approximately as **w** in **sorrow**. The exceptions to this rule include loan words, certain forms (which will be explained as they are introduced), and individual lexical items, which need to be learned (always listen carefully to the pronunciation on the recording). Examples:

Spelling	Pronunciation	Meaning
stol	[stow]	chair
bel	[bęw]	white
dolgovi	[dowgovi]	debts
poln	[pown]	full
delal	[dęlaw]	past participle of **dęlati** to work
ideal	[ideal]	ideal
stil	[st*i*l]	style

2 When **r** appears between consonants, as in **trn** 'thorn', **vrba** 'willow', **prst** 'finger', it is pronunced as schwa + **r**.

3 When not before a vowel, as in **vzęti** 'to take', **s*i*v** 'gray', **pęvka** 'female singer', **v** is pronounced approximately as **w** in **sorrow**. As the preposition **v** 'in, into', it is pronounced as **w** even before a vowel, e.g. **v avtu** 'in a car' is pronounced [wawtu].

 # Voicing and devoicing (Audio 1:9)

These consonants are paired for voicing. The first one in each pair is voiced, i.e., produced with vocal cords engaged, the second one without that engagement.

b – p   g – k   ž – š   d – t   z – s

Voiced consonants are pronounced as their voiceless counterparts at the end of the word before a pause. Examples:

Spelling	Pronunciation	Meaning
gospod	[gospǫt]	Mr., gentleman
zob	[zǫp]	tooth
mož	[mǫš]	husband, man

In clusters of consonants that are paired for voicing, the last consonant determines the voicing of the entire cluster. For example, in the word **nízka** 'low, short (f.)' the **z** is pronounced as **s** because it is followed by the voiceless consonant **k**. This rule also applies when there is no pause between the words, and the final consonant of one word forms a cluster with the initial consonant of the next word. Examples:

Spelling	Pronunciation	Meaning
lep golop	[lẹb golọp]	a pretty pigeon
drag plašč	[drak plašč]	an expensive coat
velik balon	[velig balọn]	a large balloon

Exercise

Pronounce the following place names:

Countries: **Slovẹnija, Evrọpska unija, Vẹlika Britanija, Švẹdska, Danska, Nọrveška, Avstrija, Švica, Nẹmčija** 'Germany', **Francija, Španija, Pọrtugalska, Italija, Grčija, Pọljska, Čẹška, Slovaška, Madžarska** 'Hungary', **Rusija, Bolgarija, Romunija, Srbija, Hrvaška** 'Croatia', **Bọsna in Hercegovina;**

Slovene cities: **Ljubljana, Maribor, Celje, Kranj, Kọper, Novo mẹsto, Črnọmelj, Nova Gorica, Kamnik, Slovẹnj Gradec, Velenje, Krško, Brẹžice, Metlika, Postọjna.**

Slovene mountains: **Julijske Alpe, Karavanke, Kamniške Alpe, Pọhorje, Triglav, Stol, Grintovẹc, Mangart, Jalovẹc.**

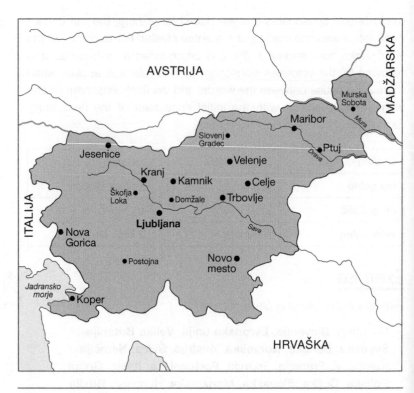

Republika Slovenija

Unit One
Dobrodošli v Sloveniji
Welcome to Slovenia

In this unit you will learn about:

- Greetings
- Introducing yourself and others
- Formal and familiar forms of address
- The present tense of the auxiliary verb 'to be'
- Personal pronouns
- Asking and answering yes/no questions

Dialogue 1

Prihod Arrival **(Audio 1:13)**

An American researcher, Ben Pintar, is greeted by his Slovene colleague, Alenka Mlakar, and her husband, Andrej, at Ljubljana Airport. Alenka is surprised to find out that Ben speaks Slovene.

BEN   Dobe̱r dan! Oprost*i*te, a ste v*i* gospa Mlakar?
ALENKA   *Ja, s*e̱*m.*
BEN   Jaz se̱m Be̱n P*i*ntar.
ALENKA   *O, gospo̱d P*i*ntar, dobrodošli v Slove̱niji! To̱ je mo̱j mo̱ž
         Andrej.
ANDREJ   Me vesel*i*.
ALENKA   Gospo̱d P*i*ntar, dobro govor*i*te slove̱nsko. Ste Slove̱ne̱c?
BEN   Ne, n*i*sem, Ameri*č*an se̱m. Mo̱j o*č*e je Slove̱ne̱c.

BEN   *Hello! Excuse me, are you Mrs. Mlakar?*
ALENKA   *Yes, I am.*
BEN   *I'm Ben Pintar.*
ALENKA   *Oh, Mr. Pintar, welcome to Slovenia! This is my husband, Andrej.*
ANDREJ   *Nice to meet you.*
ALENKA   *Mr. Pintar, you speak Slovene well. Are you Slovene?*
BEN   *No, I am not. I am American. My father is Slovene.*

Meeting at the airport

 Vocabulary

a	particle starting yes/no questions	**gospọd**	Mr.
		govoríte	you (pl.) speak
Američan	American (male)	**jaz**	I
dob<u>e</u>r dan	hello (good day)	**je**	(s/he) is
dobro	well	**me**	me
dobrodošli	welcome	**me veselí**	pleased to meet you
gospa	Mrs.	**mọj**	my

mọž	husband	sem	I am
ne	no	Slovẹnẹc	Slovene (male)
nisem	I am not	Slovẹnija	Slovenia
o	oh	v Slovẹniji	in Slovenia
oče	father	slovẹnsko	(in) Slovene
oprost*i*te	excuse me	ste	you (pl.) are
prihod	arrival	tọ	this

Language point (Audio 1:14)

Greeting people

Neutral greetings on arrival or meeting are **dobro j*u*tro** 'good morning' (for early morning, until 8 or 9), **dobẹr dan** 'hello' (literally 'good day'), and **dobẹr vẹčẹr** 'good evening'. When leaving, people normally say **na sv*i*denje** (more casually **ad*i*jo**) 'bye' or **lahko nọč** 'good night'. Among friends and particularly young people **ž*i*vjo** or **zdravo** 'hi' and 'bye' are most common on both arrival and leaving, and **čao** 'bye' on leaving. In Slovenia, people shake hands when they first meet, when they see each other after a long absence, and when they part for a long period of time or don't expect to see each other again. It is not customary to shake hands on a daily basis or repeatedly after you have met a person. Hugging and kissing is part of greeting only among people with an emotional connection, e.g., lovers, close relatives, or friends.

Exercise 1

How would you appropriately greet a store clerk on arrival and how on departure at the following times?

1 7:00 A.M.
2 10:00 A.M.
3 1:00 P.M.
4 8:00 P.M.
5 11:00 P.M.

Language points

The auxiliary verb biti 'to be'

You probably noticed in the dialogue that in introducing and identifying people and things, various present-tense forms of the auxiliary verb **biti** 'to be' are used, for instance:

Jaz sem Ben Pintar.	I'm Ben Pintar.
A ste vi gospa Mlakar?	Are you Mrs. Mlakar?
Moj oče je Slovenec.	My father is Slovene.

Biti 'to be' conjugates (changes form depending on the subject, i.e., its person and number) differently than other verbs. Its forms are given with personal pronouns in parentheses.

(jaz) sem I am	**(midva/medve) sva** we [two] are	**(mi/me) smo** we are
(ti) si you are	**(vidva/vedve) sta** you [two] are	**(vi/ve) ste** you are
(on/ona/ono) je he/she/it is	**(onadva/onidve) sta** they [two] are	**(oni/one/ona) so** they are

The negated form of **je** is **ni** 'is not'; the rest of the forms are negated by simply adding **ni-** to the beginning: **nisem, nisi, nismo,** ... Example:

Nisem Slovenec. I am not Slovene.

The category of number

Note the middle, shaded column of the auxiliary forms and the use of the auxiliary verb in the sentence:

To sta Alenka in Andrej. These are Alenka and Andrej.

Unlike English, which distinguishes forms for one (singular) and more than one (plural), Slovene has an additional set of forms for two—the dual. Consequently, the plural refers to more than two. For example:

To so Alenka, Andrej in Ben. These are Alenka, Andrej, and Ben.

Exercise 2

Complete the sentences with the correct present-tense forms of the verb **biti**.

1 Ti _____ Američan.
2 Vi _____ gospa Kovač.
3 Mi _____ Alenka, Peter in Nataša.
4 Jaz _____ Andrej Mlakar.
5 Janez in Marko _____ v Sloveniji.
6 Alenka _____ moja punca.
7 Midva _____ v Sloveniji.

Exercise 3

Negate the sentences from Exercise 2.

Language point

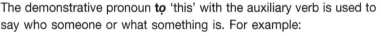

'This is', 'these are'

The demonstrative pronoun **to** 'this' with the auxiliary verb is used to say who someone or what something is. For example:

To je moj mož Andrej.	This is my husband, Andrej.
To je Slovenija.	This is Slovenia.
To sta Alenka in Andrej Mlakar.	These are Alenka and Andrej Mlakar.

Note that **to** in this context does not change depending on how many things or people are introduced, but the auxiliary verb does.

Exercise 4

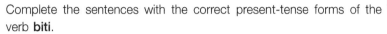

Introduce the following people:

1 Marko in Mojca
2 Miran
3 oče
4 gospod in gospa Kranjec
5 Janez, Miha, Andrej
6 Marinka Zupan

Language points

Personal pronouns

Refer to the table with the auxiliary verb **biti**. In addition to having a special set for dual, Slovene also distinguishes genders in all personal pronouns with the exception of **jaz** 'I' and **ti** 'you' (sg.). In the table, when two forms are given for a single English pronoun, e.g., **mi/me** 'we', the first form is masculine, the second feminine. Note that *masculine* dual and plural forms are used when referring to a pair or group that includes at least one male (regardless of how many women are also in the group), and that the feminine forms are reserved for pairs or groups that are exclusively female. For example:

Alenka in Andrej	→	**onadva**	the two of them
Alenka, Sonja, Ana in Andrej	→	**oni**	they
Alenka in jaz (Marta)	→	**medve**	the two of us

If this many pronouns seem overwhelming at this point, you will be happy to know that most of the time the pronouns are omitted as subjects, and the verbal form alone indicates whether the subject is **jaz** 'I', **ti** 'you', **on/ona** 's/he', and so on.

Ste Slovenec?	Are you Slovene?
Američan sem.	I am American.

However, when the subject is first introduced in the discourse, is ambiguous, or emphasized, the pronoun is used. For example:

Jaz sem Ben Pintar.	I am Ben Pintar.
Ste vi gospa Mlakar?	Are you Mrs. Mlakar?

Addressing people

When addressing people with whom you are on formal terms (strangers, people in service or official positions, superiors, unrelated older people), you use the titles **gospod** 'Sir, Mr.', **gospa** 'Madam, Mrs.', or **gospodična** 'Miss' by themselves or with last names (**gospa Mlakar**, **gospod Pintar**). In addition, you must use the plural form of the pronouns 'you' (**vi**) and 'your' (**vaš**) as well as verbs (**ste, oprostite**), so it looks like you are addressing several people when, in fact, you are talking to only one. In this case, there is no distinction of gender in the pronoun, i.e., the masculine form **vi** is used to address a man or a woman. Note how Ben talks to Alenka:

Ste vi gospa Mlakar? Are *you* Mrs. Mlakar?

This form of address is called **vikanje** after the typical pronoun **vi** that is used (when it is not omitted). **Vikanje** does not necessarily mean addressing a person with the title and the last name, which is how formality is expressed in English. For a lesser degree of formality, but still indicating respect, Slovenes use **vikanje** and the titles **gospod**, **gospa**, **gospodična** with the first name. For example:

Dober dan, gospa Majda. Kako ste? – Dobro, hvala.
Hello, Mrs. Majda. How are you? – (I am) well, thank you.

Even less formal, but still not familiar, is the address with a person's first name and the use of **vikanje**. For example:

Dobro jutro, Ben. Kako ste?
Good morning, Ben. How are [pl.] you?

As you can see, the formality is kept with **vikanje**, but its level can be varied with the use of titles and names. You will discern from the situation and by observing native speakers what level of formality to use. The rule of thumb is that you should use **vikanje** on the first encounter with people past high-school age. When people develop a closer personal or professional relationship with you, they will most likely switch to the familiar address called **tikanje** (after the typical pronoun **ti**). They might suggest you both switch to familiar address or give you permission to address them that way. In this case, the singular forms of verbs and pronouns in the second person are used, like in the following conversation between three young people. Peers up to college age always, even on the first encounter, use **tikanje**.

Dialogue 2

Kako si? How are you? (Audio 1:16)

At a loud party, Nejc runs into his friend Jan, who introduces him to his girlfriend.

NEJC   Živjo, Jan, kako si?
JAN   Dobro. Pa ti?
NEJC   V redu. In kdo je to?
JAN   To je moja punca Lara. Lara, to je Nejc.
NEJC   Zdravo. Si Sara ali Lara?
LARA   Ime mi je Lara. Lara Omahen.
NEJC   Kako se pišeš?
LARA   Omahen.

NEJC   *Hi, Jan! How are you?*
JAN   *I am well. How about you?*
NEJC   *I am fine. And who is this?*
JAN   *This is my girlfriend, Lara. Lara, this is Nejc.*
NEJC   *Hi! Are you Sara or Lara?*
LARA   *My name is Lara. Lara Omahen.*
NEJC   *What is your last name?*
LARA   *Omahen.*

Vocabulary

ali	or	**kako se pišeš?**	what is your last name?
ime	name		
ime mi je	my name is	**kdo**	who
in	and	**punca**	girl (friend)
kako	how	**v redu**	all right

Language points

Asking how one is

Kako si? (familiar)/**Kako ste?** (formal)   How are you?

You would ask this question of people you know, but not of strangers. The answer will vary, depending on how the person feels. Here are some possibilities:

Dọbro, (hvala).	Well, thanks.
Sụper.	Super.
V rẹdu.	All right/fine.
Nị slabọ.	(It's) not bad.
Grẹ.	It's going all right.
Za sịlo./Še kar.	So-so.
Slabọ.	Bad.
Zanịč.	Lousy.

First and last name

Notice the difference between familiar and formal forms in asking about one's first and last name:

> **Kakọ ti je imẹ?** (familiar)/**Kakọ vam je imẹ?** (formal) – **Imẹ mi je Janez.**
> What is your (first) name? – My (first) name is Janez.

> **Kakọ se pịšeš?** (familiar)/**Kakọ se pịšete?** (formal) – **Pịšem se Novak.**
> What is your last name? – My last name is Novak.

A more laconic style might be used by an official asking for personal information:

Imẹ?	First name?
Priịmek?	Last name?
Naslov?	Address?
Telefọn?	Phone (number)?

Asking and answering yes/no questions

To form yes/no questions, one uses the 'question word' **a** (in written or highly elevated spoken language, you will also find **ali**) immediately followed by the auxiliary verb, i.e., the word order verb–subject is used in this case, like in forming similar questions in English.

A ste vị gospa Mlakar?	Are you Mrs. Mlakar?
A si Amerịčan?	Are you American (male)?

The 'question word' is often omitted, particularly in written language:

Je to Andrej?   Is this Andrej?
Sta to Marko in Peter?   Are these Marko and Peter?
Ste Slovenka?   Are you Slovene (female)?

A positive answer to such a question consists of **ja** 'yes' (in written language **da**) and the appropriate form of the auxiliary verb or the auxiliary verb by itself:

A ste vi gospa Mlakar? – (Ja,) sem.   (Yes,) I am.

A negative answer consists of **ne** 'no' and a negated appropriate form of the auxiliary verb or this negated form by itself:

Ste Slovenec? – (Ne), nisem.   (No,) I am not.

Word order

The auxiliary verb is a clitic—a one-syllable non-stressed word that phonetically depends on the fully stressed word before or after it. You will learn about other clitics as you go along. They are important to recognize, because Slovene has a word-order rule that clitics do not occur in the initial position in a sentence unless something is left out, like **a/ali** in yes/no questions. For example:

A Ste vi gospa Mlakar?   Are you Mrs. Mlakar?

You might have noticed that when the pronoun is dropped as a subject, the position of the predicate noun changes: it takes the first position, so that the auxiliary verb can stay second, following a stressed word, e.g., **Jaz sem Američan** vs. **Američan sem** 'I am American'. However, a clitic cannot break up a phrasal unit (like an adjective + noun), so the clitic has to go after the phrase, e.g., **Samo Ben je Američan** 'Only Ben is American' or **Slaven Američan je** 'He is a famous American'.

Exercise 5

Ask these questions in Slovene. Remember to use **vikanje** when addressing people with their titles.

1 Are you Marko?
2 Is this Mrs. Kos?
3 Are you Miss Peterka?
4 Are you Borut and Mitja?
5 Are you Mr. Dolinar?

Exercise 6

Provide positive answers to questions 1–3 and negative answers to questions 4–5.

Exercise 7

Pair each sentence on the left with the appropriate response (two are extra) on the right.

1 Kako ti je ime?
2 Kako ste, gospod Zupan?
3 Je to Peter?
4 Kako se pišete?
5 Je vaš mož Slovenec?
6 Naslov?
7 Ste vi gospod Markič?

(a) Ne, to je Borut.
(b) Ne, on je Nemec.
(c) Jelovškova 23, Ljubljana
(d) Ime mi je Lea.
(e) Dobro, hvala. Pa vi?
(f) Ja, so.
(g) Ja, sem.
(h) Ni, Francozinja je.
(i) Mlakar.

Exercise 8

Complete the dialogue.

A: _____ dan, gospod Novak. Kako _____?
B: V _____ sem. In _____ si _____?
A: Dobro, _____. _____ to vaša žena?
B: Ja, _____ je Mira.
A: Jaz _____ Marko. _____ veseli.

žena wife

 Reading

Najpogostejša imena v Sloveniji

Obdobje rojstva		Moški ♂	Ženske ♀
1961–1970			
	1	Janez	Marija
	2	Jože	Irena
	3	Franc	Mojca
	4	Robert	Tatjana
	5	Andrej	Jožica
	6	Marjan	Andreja
	7	Branko	Alenka
	8	Marko	Darja
	9	Bojan	Sonja
	10	Anton	Milena

Obdobje rojstva		Moški ♂	Ženske ♀
2001–2007			
	1	Luka	Nika
	2	Jan	Sara
	3	Nejc	Eva
	4	Žan	Ana
	5	Žiga	Lara
	6	Nik	Lana
	7	Aljaž	Nina
	8	Matic	Maja
	9	Miha	Zala
	10	David	Maša

Source: Statistical records of the Republic of Slovenia.

Vocabulary

najpogọstejši	most common
obdọbje rojstva	time period of birth

Slovenes typically have only one first name (no middle name), although a combination of two first names, like **Žan Luka**, **Ana Marija**, has been more common recently than in the past. Women in the middle and younger generations often have two last names, i.e., their maiden and their husband's name, e.g., **Mọjca Novak Kovačič**. Look at the most common Slovene names from two different periods and remember which ones are male and which ones female. The ending -**a** usually indicates a female name, but some male names end in -**a** as well, e.g., **Miha**, **Žiga**, **Luka**, and these need to be memorized. It is helpful if the name in some form exists in English and you can recognize the connection to the Slovene version.

Unit Two
Družina in jezik
Family and language

In this unit you will learn about:

- Languages
- The verbs 'to speak' and 'to understand'
- Countries and nationalities
- The gender of nouns
- Possessive pronouns

Dialogue 1

Slovensko ali angleško? Slovene or English?
(Audio 1:19)

Ben is showing some photographs of his wife and son to Alenka and Andrej. They are interested in the American–Slovene make-up of Ben's family. What language do they speak at home? Does Ben's mother speak Slovene?

BEN	To je moja žena Špela in tu je moj sin Simon.
ANDREJ	Je vaša žena Slovenka?
BEN	Ja, Špela je rojena v Sloveniji.
ALENKA	A sin zna slovensko?
BEN	Simon dobro razume slovensko, a slabo govori.
ALENKA	Govorite doma slovensko ali angleško?
BEN	Žena govori slovensko, jaz govorim angleško, Simon včasih slovensko, ponavadi angleško.

Bilingual communication

ANDREJ Je tudi vaša mama Slovenka?

BEN Ne, samo oče je Slovenec, mama je Američanka. Ona ne govori slovensko, samo malo razume.

BEN *This is my wife, Špela, and here is my son, Simon.*

ANDREJ *Is your wife Slovene?*

BEN *Yes, Špela was born in Slovenia.*

ALENKA *Does your son know Slovene?*

BEN *Simon understands Slovene well, but he speaks poorly.*

ALENKA *Do you speak Slovene or English at home?*

BEN *My wife speaks Slovene, I speak English, Simon sometimes (speaks) Slovene, usually English.*

ANDREJ *Is your mother also Slovene?*

BEN *No, only my father is Slovene. My mother is American. She doesn't speak Slovene, she only understands a little bit.*

Vocabulary

a	but (when not starting a yes/no question)	**družina**	family
		jezik	language
		malo	a little bit
Američanka	American (female)	**mama**	mother
angleško	(in) English	**ponavadi**	usually
doma	at home	**razume**	s/he understands

rojena	born (f.)	tu	here
samo	only	tudi	also
sin	son	vaša	your (f.)
slabo	poorly	včasih	sometimes
Slovenka	Slovene (female)	zna	s/he knows
slovensko	(in) Slovene	žena	wife

Language point (Audio 1:21)

Countries and nationalities

Names for nationalities differ depending on the gender of the national, e.g., **Slovenec** 'male Slovene' vs. **Slovenka** 'female Slovene'. For example:

> **Je tudi vaša mama Slovenka?**   Is your mother also Slovene?
> **Samo oče je Slovenec.**   Only my father is Slovene.

To some extent, the female form can be predicted if we know the male form. For instance, if the male form ends in -**ec**, the female form will have -**ka** instead of -**ec**, like in **Slovenec** – **Slovenka**; the suffix -**ka** is added to male forms ending in -**an**, like in **Američan** – **Američanka**. In other cases, the pairs need to be learned.

Here are some names of nationalities with their respective countries:

Država country	**Državljan** male national	**Državljanka** female national
Slovenija Slovenia	**Slovenec**	**Slovenka**
Anglija England, Britain	**Anglež**	**Angležinja**
Amerika, ZDA America, USA	**Američan**	**Američanka**
Avstrija Austria	**Avstrijec**	**Avstrijka**
Hrvaška Croatia	**Hrvat**	**Hrvatica**
Italija Italy	**Italijan**	**Italijanka**
Madžarska Hungary	**Madžar**	**Madžarka**
Nemčija Germany	**Nemec**	**Nemka**
Francija France	**Francoz**	**Francozinja**
Rusija Russia	**Rus**	**Rusinja**

Exercise 1

Following are some names of students at a summer language program with their respective home countries:

> Samantha Parker (Anglija), Marco Dapit (Italija), Sandra Messner (Nemčija), Anna Szabo (Madžarska), Josip Novak (Hrvaška), Tim Smith (ZDA), Alice Bernard (Francija).

Say in full sentences what each student is by nationality.

1 Samantha _____
2 Marco _____
3 Sandra _____
4 Anna _____
5 Josip _____
6 Tim _____
7 Alice _____

Language point

To say `I speak' **and** `I understand'

You will use the verbs **govorim** 'I speak' and **razumem** 'I understand', often with some adverb qualifying your mastery of the language. Unlike in English, these adverbs normally do not come at the end of the sentence. In positive statements they will precede a present-tense verb. For example:

Dobro govorim slovensko.   I speak Slovene well.
Slabo razumem angleško.   I understand English poorly.
Malo govorim nemško.   I speak German a little bit.

In Dialogue 1, you probably noticed these two verbs with endings other than **-m**. For example:

Žena govori slovensko, jaz govorim angleško.
My wife speaks Slovene, I speak English.

Govorite doma slovensko ali angleško?
Do you (pl.) speak Slovene or English at home?

A vaš sin razume slovensko?
Does your son understand Slovene?

The ending in the present-tense verb changes depending on the person and the number of the subject. Since the subject is sometimes not explicit (if a pronoun), the verbal ending is the only indication whether the subject is the speaker (I, we), the spoken to (you) or neither (third person); single, dual, or plural. In order to conjugate verbs, that is, to be able to use them with different subjects, and/or to decipher who/what the subject is when it is not explicit, you will have to memorize what ending marks each person and number. Remember that -**m** marks the first-person singular, like in (**jaz**) **govorim, razumem**. For other persons and numbers you will replace that ending with other endings, except for the third-person singular, where you just remove the ending -**m** and do not replace it with anything (no ending). A partial present-tense conjugation of the verb **govorim** 'I speak' would then look like this:

	sg.	pl. (>2)
1	**govorim** I speak	
2	**govoriš** you speak	**govorite** you speak
3	**govori** s/he speaks	

Note that **govorite** 'you (pl.) speak' is used for speaking to more than two as well as to one person when using **vikanje**. You use these endings to conjugate almost any verb in the present tense; therefore, a partial conjugation of the verb **razumem** 'I understand' is **razumeš** 'you (sg.) understand', **razume** 's/he understands', **razumete** 'you (pl.) understand'.

You negate a verb in the present tense by putting **ne** in front of it:

razumem I understand → **ne razumem** I don't understand.

Exercise 2

(a) Say that the following people speak poorly.
(b) Say that the following people understand well.

1 Ti _____

2 Jaz _____

3 Peter _____

4 Vi _____

Language points

Languages (Audio 1:23)

The names for languages differ from the names for nationals. Adverbs ending in **-sko** or **-ško** are used for languages when talking about speaking, understanding, knowing, or learning languages. For example:

Dobro govorite anglęško.   You speak English well.

Slabǫ razumem slovęnsko, a lahkǫ govorite bolj počasi?
I understand Slovene poorly, can you speak more slowly?

Znam tudi nęmško.   I also know German.
Učim se kitajsko.   I am studying Chinese.

When you don't know a Slovene word, you would say:

Kakǫ se reče (po) slovęnsko 'lake'?
How does one say 'lake' in Slovene?

Some more languages (the roots should be familiar from the names for nationals): **francǫsko, madžarsko, italijansko, hrvaško, rusko.**

In other contexts, names of languages are nouns ending in **-ščina**: **slovęnščina, anglęščina, nęmščina, kitajščina, italijanščina.** For example:

Kitajščina je težka.   Chinese is difficult.

As an alternative, an adjective in **-ski** or **-ški** with the noun **jezik** 'language' can be used, for instance **slovęnski/anglęški/nęmški jezik.** Note that unlike names for nationals, these adjectives and names of languages are not capitalized.

Tudi angleščina je težka. Photograph by Lea H. Greenberg.

Yes/no questions

Like with the auxiliary verb, the question particle **a** (in more elevated language **ali**) is used to form yes/no questions, but it can also be omitted. However, no word-order changes, compared to statements, are necessary. For example:

Sin razume slovensko. (Your) son understands Slovene.
(A) sin razume slovensko? Does (your) son understand Slovene?

To answer the questions positively, you would use the particle **ja** 'yes' and the verb from the question (in the appropriate person):

(Ja,) razume. (Yes,) he understands.

For negative answers use the particle **ne** 'no' and a negated verb from the question. The first **ne** 'not' can be omitted. For example:

A mama govori slovensko? **(Ne,) ne govori.**
Does (your) mother speak Slovene? (No,) she doesn't speak (it).

Exercise 3

Say it in Slovene.

1 Marko understands German.
2 I speak English poorly.
3 Ana doesn't understand Italian.
4 We understand Croatian well.
5 I don't know Hungarian.
6 Does he speak Chinese?
7 Do you (sg.) speak Slovene?
8 Do you (pl.) speak French at home?

Exercise 4

Answer the questions from Exercise 3 (a) positively; (b) negatively.

Exercise 5

Choose the appropriate form to complete each sentence.

1 Nancy je _____
 (a) Anglež (b) angleščina (c) Angležinja (d) angleško
2 Petra zna _____
 (a) Nemec (b) nemščina (c) Nemka (d) nemško
3 _____ je zelo melodičen jezik.
 (a) Italijan (b) Italijanščina (c) Italijanka (d) Italijansko
4 A govorite _____?
 (a) Slovenec (b) slovenščina (c) Slovenka (d) slovensko

5 Moj sin dobro razume _____.
   (a) Madžar (b) madžarščina (c) Madžarka (d) madžarsko

Dialogue 2

Kje je . . . Where is . . . (Audio 1:25)

Before they left the airport, Ben needed a few things, but he didn't know where they were located.

BEN	Kje je stran*i*šče?
ANDREJ	Naravnost in levo.
BEN	Kje je bankomat?
ANDREJ	Tamle je izhod in desno je bankomat.
BEN	Je avto bl*i*zu?
ANDREJ	Ja, parkirišče je čez cesto in tam je moj avto.

BEN	*Where is the restroom?*
ANDREJ	*Straight ahead and left.*
BEN	*Where is an ATM?*
ANDREJ	*Over there is the exit and an ATM is to the right.*
BEN	*Is the car close by?*
ANDREJ	*Yes, a parking lot is across the street and there is my car.*

Vocabulary

avto	car		**kje**	where
bankomat	ATM		**levo**	left
bl*i*zu	close by		**naravnost**	straight
čez cesto	across the street		**parkirišče**	parking lot
desno	right		**stran*i*šče**	restroom, toilet
izhod	exit		**tamle**	over there

Language points

Absence of articles

You might have noticed there are no articles in Slovene; therefore, **izhod** may mean 'an exit' or 'the exit', depending on the context or situation.

Things can be 'he', 'she', or 'it'

We have pointed out the gender of nouns denoting people (like personal names or nationalities). In Slovene, every noun, whether denoting a person, an animal, a concrete or an abstract thing, has a gender: masculine, feminine, or neuter. The gender of a noun is usually discernible from the ending of the noun as it appears in a dictionary.

Most masculine nouns end in a consonant, like **mož**, **sin**, **izhod**, **bankomat**. The main exception to this rule are borrowed nouns like **avto** 'car', **kino** 'cinema', and many Slovene personal names, like **Marko**, **Tine**, **Jože**, **Miha**, **Sandi**.

Most feminine nouns end in -**a**, like **žena**, **punca**, **hiša** 'house', **mama**. There is a sizable group of feminine nouns ending in a consonant, like **noč** 'night', **stvar** 'thing'. In this case, the gender needs to be learned with the word.

Most neuter nouns end in -**o**, like **mesto** 'city', **jezero** 'lake', or in -**e** (if the ending is preceded by a 'soft' consonant, that is, **c**, **č**, **j**, **š**, or **ž**), like **parkirišče**, **morje** 'sea'.

The glossaries in this book only mark the gender when a masculine noun does not end in a consonant, a feminine in -**a**, or a neuter in -**o**/-**e**.

Dialogue 3

Naša hiša, njun vrt   Our house, their garden
(Audio 1:27)

Browsing through some more of Ben's photographs, Alenka is asking about the people and things in them. To whom does the garden in the picture belong?

ALENKA Kdo je to?
BEN   To je Simon in to je njegov prijatelj. Tu je naša hiša.
ALENKA Je to vaš vrt?
BEN   Ne, ni. Tu sta dedek in babica. To je njun vrt.
ALENKA In kaj je to?
BEN   To je naše mesto in tu je naše jezero.

ALENKA *Who is this?*
BEN   *This is Simon and this is his friend. Here is our house.*
ALENKA *Is this your garden?*
BEN   *No, it isn't. Here are our grandfather and grandmother.*
        This is their garden.
ALENKA *And what is this?*
BEN   *This is our city and here is our lake.*

Vocabulary

babica	grandmother	**njegov**	his
dedek	grandfather	**njun**	their (two owners)
kaj	what	**prijatelj**	friend (m.)
kdo	who	**vrt**	garden
naš	our		

Language point

Possessive pronouns like moj 'my', tvoj 'your'

1 owner	2 owners	>2 owners
moj my	**najin** our	**naš** our
tvoj your	**vajin** your	**vaš*** your
njegov his	**njun** their	**njihov** their
njen her		

* **Vaš** can also refer to one owner if using formal address, e.g., **Zna vaš sin slovensko.** Talking to a friend or an acquaintance, you would use **tvoj** instead.

Note how the ending of the possessive pronoun changes depending on the gender of the modified noun:

Je to̧ vaš vrt?	Is this your garden?
To̧ je naša hiša.	This is our house.
To̧ je naše mȩsto.	This is our city/town.

The possessive pronoun (and any adjective) must agree with the noun it modifies.

Although the endings in **naše** and **mȩsto** are not the same, the words still agree in gender: remember that the neuter ending -**o** becomes -**e** if it is preceded by **š**.

Note that the possessive pronoun can sometimes be omitted in places where it would be required in English. Some examples from Dialogue 1:

A si̧n zna slovȩnsko?	Does [your] son know Slovene?
Žena govori̧ slovȩnsko.	[My] wife speaks Slovene.

When it is clear from the context or situation to whom the relative belongs, the possessive pronoun is omitted.

Exercise 6

Say it in Slovene.

1 your (sg.) wife
2 her grandfather
3 his house
4 their city

5 our son
6 my friend
7 your (pl.) mother
8 our garden

Exercise 7

In each group, pick out the word that doesn't belong.

1	2	3	4	5
mož	moje	Slovenka	moj	hiša
sin	njihovo	Francoz	tvoj	vrt
dedek	tvoja	Angležinja	najin	babica
prijatelj	naše	Francozinja	naš	jezero

Language point

Questions with question words

In a simple present-tense question, the auxiliary (or another clitic) follows the question word:

Kdọ/kaj je tọ?	Who/what is this?
Kjẹ je bankomat?	Where is an ATM?

Notice that other verbs, too, often appear after question words (and clitics), since the subject (pronoun) is dropped:

Kjẹ govoríte slovẹnsko?	Where do you speak Slovene?
– **Doma.**	– At home.
Kakọ govorí? – Počási.	How does (s)he speak? – Slowly.

 Exercise 8

Pair the questions in the left column with the appropriate responses on the right. Provide the missing questions.

1 Kaj je to?   (a) To je moj oče.
2 A znaš angleško?   (b) Ne, Peter ne razume nemško.
3 _____   (c) Ja, dobro govorim angleško.
4 _____   (d) Moja hiša.
5 _____   (e) Ne, to ni naš vrt.

Unit Three
Kaj delate?
What do you do?

In this unit you will learn about:

- Common work and leisure activities
- Occupations
- The basic present-tense conjugation
- The verbs for 'to study'
- Numbers 1–20

Dialogue 1

Kaj ste po poklicu?   What do you do for a living?
(Audio 1:30)

Ben, Alenka, and Andrej are discussing what people in their families do.

BEN	Andrej, kaj ste po poklicu?
ANDREJ	Arhitekt sem. Veliko rišem. Ravno zdaj rišem načrt za nov hotel.
ALENKA	Je vaša žena zaposlena?
BEN	Dela doma. Prevaja in piše. Poleti igra tenis, pozimi smuča.
ANDREJ	A tudi vi smučate?
BEN	Ne, jaz ne smučam. Igram golf, včasih kolesarim.
ALENKA	In kaj dela sin?

BEN   Sin hodi še v šolo. Srednješolec je. Igra nogomet. Kaj pa
           vaša hčerka?
ALENKA   Anita je študentka. Študira pravo. Hoče biti sodnica.

BEN   *Andrej, what do you do for a living?*
ANDREJ   *I am an architect. I draw a lot. Right now I am drawing
           a plan for a new hotel.*
ALENKA   *Is your wife employed?*
BEN   *She works at home. She translates and writes. In the
           summer she plays tennis. She skis in the winter.*
ANDREJ   *Do you ski, too?*
BEN   *No, I don't ski. I play golf, sometimes I bike.*
ALENKA   *And what does your son do?*
BEN   *Our son still goes to school. He is a high-school student.
           He plays soccer. What about your daughter?*
ALENKA   *Anita is a student. She studies law. She wants to be a judge.*

Vocabulary

arhitekt	architect	prevaja	she translates
delate (delati)	you do; you work	(prevajati)	
golf	golf	ravno zdaj	just now
hčerka	daughter	rišem (risati)	I draw
hodi (hoditi)	s/he goes	smuča (smučati)	she skis
hoče (hoteti)	s/he wants	sodnica	judge (f.)
hotel	hotel	srednješolec	high-school student
igram (igrati)	I play		
kolesarim	I bike	še	still
načrt	plan	šola	school
nogomet	soccer	v šolo	to school
nov	new	študentka	college student (f.)
piše (pisati)	she writes		
poklic	occupation	študira (študirati)	she studies
po poklicu	by occupation	tenis	tennis
poleti	in summer	veliko	a lot
pozimi	in winter	za	for
pravo	law	zaposlen -a	employed

Language points

Expressing actions in the present tense

You will be pleased to know that Slovene has only one type of present tense. It is a simple (non-complex) tense, i.e., formed without the auxiliary verb, which means that both English present continuous, e.g., 'I am drawing', and present simple, e.g., 'I draw', are translated in the same way. For example:

Veliko rišem.   I draw a lot.

Ravno zdaj rišem načrt za nov hotel.
Right now I am drawing a plan for a new hotel.

Conjugation

Most present-tense verbs fall into three groups, depending on the vowel before the ending; the groups are labeled by that vowel and the first person present-tense ending, which you already know from the verb **govorim**.

-am: **delam** I do/work, **igram** I play, **študiram** I study
-em: **pišem** I write, **hočem** I want, **pijem** I drink
-im: **hodim** I walk, **kolesarim** I bike, **mislim** I think

The present-tense endings are the same for all three groups. When you apply the four endings you learned with the verbs **govorim** and **razumem** to the verb **delam**, its partial conjugation looks like this:

	sg.	pl. (>2)
1	**delam** I do	
2	**delaš** you do	**delate** you do
3	**dela** (s)he does	

The default form in translating isolated present-tense Slovene verbs is the simple present (but depending on the context, they may be translated with the simple or continuous present).

Dictionaries will provide the infinitive form, mostly ending in **-ti**, e.g., **delati** 'to do/work', **igrati** 'to play', **pisati** 'to write', from which it is sometimes difficult to discern the present-tense form. In many cases the part preceding **-ti** (the stem) will be the same in the present tense (**delati delam**, **igrati igram**) and you only need to know the endings in order to conjugate the verb. However, that should not be assumed, as often the vowel preceding **-ti**, the consonant before that vowel, or the stress differ in the infinitive and the present tense, like in **pisati pišem**. In that case, glossaries in this book list both the infinitive and the first-person present e.g., **pisati pišem**. To save space, the difference between the infinitive and present-tense stem is marked as follows: the vertical line in the infinitive shows from what point the two forms differ, e.g., **ri|sati -šem**. When there is no difference between the infinitive and the present-tense stems (the verb is regular), only the infinitive is given, e.g., **delati**.

Some infinitives end in **-či**, e.g., **reči** 'to say', **teči** 'to run'. Although they will all fall into the **-em** group in the present tense, consider them all 'irregular' and always learn the first-person present with the infinitive.

Double negative

Slovene uses a double negative. If there is a negative adverb (e.g., **nikoli** 'never', **nikjer** 'nowhere') or a pronoun (**nihče** 'nobody', **nič** 'nothing') in the sentence, the verb must be negated, too. For example:

Nikoli ne smučam.   I never ski.
Nihče ne smuča.   Nobody skis.

Exercise 1

Complete the sentences with the correct present-tense forms.

1 Ti poleti _____. (kolesariti)
2 Luka _____. (prevajati)
3 Jaz _____. (smučati)
4 Vi _____ doma. (delati)

5 Jaz _____ počasi. (govoriti)
6 A ti _____ pravo? (študirati)
7 Vi _____ roman ('novel'). (pisati)
8 Andreja _____ tenis. (igrati)

Exercise 2

Rewrite the sentences 1–5 from Exercise 1 so that they include the adverb **nikoli**, e.g., **Ti poleti nikoli** . . .

Language point

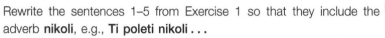

Occupations

When you want to know someone's **poklíc** 'occupation', the question is:

Kaj ste/si po poklícu?   What do you do for a living?
Literally: 'What are you by occupation?'

You will often recognize words for action, place of action, or something else related to the job in the names for occupations, which will help you learn this vocabulary. In most cases, both male and female forms need to be learned, except in cases of traditionally male or female occupations. Some examples:

dẹlati	to work	**dẹlavẹc, dẹlavka**	worker
pisati	to write	**pisatelj, pisateljica**	writer
prodajati	to sell	**prodajalẹc, prodajalka**	sales clerk
prevajati	to translate	**prevajalẹc, prevajalka**	translator
kuhati	to cook	**kuhar, kuharica**	cook
učíti	to teach	**učítelj, učíteljica**	teacher
sodíti	to judge	**sodník, sodníca**	judge
računalnik	computer	**računalničar, računalničarka**	computer expert
knjížnica	library	**knjížničar, knjížničarka**	librarian
podjẹtje	enterprise	**podjẹtnik, podjẹtnica**	entrepreneur
srẹdnja šọla	high school	**srednješọlec, srednješọlka**	high-school student

Many Slovene names for occupations will be easier to learn because of their recognizable common origin with English, for instance:

arhitẹkt, arhitẹktka
profẹsor, profẹsorica
študent, študentka
biolọg, biolọginja: a large group of occupations ending in
  -olọg(inja) '-ologist'

As in English (think of Smith, Miller, Cooper, Wright), you will often come across Slovene last names that are originally names for occupations, some already obsolete, like **Kovač** 'blacksmith', **Mlínar** 'miller', **Sítar** 'sieve maker', **Sọdnik** 'judge', **Zupan** 'mayor', **Žagar** 'sawyer', or **Kolar** 'wheel maker'.

Kolar

Exercise 3

The letters on the business cards on the line for one's occupation got scrambled. Unscramble them and complete the sentences saying what each person's occupation is.

Petra Lavrič alpevakrja	Simona Pintar luicitejač	Tomaž Perko ilbogo	Sonja Mali opesricrfoa
Miran Jesenovec ahkru	Vesna Strojan kropajalad	Damjan Kocjan kirničžnja	Katja Kos ndjecpaiot

1 Petra je _____   5 Miran je _____
2 Simona je _____   6 Vesna je _____
3 Tomaž je _____   7 Damjan je _____
4 Sonja je _____   8 Katja je _____

Language point

'To study'

The cognate verb **štud*i*rati** is used when talking about studying in college (**fakult*ẹ*ta**) in general, for example, **An*i*ta štud*i*ra = An*i*ta je študentka**, studying something as a major or minor subject in college, or deeply examining something. Similarly, the word **š*t*udent(ka)** has a narrower meaning than the word 'student' in English, as it only refers to a college or graduate student. A student of **osnovna š*ọ*la** 'elementary school' is called **uč*ẹ*n*ẹ*c** or **osnovnoš*ọ*l*ẹ*c/osnovnoš*ọ*lka**; a student of **sr*ẹ*dnja š*ọ*la** 'high school' is called **dij*a*k(inja)** or **srednješ*ọ*l*ẹ*c/srednješ*ọ*lka**. For studying something that is not one's academic or scholarly discipline, like studying a language to gain proficiency, the verb **uč*i*ti se** is used. For example:

> **S*i*mon se uč*i* šp*a*nsko in n*ẹ*mško.**
> Simon studies Spanish and German (but not as major or minor subjects in college).

Exercise 4

Pair the questions in the left column with the appropriate responses on the right. One response is extra.

1 Kaj delaš poleti?   (a) Profesorica je.
2 Kaj dela vaš sin?   (b) Ne, hodim še v srednjo šolo.
3 A si študentka?   (c) Ne, jaz ne smučam.
4 A vi smučate?   (d) Ja, veliko rišeš.
5 Kaj je po poklicu?   (e) Kolesarim in igram golf.
                             (f) Študira pravo.

Exercise 5

Answer the following questions about Dialogue 1.

1 Kaj je po poklicu Andrej?
2 Kaj dela?
3 Kje dela Benova ('Ben's') žena?
4 Kaj dela pozimi?
5 A Ben smuča?
6 Hodi njegov sin v osnovno ali v srednjo šolo?
7 Je Alenkina ('Alenka's') hčerka zaposlena?
8 Kaj hoče biti Anita?

 Dialogue 2

 Naslov in telefonska številka   Address and phone number **(Audio 1:33)**

Ana wants to drop off some notes at Lara's house, but she doesn't have her phone number or address, so she turns to Lara's boyfriend, Jan, for help.

ANA   Jan, ti najbrž veš, kje živi Lara.
JAN   Njen naslov je Levstikova petnajst. Tudi Eva in Vesna
      stanujeta tam.
ANA   Vedno so skupaj. Skupaj študirajo, skupaj žurirajo . . .
JAN   Ja, zelo dobro se razumejo.
ANA   A imaš tudi Larin telefon?
JAN   Ja, tu je, izvoli: pet-osem-dve šest-sedem-devet.
ANA   Hvala.
JAN   Ni za kaj.*

ANA   *Jan, you probably know where Lara lives.*
JAN   *Her address is Levstikova 15. Eva and Vesna also live there.*
ANA   *They are always together. They study together, they party
      together . . .*
JAN   *Yes, they get along very well.*
ANA   *Do you also have Lara's phone [number]?*
JAN   *Yes, here it is: 582–679.*

ANA *Thank you.*
JAN *You are welcome.*

---

* 'you are welcome, don't mention it' (answer to 'thank you').

Vocabulary

hvala	thank you	**stan|ovati -*uj*em**	to reside
im|eti -am	to have	**vedno**	always
najbrž	probably	**vem (vedeti)**	I know (a fact)
ni za kaj	no problem	**zelo**	very
raz|umeti se -*um*em	to get along	**živ|eti -*im***	to live
skupaj	together	**žurirati**	to party

Language point

Present-tense conjugation in dual and plural

You already know the second-person plural (e.g., **igrate**, **govorite**), which you learned along with singular forms, mostly because it is used not only for addressing several people, but also for addressing just one person if using **vikanje**. In Dialogue 2 you learn other non-singular forms of verbs. For example:

Eva in Vesna *stanujeta* tam.   Eva and Vesna live there.
Lara, Eva in Vesna skupaj   Lara, Eva, and Vesna study
   študirajo.   together.

Here are the rest of the forms you need to know to complete the present-tense conjugation:

	Du.	Pl. (>2)
1	**delava** we [two] do	**delamo** we do
2	**delata** you [two] do	
3	**delata** they [two] do	**delajo** they do

Again, you won't always be able to derive these forms correctly from the infinitive, since in many cases the infinitive and present-tense stems (the part before -**ti** or the ending) differ. Take, for example, the verbs **živeti** 'to live' and **stanovati** 'to reside': you need to remember that their first-person present-tense forms are **živim** and **stanujem**, respectively. Remove the first-person ending and replace it with the appropriate dual or plural ending, depending on the subject. For example:

živim → (one) **živijo**   they live
stanujem → (onidve) **stanujeta**   they (two) reside

Exercise 6

Fill in the correct present-tense forms.

1 Eva, Vesna in Peter _____ tam. (živeti)
2 Mi slabo _____ slovensko. (govoriti)
3 Oni skupaj _____. (študirati)
4 Vidva se dobro _____. (razumeti)
5 A tu _____ Marko in Sonja? (stanovati)
6 Kje vi običajno _____? (žurirati)

Language point

Vocabulary building (Audio 1:36)

Numbers 1–20

Numbers (**številke**) are essential for communicating many everyday things, like addresses and phone numbers, for example. Learn to count from 0 to 20:

0 **nič**	7 **sedem**	14 **štirinajst**
1 **ena**	8 **osem**	15 **petnajst**
2 **dve**	9 **devet**	16 **šestnajst**
3 **tri**	10 **deset**	17 **sedemnajst**
4 **štiri**	11 **enajst**	18 **osemnajst**
5 **pet**	12 **dvanajst**	19 **devetnajst**
6 **šest**	13 **trinajst**	20 **dvajset**

Hišna številka

Exercise 7

Write down the following words as numbers:

1 pet
2 dvajset
3 štirinajst

4 sedemnajst
5 devet
6 osem

7 trinajst
8 nič
9 enajst

Language point

Expressions of politeness

Oprosti/oprostite means 'excuse me' and 'I'm sorry'. It is not used, though, to get someone to give you space or get out of your way; for that people will say **Samo malo, prosim** [literally] 'just a little bit (of room), please'.

The answer to **hvala (lepa)** 'thank you (very much)' is **prosim** [literally] 'please' or **ni za kaj** 'you are welcome/don't mention it'.

The expression **izvoli(te)** is used (1) when offering or handing something (like in Dialogue 2, when Jan gives Ana the phone number); (2) as a polite command or encouragement to do something, like 'please do/go ahead'; (3) as an invitation to enter.

Reading

Vizitka business card

<u>Arhitekturni biro Pivec d.o.o.</u>
projektiranje in inženiring

Andrej Mlakar
arhitekt

Doma: Slamnikova 43, 1230 Domžale

Biro: Jelenova 115, 1000 Ljubljana

tel./faks: +386 1 58 23 47

gsm: +386 41 123 45 67

e-mail: amlakar@biropivec.si

Note that in a Slovene **naslov**, the name of the street comes before the number; the four-digit postal code precedes the city/town name.

Oglas advertisement

PREVAJALSKA AGENCIJA BESEDA

Kontaktni podatki: Darinka Kos, Cankarjeva ulica 45, 2000 Maribor
GSM: 059 925 1432
e-mail: darinka.kos@siol.net

Prevajamo strokovna besedila: ekonomija, tehnika, pravo
(nemško<>slovensko)

Vocabulary

podatki	information
strokovna besed/la	technical texts

Exercise 8

1 Where is Andrej's office located?
2 Where does he live?
3 What kind of business is the advertisement for?
4 What services does it offer?

Unit Four
Mesto in opravki
The city and errands

In this unit you will learn about:

- Talking about more than one thing
- Saying what things are like
- Colors
- The nominative case
- Adjective–noun agreement

Dialogue 1

Banke so danes zaprte   Banks are closed today
(Audio 1:38)

Andrej is taking Ben and another American, Tom, around town on a Saturday afternoon. The two Americans would like to run some errands. Can they get them done?

BEN	Andrej, a je tu blizu kakšna banka?
ANDREJ	Tista rumena stavba čez cesto je banka.
BEN	Midva morava zamenjati denar.
ANDREJ	Banke so danes zaprte.
BEN	Kaj pa pošta? A lahko na pošti zamenjava denar?
ANDREJ	Ne, popoldne tudi pošta ni odprta. Čez cesto je nov bankomat.
BEN	In kje lahko kupiva znamke?

Pošta

ANDREJ Vidita tisti sivi kiosk na levi? Kioski so odprti. Tam prodajajo znamke.

BEN Tudi internetna kavarna je odprta. A lahko pogledava e-pošto in pošljeva kratko sporočilo domov?

ANDREJ Seveda, kar izvolita.

BEN *Andrej, is there a bank nearby?*

ANDREJ *That yellow building across the street is a bank.*

BEN *We [two] have to exchange some money.*

ANDREJ *Banks are closed today.*

BEN *What about a post office? Can we exchange money at the post office?*

ANDREJ *No. The post office is not open in the afternoon either. A new ATM is across the street.*

BEN *And where can we buy stamps?*

ANDREJ *Do you see that grey kiosk on the left? Kiosks are open. They sell stamps there.*

BEN *The Internet café is also open. Can we look at email and send a short message home?*

ANDREJ *Of course, just go ahead.*

Vocabulary

banka	bank	popoldne	in the afternoon
denar	money	poslati pošljem	to send
domov	(to) home	pošta	post office, mail
kakšen	some, any	na pošti	at the post office
kar izvolita	just go ahead	prodajati	to sell
kavarna	café	seveda	of course
internetna k.	cyber café, Internet café	siv	gray
		sporočilo	message, note
kratek	short	stavba	building
kupiti kupim	to buy	tam	there
lahko	can, may	tisti	that
morati	must	vidleti -im	to see
nov	new	zamenjati	to exchange
odprt	open	zaprt	closed
opravek	errand	znamka	stamp
pogledati	to look at		

Language points

What are cases?

In Slovene the forms (mostly endings) of nouns, adjectives, and pronouns change depending on their function in the sentence or phrase.
In Dialogue 1, for instance, the noun **pošta** 'post office; mail' also
appears as **pošti** and **pošto**:

Pošta ni odprta.	The post office is not open.
A lahko pogledam e-pošto?	Can I look at (my) email?
A lahko na pošti zamenjam denar?	Can I exchange money at the post office?

These different forms of the same noun, which function in the above
sentences as the subject, direct object, and with a preposition denoting location, are called cases. Slovene has six cases, each of them
fulfilling several functions.

Nominative singular of nouns

The nominative case (singular) is the form in which nouns appear in the dictionary. Its name suggests that it is used for naming things and people, like making lists or pointing something out. For example:

To je *hotel*.	This is a hotel.
To je *banka*.	This is a bank.
To je *mesto*.	This is a city.

Other common uses of the nominative case:

(a) the subject of the sentence:

Pošta ni odprta.	The post office is not open.
Žena piše in prevaja.	(My) wife writes and translates.

(b) a complement after the auxiliary verb **biti** in equational sentences:

Prijatelj je *arhitekt*.	(My) friend is an architect.

(c) calling or addressing people:

Kako si, *Tomaž*?	How are you, Tomaž?

Nominative plural and dual of nouns

Just as in the singular (e.g., **hotel, banka, mesto**), nominative endings in the plural differ depending on the gender of the noun. Look at the nouns in these sentences:

To so *hoteli*.	These are (the) hotels.
Kje so *banke*?	Where are (the) banks?
To so *mesta*.	These are (the) cities.

The nominative plural ending for most masculine nouns is -**i**. That ending is added to the nominative singular of the noun ending in a consonant: **hotel + -i → hoteli**.

Feminine nouns ending in -**a** in the nominative singular end in -**e** in the nominative plural, e.g., **banka + e → banke**.

Neuter nouns end in -**a** in the nominative plural, e.g., **mesto + a → mesta**.

Always remember to remove the ending of the dictionary (nominative singular) form before adding a new one, unless the dictionary form ends in a consonant (in our tables we mark the absence of a vowel ending with a dash (—).

Here is an overview of basic nominative endings for nouns. Exceptions will be discussed later in the book.

	Masculine	Feminine	Neuter
N sg.	k*i*osk	banka	m**ẹ**sto
N pl.	k*i*oski	banke	m**ẹ**sta
N du.	k*i*oska	banki	m**ẹ**sti

	m.	f.	n.
sg.	—	-a	-o/-e
pl.	-i	-e	-a
du.	-a	-i	-i

The table includes the nominative *dual* of nouns. Spoken language in certain categories (like feminine and neuter nominative) uses plural forms for two, although that is not acceptable in standard written language. That does not mean you do not need to learn them, but they are not essential for everyday oral communication.

The fleeting vowel e

The majority of nouns that have a vowel written as **e**, but pronounced as a schwa (like the 'o' in 'hammock' or 'second') in the final syllable, drop this **e** whenever an ending is added. Particularly numerous are nouns ending in -**ẹc** or -**ẹk**, like **učenẹc** 'pupil', **kovčẹk** 'suitcase', **dẹdẹk** 'grandfather'. Their plural forms are **učenci, kovčki, dẹdki**. In this book, **e** is always underlined when pronounced as schwa (**polglasnik**). In vocabulary lists and examples the schwa appears in normal rather than bold print when it is fleeting.

Exercise 1

Rewrite the following sentences in the plural. Remember that **to** is used in this construction for 'this' and 'these'.

1 To je pošta.
2 To je mesto.
3 Tam je kiosk.
4 Tu je znamka.

5 Tu je sporočilo.
6 A je to šola?
7 Kje je jezero?
8 Tu je kavarna.

Language points

Adjective-noun agreement

As we have already mentioned with the possessive pronouns, adjectives must agree with the noun they modify in gender, number, and case. That does not mean that endings on the noun and corresponding adjective will always be identical, as adjectives and nouns often have different endings to express the same category. Adjectival endings are thus sometimes the same as endings on the noun and sometimes different. In the nominative case, the endings are, for the most part, the same on adjectives and nouns. Look at the adjective **nov -a -o** 'new' with different nouns in these sentences:

T*i*sta *nova stavba* je banka.	That new building is a bank.
Čez c*ę*sto je *nov bankomat.*	There is a new ATM across the street.
T*u* je *novo sporočilo.*	Here is a new message.

The adjective must agree with the noun it modifies not only when it stands immediately in front of it, but also as a complement after the auxiliary verb **b*i*ti**. Here are some examples in the plural:

K*i*oski so *odprti.*	Kiosks are open.
Banke so *zaprte.*	The banks are closed.
Sporoč*i*la so *kratka.*	The messages are short.

Adjectives with the fleeting ɘ

Some adjectives have a schwa in the final syllable of the nominative singular masculine, and just as in masculine nouns, such a schwa drops when an ending is added. Here are some examples with their opposites:

d*ǫb*ęr	dobra	good	slab -a
krat*ę*k	kratka	short (in length)	dolg -a
majh*ę*n	majhna	small	velik vel*i*ka
tež*ę*k	težka	heavy; difficult	lah*ę*k lahka

Masculine singular adjectives ending in -i

You may have noticed that some masculine singular adjectives, like adjectives in -**ski** and -**ški**, end in -**i** rather than in a consonant, e.g., **slovenski (jezik)**, **angleški (slovar** 'dictionary'). In other forms these adjectives replace that -**i** with other endings, e.g., **slovenski, slovenska, slovensko**.

Qualitative adjectives that do end in a consonant in the masculine singular, can have -**i** added to express definiteness (where you would use 'the' in front of an adjective in English) or when they follow a demonstrative or possessive, like **tisti sivi kiosk** 'that gray kiosk', **moj novi računalnik** 'my new computer'. Adjectives **majhen** and **velik** have special definite forms **mali** and **veliki**.

Adverbs derived from adjectives

You might have noticed adverbs (words modifying verbs and adjectives, but not nouns) that look like the neuter singular form of adjectives:

> **Simon dobro razume slovensko, a slabo govori.**
> Simon understands Slovene well, but he speaks poorly.

Most qualitative adjectives can have adverbs derived from them that are identical in form to the nominative neuter singular adjectives. Sometimes, however, they differ in stress, i.e., the adverb will be stressed on the final -**o** as opposed to the stem stress in the adjective, as in **slabo delo** 'poor work/job' vs. **slabo dela** 's/he works poorly'; similarly **težko** – **težko**, **lahko** – **lahko**, **lepo** 'beautiful' – **lepo**.

English equivalents of these adverbs are most often adverbs in -**ly**. Unlike adjectives, adverbs do not change form.

Exercise 2

Say that the following things are large, first in the singular, then in the plural.

1 hiša   4 stavba
2 parkirišče   5 banka
3 mesto   6 hotel

Exercise 3

Complete the sentences with the correct form of the adjective indicated.

dob̯er

1 Andrej je _____ arhitekt.
2 Tu so _____ muzeji.
3 Anita je _____ študentka.

tež̯ek

4 A so ti _____ kovčki vaši?
5 Slovenščina ni _____.
6 _____ torbe* so doma.

* **torba** 'bag'.

Language point

`Is there a ... nearby?`

When looking for things around town, this type of question comes in handy:

A je tu blízu kakšna banka?   Is there a bank nearby?

Kakšna 'some, any' is used to indicate that you are looking for any bank, not a specific one. It needs to agree with the noun it modifies, which means you will use **kakš̯en** with a masculine noun, **kakšno** with a neuter:

A je tu blízu kakš̯en kiosk?   Is there a news stand nearby?
A je tu blízu kakšno igrišče?   Is there a playground nearby?

Other things you could be looking for:

ambulanta	clinic	**galerija**	art museum, gallery
avtobusna postaja	bus station	**gledališče**	theater
baz̯en	swimming pool	**kavarna**	café
bolnica	hospital	**kino**	movie theater, cinema
cerk̯ev	church	**knjižnica**	library

lekarna	pharmacy	**potovalna agencija**	travel agency
muzej	museum	**restavracija**	restaurant
park	park	**šola**	school
parkirišče	parking lot	**trgovina**	store
pokopališče	cemetery	**železniška postaja**	train station

Smerokazi

Exercise 4

Your friend is looking for some information about facilities in town on a Saturday afternoon. Tell her about each facility, according to the information in the chart.

		Closed	Good	New
1	library	✔		
2	art galleries		✔	
3	swimming pool			✔
4	cyber café			✔
5	post office	✔		
6	banks	✔		
7	restaurant 'Jelen'		✔	
8	museums	✔		

Language points

'Also' **and** 'either'

The particle **tudi** is used for both 'also' and 'either', as in these two sentences:

Popoldne tudi pọšta nị odprta.
In the afternoon, the post office is not open, either.

Tudi internẹtna kavarna je zaprta.
The Internet café is also closed.

Note the word order: the particle **tudi** does not come at the end, but immediately in front of the word or phrase in focus.

The possibility of doing something

To say that one can or may do something, the adverb **lahkọ** is used with the verb in the present tense:

Tukaj lahkọ zamẹnjata denar.   Here you can exchange money.
Kjẹ lahkọ kupiva znamke?   Where can we buy stamps?

Exercise 5

Say it in Slovene, with the verbs first in the plural, then in the dual.

1 Where can they buy stamps?
2 We can exchange money over there.
3 Where can they look at email?
4 Here you can send a note home.

Dialogue 2

Kjẹ je Larina hị̌ša?   Where is Lara's house? **(Audio 1:41)**

Ana and her friend, Jera, are looking for Lara's house. Jera knows what Lara's house looks like.

ANA   Mogǫče je tǫ Larina híša.
JERA   Larina híša je zelena in nova. Ta híša je stara.
ANA   Potęm je najbrž tísta híša na dęsni.
JERA   Ja, žę vídim: Lęvstikova 15.
ANA   Zelǫ velíka híša.
JERA   Tu ne živíjo samǫ Lara in njęni prijateljici. Spodaj živíjo Larini starši in brat. Larino stanovanje je zgoraj.

ANA   *Perhaps this is Lara's house.*
JERA   *Lara's house is green and new. This house is old.*
ANA   *Then it is probably that house on the right.*
JERA   *Yeah, I see: Levstikova 15.*
ANA   *A very large house.*
JERA   *It is not only Lara and her two friends who live here. Lara's parents and brother live downstairs. Lara's apartment is upstairs.*

Vocabulary

brat	brother	**stanovanje**	apartment
Larin(a)	Lara's	**star**	old
mogǫče	perhaps	**starši** (pl.)	parents
na dęsni	on the right	**zelen**	green
najbrž	probably	**zgoraj**	upstairs
potęm	then	**žę**	already
spodaj	downstairs		

Language point

Asking what things are like

To ask what something or someone is like, the question word **kakšęn** is used, which is a different **kakšęn** than in **Je tu kakšna šǫla?** 'Is there a school here?': they are spelled the same, but this one has a long **a** instead of a short one. It is an adjective; therefore, it needs to agree with the noun the question is about. For example:

Kakšna je vaša hiša? Bęla, velika in stara.
What is your house like? White, large, and old.

Kakšen also corresponds to 'what kind/type of', for instance:

Kakšno męsto je Ljubljana? Zelo prijętno.
What kind of city is Ljubljana? Very pleasant.

Kakšen priimek je Rossi? Italijanski.
What kind of last name is Rossi? Italian.

This is a good example of how translating word-for-word can take you in the wrong direction. None of the sentences starts with **kaj** 'what' in Slovene. You must learn to 'translate' concepts and ideas instead of words, as quite often there is no parallel construction to express the same idea in the target language.

Exercise 6

Ask the questions about the features italicized in the answers.

1 <u>Kakšno je tvoje stanovanje</u>? Moje stanovanje je *majhno*.
2 _____? Kioski so *sivi*.
3 _____? Sonjina hiša je *zelena in nova*.
4 _____? Ta profesor je *dober*.
5 _____? Slovenske hiše so *velike*.
6 _____? Njegov priimek je *zelo dolg*.

Language points

Possessive adjectives from personal names

Possessive adjectives (these answer the question word **čigav** 'whose') have typical suffixes **-ov/ev** or **-in** (the equivalent of English possessive ''s'). When derived from a personal name such an adjective can be used to express that person's possession, like *Larina* hiša 'Lara's house' or *Larini* starši 'Lara's parents'. On the other hand, some uses of these possessive adjectives in Slovene are unlike in English. The plural masculine forms derived from family names are used to say 'members of that family'. For example:

Novak → **Novakovi**   the Novak family, the Novaks

You will also find possessive adjectives ending in -**ova**/-**eva** in many Slovene street names, e.g., **Lẹvstikova**, **Vọdnikova**. The ending is feminine as the adjective agrees with the implied (even if mostly left out) nouns **u**lica 'street', e.g., **Lẹvstikova u**lica [literally] 'Levstik's Street' or **cẹsta** 'road', e.g., **Vọdnikova cẹsta** 'Vodnik's Road'.

Vocabulary building

Colors

Note how things are described and identified with **barve** 'colors'. For example:

Larina hiša je *zelena* in **nova.**
Tista *rumena* stavba čez cẹsto je banka.

Learn some of the most common **barve**:

bẹla	white	**rdẹča**	red
črna	black	**rjava**	brown
zelena	green	**oranžna**	orange
plava, mọdra	blue	**vijọlična**	purple
rumena	yellow	**s**iva	gray

Some expressions for location

Some useful expressions for location in the immediate environment:

tu, tukaj	here	**na dẹsni/dẹsno**	(on the) right
tam(le)	(over) there	**na lẹvi/lẹvo**	(on the) left
blizu	close by	**spodaj**	downstairs
daleč	far away	**zgoraj**	upstairs
čez cẹsto	across the street		

Exercise 7

Unscramble the words and add the missing ones to complete this chart for mixing colors.

1 aderč + maruen = _____
2 eabl + _____ = asiv

3 _____ + daorm = ezaenl
4 romad + derač = _____

Exercise 8

Complete the sentences as indicated in the parentheses.

1 Banka je tista bela hiša _____. (across the street)
2 A vidiš tisti sivi kiosk _____? (on the right)
3 A Lara stanuje _____ ali _____? (downstairs, upstairs)
4 Galerija je _____. (close by)
5 Tudi muzej ni _____. (far away)
6 Vodnikova ulica je _____. (on the left)

Reading

Razglednica   postcard **(Audio 1:43)**

Dragi Simon,

zdaj govorim samo slovensko,
zato tudi pišem slovensko.

Tu je lepo. Mlakarjevi so zelo
prijazni. Na razglednici vidiš
Kamnik – prijetno staro
mestece. Tu so ozke ulice,
majhne trgovine in butiki, zanimiv
renesančni grad in muzej. Čisto
blizu so Kamniške Alpe.

   Lep pozdrav,

      Oči

Simon Pint...
    123...
C...

Kamnik

Vocabulary

dragi	dear
grad	castle
mestece = majhno mesto	
oči	daddy
ozek	narrow
pozdrav	greeting
prijazen	friendly
zanimiv	interesting
zato	therefore

Vocabulary note

Kamniški – adjective from **Kamnik**: adjectives in **-ski** and **-ški** are derived from place names, e.g., **London** – **londonski**, **Ljubljana** – **ljubljanski**, **Pariz** – **pariški**.

Unit Five
Želite, prosim?

May I help you?

In this unit you will learn about:

- Ordering in a café
- Requesting a hotel room
- The direct object accusative of nouns and adjectives
- The accusative used with the preposition **za**
- Masculine nouns ending in -**o**
- Numbers 21–100
- Money

Dialogue 1

V kavarni   At the café (Audio 1:45)

Alenka, Andrej, and Ben are tired after walking around town on a summer day. Where do they stop? What does Alenka recommend? What does Ben order?

ALENKA	Malo sem utrujena.
ANDREJ	A gremo na kavo? Tamle je kavarna Luna. Lahko sedimo zunaj.
BEN	Dobra ideja. Dan je lep in kava se vedno prileže.
ALENKA	Tukaj imajo tudi imenitne slaščice. Priporočam čokoladno torto.

ANDREJ	Če sta žejna, lahko naročimo radensko.*
ALENKA	Ja, cel liter. Želita mogoče vino ali pivo?
BEN	Za alkohol je še prezgodaj. Samo radensko in kakšen sok.

When the waitress comes . . .

NATAKARICA	Dober dan. Želite, prosim?
ANDREJ	Eno kavo s smetano, eno radensko in en gosti sok. Pa tri kozarce za mineralno, prosim.
NATAKARICA	Pa vi, gospa?
ALENKA	Jaz bi rada kapučino in čokoladno torto.
NATAKARICA	In za gospoda?
BEN	Enako kot za gospo. Je mineralna voda mrzla?
NATAKARICA	Je. Lahko prinesem tudi led.
BEN	Hvala.

ALENKA	*I am a little tired.*
ANDREJ	*Let's go for coffee. Café 'Luna' is over there. We can sit outside.*
BEN	*Good idea. It is a nice day and coffee always tastes good.*
ALENKA	*They also have excellent pastries here. I recommend the chocolate cake.*
ANDREJ	*If you are thirsty, we can order mineral water.*
ALENKA	*A whole liter. Do you perhaps want wine or beer?*
BEN	*It is still too early for alcohol. Just mineral water and some kind of juice.*

When the waitress comes . . .

WAITRESS	*Hello. May I help you?*
ANDREJ	*A coffee with cream, one mineral water and one pulpy juice. And three glasses for the water, please.*
WAITRESS	*And you, madam?*
ALENKA	*I would like a cappuccino and chocolate cake.*
WAITRESS	*And for the gentleman?*
BEN	*The same as for the lady. Is the mineral water cold?*
WAITRESS	*Yes, it is. I can also bring ice.*
BEN	*Thank you.*

---

* **Radenska**: most common local brand of mineral water.

Kava in torta

Vocabulary

alkohọl	alcohol	**prezgọdaj**	too early
cẹl	whole	**prilẹ|či se -žem**	to do (feel) good
če	if	**prines|ti -em**	to bring
čokoladẹn	chocolate (adj.)	**priporọčati**	to recommend
enako kot	the same as	**s**	with
gọst	thick, pulpy	**sed|ẹti -ím**	to sit
grẹm (íti)	I go (to go)	**slaščíca**	sweet, pastry
ideja	idea	**smẹtana**	cream
imenítẹn	excellent	**sọk**	juice
kava	coffee	**tọrta**	cake
kozarẹc	glass (drinking)	**utrujẹn**	tired
lẹd	ice	**víno**	wine
líter	liter	**voda**	water
mrzẹl	cold	**mineralna v.**	mineral water
naročíti	to order	**za**	for
natakarica	waitress	**zunaj**	outside
pa	and	**žejẹn**	thirsty
pívo	beer	**žel|ẹti -ím**	to want

Language points

The accusative case

The most common use of the accusative case is for the direct object, which is the thing or person directly affected by the subject's action. The verbs in the dialogue that require a direct object are **im|ęti -am** 'to have', **žel|ęti -im** 'to want', **priporǫčati** 'to recommend', **naroč/ti**, 'to order', **prines|ti -em** 'to bring'. In conversational language, nouns are often direct objects of the verbs that are just implied, because they are understood from the context, as in the dialogue above:

Ja, (lahkǫ naročimo) cęl liter.
Yes, (we can order) a whole liter.

(Želim) En gǫsti sǫk in eno kavo s smętano.
(I want) one pulpy juice and a coffee with cream.

Although the verbs **naroč/mo** and **žel/m** are left out, the nouns **liter**, **kozarce**, **kavo**, and **sǫk** are still direct objects and therefore, the accusative case must be used.

Accusative singular

The accusative singular of masculine and neuter nouns and adjectives is the same as the nominative singular unless a masculine noun (or phrase) denotes something animate, i.e., a man or animal. In the following pairs of sentences the nouns **sǫk** and **vino** appear first as a subject (nominative) and then as a direct object (accusative):

Gǫsti sǫk je mrzel. Želim gǫsti sǫk.
The pulpy juice is cold. I want pulpy juice.

Bęlo vino je dobro. Natakar prinese bęlo vino.
White wine is good. The waiter brings white wine.

The accusative singular of feminine nouns and adjectives is different than the nominative, as it ends in **-o** instead of **-a**. Compare the nouns and adjectives used as a subject and as a direct object in these two sentences:

Čokoladna tǫrta je dobra. Priporǫčam čokoladno tǫrto.
Chocolate cake is good. I recommend chocolate cake.

Accusative plural and dual

Most of the accusative endings in the plural and dual are the same as in the nominative.

The only difference is in the masculine plural where the accusative ends in **-e** (not in **-i** as in the nominative). For example:

> **Kozarci in kapučini so na mizi. Natakarica prinese kozarce in kapučine.**
> Glasses and cappuccinos are on the table. The waitress brings glasses and cappuccinos.

Requesting things

To ask for things, you can simply use the accusative case of the noun (and adjective) denoting the thing you desire with **prosim**, for instance:

> **Čokoladno torto, prosim.**   Chocolate cake, please.

A very formal way of saying what you want is with the verb **želeti** and the accusative, as in **Želim gosti sok.** The more common way is with the expression **rad(a) bi** 'I (you/s/he) would like' plus the accusative. For example:

> **Rad bi temno pivo.**   I (you/he) would like a dark beer.
> **Rada bi navadno vodo.**   I (you/he) would like regular water.

Rad changes the ending like an adjective, depending on the gender and number of the subject: use **rad** if the person desiring something is male and **rada** if female. With dual and plural subjects you would use the endings you learned for dual and plural nominative adjectives. For instance, you know that the adjectival nominative ending **-i** appears in feminine dual and masculine plural; therefore, **Radi bi temno pivo** 'We (you/they) would like a dark beer' can be used if two women are ordering or more than two people of which at least one is male are ordering. With this expression, the category of person can be ambiguous if the subject is not explicit (e.g., a dropped pronoun). Given the context, it should be clear whether **rad bi** means 'I would like . . .' or 'you would like . . .' or 'he would like . . .'.

Word order

The particle **bi** is a clitic like the auxiliary verb, meaning that it will occur in second position and unstressed, unless it is used in a yes/no question. As a consequence, the position of **rad** in the sentence varies: when there is no fully stressed word or phrase to appear in the first position, like no explicit subject, **rad** will appear before **bi**, as in **Rad bi čokoladno torto**; in the opposite case it will appear after **bi**, for instance, **Jaz/Janez bi rad čokoladno torto**. It does not necessarily follow immediately after **bi**: **Janez bi res rad čokoladno torto** 'Janez would really like chocolate cake.'

Brand names used as common names

Some very commonly used brands have become common names for things. For instance, instead of using the phrase **mineralna voda** for 'mineral water' people will more likely use the word **radenska**, which is the most widely used brand of mineral water in Slovenia. Similar examples are **vim** 'scrubbing powder' or **vileda** 'sponge cloth'.

Exercise 1

Order the following things using the accusative and **prosim**:

1 coffee
2 juice
3 mineral water

4 white wine
5 beer
6 cappuccino

Exercise 2

Using the correct form of the expression **rad bi**, say that the following people would like the items from Exercise 1.

1 Ana
2 Miran
3 Peter in Sonja

4 Metka, Marko in Matjaž
5 mama in oče
6 Andreja in Tjaša

Language points

The accusative of animate masculine nouns

The accusative of masculine nouns denoting people or animals (animate nouns) in the singular differs from the accusative of inanimate nouns, as it ends in -**a**. Compare these two sentences:

Janez ima kozar<u>e</u>c. Janez ima prijatelja.
Janez has a glass. Janez has a friend.

Animacy plays a role only in the *masculine singular*, i.e., the accusative endings of animate and inanimate masculine nouns differ in the singular, but are the same in the plural (or dual), for instance:

Janez ima kozarce. Janez ima prijatelje.
Janez has glasses. Janez has friends.

The modifier (adjective) in the phrase referring to a single male person or animal is also affected: it is not like the nominative nor has it the same ending as the noun it modifies, for instance:

Janez ima dobrega prijatelja. Janez has a good friend.

At this point, try to pay attention to animacy in masculine singular nouns and memorize the nominal ending -**a**; we will get back to this adjectival ending when we talk about the genitive case of adjectives.

Here is an overview of basic accusative endings for nouns. Adjectival endings are the same, except if a singular masculine noun is animate. The forms (endings) that differ from the nominative are shaded.

	Masculine	Feminine	Neuter
A sg.	**k*i*osk** **prijatelja**	**banko**	**jezero**
A pl.	**kioske**	**banke**	**jezera**
A du.	**kioska**	**banki**	**jezeri**

	m.	f.	n.
sg.	— **-a**	-o	-o/-e
pl.	-e	-e	-a
du.	-a	-i	-i

The accusative case with the preposition
za 'for'

Other uses (besides the direct object) of the accusative case are
with several prepositions, which you will learn gradually. One of them
is the preposition **za** when it means 'for' (you will learn another meaning later). For example:

> **In (kaj prinesem) za**   And (what should I bring) for
>   **gospǫda?**   the gentleman?
> **Isto kot za gospǫ.**   The same as for the lady.

> **Natakarica prinese tri kozarce za goste.**
> The waitress brings three glasses for guests.

Exercise 3

Fill in the blanks with the appropriate form of the noun indicated in the
parentheses:

1 Natakarica prinese _____ (a cake) za _____ (Alenka).
2 Tu je _____ (beer) za _____ (Andrej).
3 Za _____ (Ben) lahko naročimo _____ (coffee).
4 A poznaš ('know') mojega _____ _____ (friend, Miran)?
5 Prosim _____ (a glass) za _____ (gentleman).

Exercise 4

Once you know the vocabulary from Dialogue 1 well, translate these
sentences into Slovene.

1 Alenka is tired.
2 Ben and Alenka are thirsty.
3 Is the beer cold?
4 They have very good coffee here.
5 We can order mineral water and juice.
6 I would like coffee with cream and chocolate cake.
7 Can you bring (some) ice?
8 The waitress brings cake for Alenka and Ben.
9 It is still too early for wine.

Dialogue 2

Račun, prosim   Check (bill), please **(Audio 1:48)**

A guest wants to pay for himself and some friends in a café.

GOST   A lahko plačam, prosim?
NATAKAR   Seveda, samo trenutek. Dvakrat kapučino – dva evra
štirideset, enkrat kava s smetano – evro dvajset, trikrat
sok – štiri evre šestdeset in enkrat radenska – evro
trideset. Devet evrov petdeset centov, prosim.
GOST   Izvolite. *(Hands him 10 euros.)* Je že v redu.
NATAKAR   Hvala. Na svidenje.

GUEST   *Can I pay, please?*
WAITER   *Of course, just a minute. Two cappuccinos – €2.40, one*
coffee with cream – €1.20, three juices – €4.60, and one
mineral water – €1.30. €9.50, please.
GUEST   *Here you go. (Hands him 10 euros.) Keep the change.*
WAITER   *Thank you. Bye.*

Vocabulary

enkrat, dvakrat,	one, two, three . . .	**račun**	bill
trikrat . . .	times	**trenutek**	moment
plačati	to pay		

Language points

Counting orders of drinks or food

Note that orders of drinks or food are expressed with numerals + **krat**
'times', i.e., **dvakrat kapučino** 'two orders (cups) of cappuccino';
enkrat sok 'one order (glass/bottle) of juice', **trikrat čokoladna torta**
'three orders (pieces) of chocolate cake'. An alternative is using numerals
alone with these nouns, like **dva kapučina, en sok, tri torte.**

Vocabulary building (Audio 1:49)

Numbers 21–100

In counting from 21 to 29 (and in every subsequent ten) ones precede tens (unlike in English), as if to say 'one-and-twenty'. To count by tens from 30 to 90, put together the words you learned for numerals 3 to 9 with **deset**.

21	enaindvajset	27	sedemindvajset	60	šestdeset
22	dvaindvajset	28	osemindvajset	70	sedemdeset
23	triindvajset	29	devetindvajset	80	osemdeset
24	štiriindvajset	30	trideset	90	devetdeset
25	petindvajset	40	štirideset	100	sto
26	šestindvajset	50	petdeset		

Exercise 5

Write down the following words as numbers:

(a) petintrideset
(b) oseminšestdeset
(c) štiriindvajset
(d) sedeminpetdeset

(e) devetindevetdeset
(f) šestinštirideset
(g) triinsedemdeset
(h) dvainosemdeset

Language points

Denar 'money'

Slovenes use **evro** 'euro'; its hundredth part is **cent** 'cent'. In saying prices of things the number is used with the appropriate form of the words **evro** and **cent** (which is often omitted, particularly with numbers higher than 10), e.g., **en evro triindvajset (centov)**. The accusative singular, dual or plural, respectively, of **evro** or **cent** is used with numerals 1–4, forms ending in **-ov** with numerals 5–100; therefore, **en evro/cent, dva evra/centa, tri/štiri evre/cente, pet evrov/centov**. To find out the **cena** 'price/cost' of something, the question is **Koliko stane(-ta/-jo) . . . ?** 'How much is/are . . . ?' When paying, you will often be asked for **drobiž** 'change', e.g., **A imate drobiž?** 'Do you have change?' or **Drob*i*ž, pr*o*sim** 'Change, please.' **Drob*i*ž** is also something that most people would leave as a **napitn*i*na** 'tip' in a café or a restaurant. There is no set rule about tipping: it is not expected, but it is appreciated, and most people will leave the change or round up the bill, which can amount to anywhere from 5 to 20 percent, for the tip. For instance, in Dialogue 3, where the total bill is 9.50, the guest leaves the 50 cents change from 10 euros.

*E*vro **and other masculine nouns in** -o

The noun ***e*vro** is masculine, even if it does not end in a consonant. A sizable group of borrowed masculine nouns end in unstressed -o, e.g., **avto** 'car', **r*a*dio** 'radio', **k*i*no** 'movie theater', **st*u*dio** 'studio'. In standard language, Slovene names in -o, like **M*a*rko, Sr*e*čo**, fall into this group as well. These nouns are treated like regular masculine nouns; therefore, in cases other than the nominative and non-animate accusative singular they have the same endings as masculine nouns ending in a consonant, e.g., **dv*a* *e*vra/centa, tr*i* *e*vre/cente**.

Exercise 6

A What would the guest say in the following situations:

1 He wants to know how much a large beer costs.
2 She wants to pay.
3 She hands the waiter the money.
4 He wants the waiter to keep the change.

B What would the waiter say in the following situations:

5 He would like to know what the guest wants.
6 He offers to bring ice.
7 He wants to collect €4.30 from the guest.
8 He wants the guest to give him the (exact) change.

Dialogue 3

A imate prosto sobo? Do you have a room available? **(Audio 1:52)**

Andrej is helping Ben's friend Tom to find a hotel room. They are at the hotel front desk. What do they find out?

ANDREJ	Dober dan. Oprostite, a imate prosto sobo?
RECEPTOR	Kakšno sobo pa želite?
ANDREJ	Gospod bi rad enoposteljno sobo za tri dni.
RECEPTOR	Samo trenutek . . . Ja, imamo prosto enoposteljno sobo.
ANDREJ	In koliko stane?
RECEPTOR	Enoposteljna soba stane osemdeset evrov na noč.
ANDREJ	A ta cena vključuje zajtrk?
RECEPTOR	Ja, vključuje. Tudi parkiranje in internet sta brezplačna.

ANDREJ	*Hello. Excuse me, do you have a room available?*
RECEPTIONIST	*What kind of room would you like?*
ANDREJ	*The gentleman would like a single room for three days.*
RECEPTIONIST	*Just a moment . . . Yes, we do have a single room available.*
ANDREJ	*And how much does it cost?*
RECEPTIONIST	*A single room is €80 a night.*
ANDREJ	*Does this price include breakfast?*
RECEPTIONIST	*Yes, it does. The Internet and parking are free as well.*

Vocabulary

brezplačen	gratis	**soba**	room
na noč	per night	**enoposteljna s.**	single room
parkiranje	parking	**vključuje (vključevati)**	(it) includes
prost	available	**zajtrk**	breakfast

Reading

Cen/k price list

Kavarna Luna

Kava in topli napitki			**Brezalkoholne pijače**		
Espresso	1,00 €		Coca Cola	0,25 l	1,60 €
Kapučino	1,20 €		Fanta	0,25 l	1,60 €
Kava z mlekom	1,20 €		Cockta	0,25 l	1,60 €
Kava s smetano	1,20 €		Radenska	0,5 l	1,30 €
Kakav	1,60 €		Ledeni čaj	0,5 l	1,80 €
Vroča čokolada	1,80 €		Sadni sok	0,2 l	1,60 €
Vroča čokolada s smetano	2,00 €		Limonada	0,2 l	1,40 €
Čaj (sadni, zeliščni, pravi)	1,50 €				

Vocabulary

brezalkoholna pijača	non-alcoholic drink
Cockta [kokta]	a Slovene brand of soft drink
kakav	cocoa

mleko	milk
sadni čaj	fruit-flavored tea
topli napitek	warm beverage
vroča čokolada	hot chocolate

Vocabulary note

A decimal comma, not a decimal point, is used to separate the integer from the fractional part of decimal numerals, e.g., euros from cents, liters from deciliters.

Exercise 7

What would a waiter say to collect the money for the following orders of drinks at the coffee shop 'Luna'? Write out the amounts in words.

1 coffee with cream, fruit tea
2 3x cappuccino
3 3x mineral water, hot chocolate
4 juice, lemonade
5 iced tea, herbal tea, coffee with milk
6 5x juice

Unit Six
Urniki
Schedules

In this unit you will learn about:

- Daily activities and schedules
- Telling the time
- Time expressions
- Saying where one is going
- Verbs of motion

Dialogue 1

Kdaj greste v službo? When do you go to work? **(Audio 1:55)**

Early in the morning, Ben and Andrej are discussing Andrej's schedule and Ben's plans for Thursday. When does Andrej usually get up? How does he go to work? Where is Ben planning to go?

BEN   Koliko je ura?

ANDREJ   Ura je pet.

BEN   A vedno tako zgodaj vstanete?

ANDREJ   Ne, ponavadi vstanem ob šestih. Ampak danes je
       ponedeljek. Ob ponedeljkih imam sestanek že ob pol
       osmih.

BEN   In kdaj greste drugače v službo?

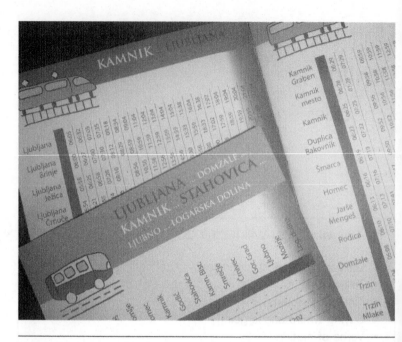

Vozni redi

ANDREJ   Vlak odpelje ob petnajst do osmih. V Ljubljano pridem
         ob četrt čez osem.
BEN   Se vsak dan vozite z vlakom?
ANDREJ   Ne, ob četrtkih gresta zjutraj v Ljubljano tudi Alenka in
         Anita. Takrat se skupaj peljemo z avtom.
BEN   Ravno prav. V četrtek grem v Maribor. Tam imam
         predavanje ob enajstih. Mogoče se lahko peljem z vami v
         Ljubljano, potem pa naprej v Maribor z vlakom.
ANDREJ   Seveda, ni problem.

BEN   *What time is it?*
ANDREJ   *It's five o'clock.*
BEN   *Do you always get up this early?*
ANDREJ   *No, I usually get up at six. But today is Monday. On
         Mondays I have a meeting as early as seven thirty.*
BEN   *And when do you normally go to work?*
ANDREJ   *The train leaves at a quarter to eight. I arrive in Ljubljana
         at a quarter after eight.*
BEN   *Do you ride the train every day?*

ANDREJ   *No, on Thursdays Alenka and Anita go to Ljubljana in the*
         morning as well. Then we go together by car.
BEN   *How convenient. I'm going to Maribor on Thursday. I have*
         a lecture there at eleven. Perhaps I can ride with you to
         Ljubljana, and then (continue) to Maribor by train.
ANDREJ   *Of course, no problem.*

Vocabulary

četrt	quarter	**tako**	so
četrtek	Thursday	**takrat**	at that time
čez	past (hour)	**ura**	hour
do	till	**ura je ...**	it is ... o'clock
drugače	otherwise	**koliko je ura?**	what time is it?
kdaj	when		
naprej	on (forward)	**v (+A)**	(in)to
ni problem	not a problem	**vlak**	train
ob	at; by, near	**voziti se vozim se**	to ride
odp|eljati -eljem	to depart, to drive away	**vsak**	every
ponedeljek	Monday	**vstati vstanem**	to get up
ob ponedeljkih	on Mondays	**z**	with, by
predavanje	lecture	**z vami**	with you
pridem (priti)	I come, arrive	**z vlakom**	by train
ravno prav	how convenient	**zgodaj**	early
služba	work (job)	**zjutraj**	in the morning

Vocabulary note

Maribor: the second largest city in Slovenia (pop. a little over 100,000), in north-eastern Slovenia.

Language points

Telling the time (Audio 1:57–60)

On the hour

The answer to the question **Kọliko je ura?** 'What time is it?' is **Ura je** + number, for instance, **Ura je ena/dvẹ/tri** . . . 'It is one/two/three o'clock.' In casual communication the twelve-hour clock is used, while in announcements, schedules, or official documents, i.e., wherever one wants to avoid ambiguity, Slovenes use the twenty-four-hour clock. So, instead of **Ura je dvẹ** 'It is two P.M.' you will hear **Ura je štirinajst**. Note that the question and answer about time are worded entirely differently than in English.

Half hour, minutes past and till the hour

If using the twenty-four-hour clock, the hour number is followed by the number of minutes past that hour when telling the time between full hours:

17.25 = sẹdemnajst (in) pẹtindvajset	five twenty-five P.M.
21.43 = enaindvajset (in) triinštirideset	nine forty-three P.M.

Note that hours and minutes, when written with numbers, are separated by a period (full stop).

In everyday speech, where the twelve-hour clock is used, the time between full hours is expressed in terms of minutes past the hour for the first half hour. You need to know the numbers and the preposition **čez** 'past, after':

9.10 = desẹt čez devẹt	ten after nine
15.20 = dvajset čez tri	twenty after three (P.M.)
17.15 = pẹtnajst čez pẹt	fifteen after five (P.M.)

To tell the time between the bottom of the hour and the next full hour you say the number of minutes + preposition **do** 'till' + the numeral representing the next full hour. That numeral needs to be put in a case form; for now it will be easiest if you memorize **(do) dvẹh/trẹh** 'till two/three', and add the ending **-ih** to the rest of the numerals (note the fleeting **e** in **sedẹm** and **osẹm**), e.g., **(do) enih, štirih, sedmih, osmih, desetih**.

Some examples of time between the bottom of the hour and next full hour:

6.50 = desęt do sedmih   ten to seven
12.35 = pętindvajset do enih   twenty-five to one (P.M.)
22.45 = pętnajst do enajstih   fifteen to eleven (P.M.)

Instead of **pętnajst** 'fifteen (minutes)' you can say **četrt** 'quarter', e.g., **četrt čez pęt** 'quarter after five', **četrt do enajstih** 'quarter to eleven'.

The bottom of the hour is **pol** 'half' followed by the numeral representing the *next* full hour, so it is like saying 'half of (the next hour)'. The numeral has the same form as you would use with **do: pol enih** 'twelve thirty', **pol dvęh** 'one thirty', **pol osmih** 'seven thirty'.

The noun ura

The noun **ura** corresponds to English 'hour', but it also means 'clock' and 'watch'. But when someone asks you **A imate uro?** 'Do you have a watch?', (s)he is not actually interested in whether you own a watch, but wants to find out what time it is. **Ura** can also mean 'lesson', e.g., **ura klavirja** 'piano lesson', **ura balęta** 'ballet lesson'.

Exercise 1

The times are written out in words. Fill in the prepositions **do** or **čez** where appropriate.

1 6.50   deset _____ sedmih   5 20.45 četrt _____ devetih
2 9.30   pol _____ desetih   6 23.20 dvajset _____ enajst
3 12.15 četrt _____ dvanajst   7 3.55 pet _____ štirih
4 18.05 pet _____ šest   8 4.30 pol _____ petih

Exercise 2

Say (casually) what time it is.

1 5.30   5 19.10
2 10.15   6 21.35
3 13.00   7 16.45
4 15.20   8 23.40

Dialogue 2

 Kam takǫ hitíš? Where are you hurrying? (Audio 1:61)

Nejc bumps into Lara in the city. He hasn't seen her much lately. Why?

NEJC Živjo, Lara. Kam takǫ hitíš?

LARA Tečem na faks. Predavanje imam opoldne, a grem prej še v knjížnico.

NEJC Kje si? Zadnje čase te sploh ne vídim.

LARA Ta semęstęr imam grozno natrpan urnik. Predavanja vsak dan dopoldne in popoldne, dvakrat na tęden tudi prakso.

NEJC Imaš kdaj čas za kavo ali kosílo?

LARA Ja, lahkǫ gręva na kosílo jutri ali v pętek.

NEJC V redu, v pętek. Se prej še slíšiva. Čao!

LARA Čao!

NEJC *Hi, Lara. Where are you hurrying like this?*

LARA *I am running to school [college]. I have a lecture at noon, but I am going to the library first.*

NEJC *Where have you been? I haven't seen you lately.*

LARA *I have a terribly crowded schedule this semester. Lectures every day in the morning and in the afternoon and also an internship twice a week.*

NEJC *Do you ever have time for coffee or lunch?*

LARA *Yes, we can go to lunch tomorrow or on Friday.*

NEJC *OK, on Friday. We'll be in touch before then. Bye!*

LARA *Bye!*

 Vocabulary

čas	time	**hit|ęti -im**	to hurry
dopoldne	before noon	**jutri**	tomorrow
faks	college (coll.)	**kam**	where to
grozno	terribly	**kdaj**	sometime, ever

kos*i*lo	lunch	**sl*i*š|ati -im**	to hear
nat*r*pan	crowded	**sploh**	at all
opoldne	at noon	**te** (A)	you
p*ete*k	Friday	**te|či -čem**	to run
popoldne	afternoon	**t*e*den**	week
pr*a*ksa	internship	**na t*e*den**	per week
prej	beforehand	**z*a*dnje č*a*se**	recently
sem*este*r	semester		

Language points

The verb *i*ti, gr*e*m `to go´ **and other verbs of motion**

The verb *i*ti, **gr*e*m** is used when we mean movement in one direction with a particular destination; when we mean movement in more than one direction and/or multiple times, we need to use the verb **hod*i*ti hodim**, e.g., **S*i*n h*o*di še v š*o*lo** 'My son still goes to school.'

These examples in our texts denote one-time movement with a particular destination:

Kd*a*j gr*e*ste v slu*ž*bo? When do you go to work?
Prej gr*e*m še v knj*i*žnico. I am going to the library first.

The verb **gr*e*m** conjugates like regular **-em** verbs, but has endings **-ste/-sta** instead of **-te/-ta**, i.e., **gr*e*ste, gr*e*sta** in the second-person plural and second- and third-person dual. Here is a complete conjugation:

	sg.	du.	pl.
1	gr*e*m	gr*e*va	gr*e*mo
2	gr*e*š	gr*e*sta	gr*e*ste
3	gr*e*	gr*e*sta	gr*e*jo

Several verbs of motion make the distinction between movement in one direction and movement in more than one direction. Here are the most common examples:

	One-directional	Multi-directional
to go	*i*ti gręm	hod*i*ti hǫdim
to drive/ride	peljati (pęljem) se	voz*i*ti se
to fly	letęti let*i*m	lętati
to run	teči tečem	tękati
to carry	nesti nesem	nos*i*ti nǫsim

'Where to?'

With verbs of motion you often need to say **kam** 'where to' you are
going (driving, flying, . . .). This is expressed with the preposition **v**
'(in)to' or **na** '(on)to' + the accusative. For example:

Pęljem se v Ljubljano.   I am driving/riding to Ljubljana.
Tečem na faks.   I am running to school [college].

The preposition **v** is generally used with the accusative when talking
about movement into and **na** when talking about movement onto a
place or object, e.g., **Gręm v h*i*šo** 'I am going into the house' vs. **Gręm
na h*i*šo** 'I am going on top of the house.' But certain nouns require **na**
even for the meaning 'into', for instance nouns denoting events, like
koncert, razstava 'exhibit', **predavanje** 'lecture', **sestanęk** 'meeting';
institutions of higher education, like **univerza** 'university', **fakultęta,
faks** [coll.] 'college', **akadem*i*ja** 'academy', **inštit*u*t** 'institute'; institutions
and offices: **pǫšta, ǫbčina** 'county office', **polic*i*ja** 'police station'.
Sometimes you can use either preposition, but with different meanings
of the same noun, as with the noun **mǫrje**: **v mǫrje** has a concrete
meaning of moving into the sea (water), **na mǫrje** means 'to the coast'.
    Certain groups of place names (besides mountains) also require
na, such as names of islands, countries, and regions ending in **-ska**,
-ška, or individual names of towns (these need to be memorized).
For example:

Gręmo na Hvar.   We are going to the island of Hvar.
Pot*u*jejo na Madžarsko.   They are traveling to Hungary.
Pęljeta se na Goręnjsko.   They [two] are driving to Upper Carniola.
Let*i*m na D*u*naj.   I am flying to Vienna.

You will also use **na** + the accusative of nouns denoting meals, foods, and drinks to say 'to go for . . .'. The question **A greš/grẹva na kavo?** 'Are you/we going for coffee?' is an invitation 'Let's go for coffee.'

Exercise 3

Say that the following people are going to the places indicated in parentheses.

1 Jana (knjižnica)
2 Peter in Marko (park)
3 vi (šola)
4 jaz (mesto)

5 prijatelji (kino)
6 midva (koncert)
7 vidva (fakulteta)
8 ti (sestanek)

Exercise 4

Answer the following questions about Dialogue 2.

1 Kam teče Lara?
2 Kdaj ima predavanje?
3 Kam gre pred predavanjem?
4 Kakšen je ta semester njen urnik?
5 Kaj ima vsak dan in kaj dvakrat na teden?
6 A ima kdaj čas za kosilo?
7 Kdaj gre Nejc lahko na kosilo?

Language point

Vocabulary building (Audio 1:64–68)

Days of the week

ponedẹljek	Monday	**pẹtek**	Friday
torẹk	Tuesday	**sobọta**	Saturday
srẹda	Wednesday	**nedẹlja**	Sunday
četrtẹk	Thursday		

Note that days of the week are not capitalized.

To say that something happens on a particular Monday (Tuesday, Wednesday . . .), the preposition **v** + accusative is used: **v ponedẹljek, v torẹk, v srẹdo,** . . . . But to say on Mondays (Tuesdays, Wednesdays . . .), a different preposition and form are used: **ob ponedęljkih, ob torkih, ob sredah, ob četrtkih**. The endings are -**ih** (masculine) and -**ah** (feminine). Some examples from the dialogues:

> **Ob ponedęljkih imam sestanek žę ob pol osmih.**
> On Mondays, I have a meeting as early as 7:30.

> **Ob četrtkih gręsta zjutraj v Ljubljano tudi Alęnka in Anita.**
> On Thursdays, Alenka and Anita go to Ljubljana in the morning as well.

Some more expressions answering the question kdaj **'when'**

When talking about routines and schedules, these time expressions will come in handy:

zjutraj	in the morning
dopoldne	before noon
opoldne	at noon
popoldne	in the afternoon
zvečer	in the evening
ponoči	at night
opolnoči	at midnight
zgǫdaj	early
pozno	late
kasneje/pozneje	later
prej	earlier; beforehand
potęm	after that
danes	today
jutri	tomorrow
pojutrišnjem	the day after tomorrow

The following words express **kakǫ pogǫsto** 'how frequently' something happens: **vędno** 'always', **ponavadi** 'usually', **pogǫsto** 'frequently', **včasih** 'sometimes', **rędko** 'rarely', **nikǫli** 'never', **vsak dan** 'every day'.

To answer the question **ob katęri uri** 'at what time', the preposition **ob** is used with the time unless it is on the hour. For example:

> **ob 17.15 = ob pętnajst čez pęt**   at 5:15 P.M.
> **ob 22.50 = ob desęt do enajstih**   at 10:50 P.M.

To say 'at [number] o'clock' use the preposition **ob** followed by the number in the same form as used with **pol**. When the hour is written with a number, the number is followed by an **h**. For example:

ob 11h = ob enajstih at 11:00 A.M.
ob 15h = ob treh at 3:00 P.M.

When there is doubt over whether one is talking about the afternoon or the morning, **zjutraj/dopoldne** or **popoldne/zvečer** is added to the hour, e.g., **ob treh popoldne** 'at 3:00 P.M.', **ob deset do enajstih zvečer** 'at 10:50 P.M.'

Exercise 5

Luka is a pilot and flies to a different city every day. Following is his schedule for this week. Say in six sentences where Luka is flying each day; the first sentence is done for you.

P	Rim	1 V ponedeljek leti v Rim.
T	Moskva	2
S	Pariz	3
Č	Praga	4
P	Berlin	5
S	Kreta	6

Exercise 6

Sara's school schedule is given below. Provide short answers to her mother's questions.

	7.50	8.40	9.30	10.20	11.10	12.00*
ponedeljek	NEM	BIO	SLO		INF	FIZ
torek	SLO	MAT		BIO	KEM	ZGO
sreda	MAT	SLO	ANG		FIZ	KEM
četrtek	GEO	ZGO	NEM	ANG		SLO
petek	MAT	SLO	KEM		NEM	BIO

* Slovene school periods are 45 minutes long.

1 Kdaj imaš fiziko? Ob _____ ob _____ in ob _____ ob _____.
2 Kdaj imaš matematiko?
3 Kdaj imaš kemijo?
4 Kdaj imaš biologijo?
5 Kdaj imaš nemščino?
6 Kdaj imaš zgodovino ('history')?

Reading

Dęlovni čas Hours of operation

AMBULANTA		SISTEMATSKI PREGLEDI
PON	12.00–20.00	
TOR	10.30–13.30	07.00–10.30
SRE	13.00–19.00	
ČET	13.00–14.00	07.00–13.00
PET	07.00–12.00	

Vocabulary

sistemątski pregled   physical (exam)

Od kdaj do kdaj **'from when to when?'**

To say from what hour to what hour something takes place, use the prepositions **od** 'from' and **do** 'till' followed by the number in the same form as used with the preposition **ob**. Make sure to keep these prepositions apart, since they look a lot alike, but each has a different meaning. For example:

Ambulanta je ob ponedęljkih odprta od dvanajstih do osmih.
On Mondays, the clinic is open from twelve to eight.

Ob torkih je odprta od pol enajstih do pol dveh.
On Tuesdays it is open from 10:30 to 1:30.

Exercise 7

Based on the information from the posted hours, answer the following
questions. Write out the times in words.

1 Kdaj je ambulanta odprta ob sredah, četrtkih in petkih?
2 Kdaj so sistematski pregledi?

Unit Seven
Dober tek!

Bon appétit!

In this unit you will learn about:

- Food and meals
- Expressing likes and dislikes
- The genitive case
- Offering, declining food
- Complimenting and toasting

Dialogue 1

Kaj radi jęste? What do you like to eat? **(Audio 1:69)**

Alenka is getting ready to go grocery shopping. She would like to know her guest's food preferences. What does Ben like to eat for breakfast? Does he like orange juice?

ALENKA	V trgovino moram. Hladilnik je skoraj prazen. Ben, kaj imate radi za zajtrk?
BEN	Doma za zajtrk ponavadi jem žitarice, jogurt in banano. Tu imam raje kruh. Črni kruh je odličen. Mi nimamo takega kruha.
ALENKA	Kaj imate radi zraven?
BEN	Sir ali skuto. Vaša skuta je posębno okusna.

ALENKA Sir še imam, skute pa nimam. Kaj pa jajca? A bi mogoče
ocvrto ali mehko kuhano jajce za zajtrk?

BEN Jajc nimam posebno rad. Špela včasih naredi palačinke.

ALENKA Tudi jaz lahko naredim palačinke. Pogledati moram,
če imam dovolj bele moke. Kupiti moram tudi mleko in
marmelado.

ANDREJ Prinesti moraš tudi kavo. Mislim, da nimamo več
brezkofeinske kave.

ALENKA In pijače? Kaj radi pijete, Ben? Morda pomarančni sok?

BEN Pomarančnega soka ne maram. Rad imam slovenske
goste sokove. Najraje imam marelični ali breskov sok.

ALENKA Dobro. Zdaj pa potrebujem že listek.

ALENKA *I must go to the market. The refrigerator is almost empty.*
Ben, what do you like for breakfast?

BEN *At home I usually eat cereal, yogurt, and a banana. Here*
I prefer bread. The dark [wheat] bread is excellent. We
don't have bread like that.

ALENKA *What do you like with it?*

BEN *Cheese or cottage cheese. Your cottage cheese is*
especially tasty.

ALENKA *I still have cheese, but I don't have any cottage cheese.*
What about eggs? Would you perhaps like a fried or a
soft-boiled egg for breakfast?

BEN *I don't particularly like eggs. Špela sometimes makes*
crêpes.

ALENKA *I can make crêpes, too. I have to check whether I have*
enough white flour. I must also buy milk and jam.

ANDREJ *You must also bring coffee. I think we don't have any*
more decaffeinated coffee.

ALENKA *What about drinks? What do you like to drink, Ben?*
Orange juice perhaps?

BEN *I don't like orange juice. I like Slovene juices with pulp.*
I like apricot or peach juice the most.

ALENKA *OK, now I already need a list.*

Dober zajtrk

Vocabulary

breskov	peach (adj.)	**okusen**	tasty
brezkofeinski	decaffeinated	**palačinka**	crêpe
da	that (conj.)	**pijača**	drink
dovolj	enough	**piti -jem**	to drink
hladilnik	refrigerator	**pomarančni**	orange (adj.)
jajce	egg	**posebno**	especially
jem (jesti)	I eat (to eat)	**potrebujem**	I need
jogurt	yogurt	**(potrebovati)**	
kruh	bread	**prazen**	empty
črni kruh	wholewheat b.	**prine|sti -sem**	to bring
kuhan	boiled	**rad**	gladly
mehko kuhan	soft-boiled	**rad imeti**	to like
listek	(shopping) list	**sir**	cheese
marati	to like, care for	**skoraj**	almost
marelični	apricot (adj.)	**skuta**	cottage cheese
marmelada	jam	**več**	any more (with
moka	flour		negated verb)
narediti	to make	**zraven**	alongside
ocvrt	fried	**žitarice** pl.	cereal

Language points

Negating the verb imęti 'to have'

The verb **im|ęti -am** in the present tense is negated by putting **n-** at the beginning of the present-tense forms, e.g., **imam** → **n***i***mam, imaš** → **n***i***maš, imamo** → **n***i***mamo**, etc. Note the change in the place of stress.

The genitive case

You might have noticed in the dialogue that a direct object is not in the accusative if the verb is negated. For example:

Prinesti mǫraš kavo.	You must bring coffee.
N*i***mamo brezkofe***i***nske kave.**	We don't have decaffeinated coffee.

When the verb is negated, the direct object is in the genitive case. This is just one of several uses of this case, which will be discussed further in the book.

Genitive singular

The genitive singular ending of masculine and neuter nouns is **-a**. It differs from the adjectival ending, which will be discussed later. For example:

N*i***mam kru*ha, s*i*ra in mlęka.**	I don't have juice, cheese, and milk.
Ne maram pomarančnega sǫka.	I don't like orange juice.

The genitive singular ending of feminine nouns and adjectives is **-e**, as in **brezkofe***i***nske kave** 'decaffeinated coffee', **bęle mǫke** 'white flour'.

Genitive plural and dual

The genitive plural and dual endings of nouns are the same. The majority of masculine nouns in the genitive plural add the ending **-ov** or **-ev** (after a 'soft' consonant) to the nominative singular form, just as in **centov, evrov**. You are familiar with this form because the genitive plural is also used after the numerals 5–100.

The majority of feminine and neuter nouns have the so-called 'zero' ending in the genitive plural and dual, i.e., they lose the `ending they have in the nominative singular and do not replace it with anything. The following are some examples of nouns in the nominative singular and genitive plural:

Tu je . . .		Tu je pet . . .
hruška	pear	**hrušk**
pomaranča	orange	**pomaranč**
jagoda	strawberry	**jagod**
banana	banana	**banan**
jabolko	apple	**jabolk**
jajce	egg	**jajc**

Here is an overview of basic genitive endings for nouns.

	Masculine	Feminine	Neuter
G sg.	**kioska**	**banke**	**jezera**
G pl.			
	kioskov	**bank**	**jezer**
G du.			

	m.	f.	n.
sg.	-a	-e	-a
pl.	-ov*	—	—
du.			

* **-ev** when preceded by **c, č, j, š,** or **ž**

Exercise 1

Create mini-dialogues with one person requesting the items listed and the other answering that s/he unfortunately (**žal**) does not have the requested item.

Example:

1 cheese **Sir, prosim – Žal nimam sira.**
2 milk
3 pancakes
4 eggs
5 jam
6 apples
7 bread
8 cottage cheese

Language point

The verbs p*i*ti 'to drink' **and** j*ę*sti 'to eat'

The verb **p*i*ti** 'to drink', **p*i*jem** extends its stem in the present tense with **j**, but otherwise conjugates like an **-em** verb. The verb **j*ę*sti** 'to eat', **j*ę*m** has endings **-ste/-sta** instead of **-te/-ta** in the second-person plural and second- and third-person dual (like **gr*ę*m**).

	sg.	du.	pl.
1	j*ę*m	j*ę*va	j*ę*mo
2	j*ę*š	j*ę*sta	j*ę*ste
3	j*ę*	j*ę*sta	j*ę*jo

Exercise 2

Complete the sentences with the appropriate present-tense form of **piti** or **jesti**.

1 Jaz _____ torto, ona _____ marelični sok.
2 Oni radi _____ kruh za zajtrk.
3 Midva zjutraj vedno _____ kavo.
4 A Peter pogosto _____ pivo?
5 Marko in Alenka običajno _____ doma.
6 Ti nikoli ne _____ zelenjave ('vegetables').

Language points

Expressing the necessity of doing something

To say that one must do something, use the present tense of the verb **m*ǫ*rati** 'must' with the infinitive of the verb expressing the necessary action, for instance:

Al*ę*nka m*ǫ*ra kup*i*ti ml*ę*ko in marmel*a*do.
Alenka must buy milk and jam.

Prinesti m*ǫ*raš t*u*di kavo. You must also bring coffee.

The infinitive in everyday spoken language loses its final -**i**; therefore, in the sentences above, you will hear people say **mǫram kupit** and **prinest mǫraš**. Although **mǫrati** is not a clitic, it tends to occupy second place if no emphasis is placed on it; therefore, the infinitive will precede **mǫrati** if no other element is available to occupy the first place, as in **Prinesti mǫraš tudi kavo.**

When saying that one needs to go somewhere, the verb *iti* can be omitted, for instance:

V trgovino mǫram.   I must [go] to the market.

Since the destination is given, it is implied that what the person needs to do is go there.

Things we like and people we love

To say that one likes (is fond of) something, use the word **rad** in the appropriate form, just as you learned in Unit 5, and the present tense of the verb **imęti** with the accusative. For example:

Rada imam sir ali skuto.	I [f.] like cheese or cottage cheese.
Bęn ima rad mlęčne izdęlke.	Ben likes milk products.
A imaš rad palačinke?	Do you like pancakes?

The same word-order rule applies in positioning **rad** before or after **imęti** as you learned with **rad bi**, i.e., **imęti** remains in the second position like a clitic.

To say that one prefers something, replace **rad** with **raje**, which does not change form depending on the gender of the subject. For example:

Bęn ima raje kruh.   Ben prefers bread.

Alęnka, kaj imaš raje: pomarančni ali maręlični sǫk?
Alenka, what do you prefer: orange or apricot juice?

To say that you like something most, you add **naj** to **raje** → **najraje**:

Najraje imam maręlični sǫk.	I like apricot juice the most.
Kaj imaš najraje za zajtrk?	What do you like most for breakfast?

When the direct object is a person, **imeti rad** expresses affection for the person, not just liking, so make sure you know the difference. For example:

Rada imam Janeza. I love Janez.

To say 'I love you [sg.]' you would use the accusative of **ti** 'you' as direct object, i.e., **rad(a) te imam** or, less commonly, **lju̯bim te**, which is too literary for everyday use.

Exercise 3

Translate the following sentences into Slovene.

1 My friend likes orange juice.
2 Do you like crêpes?
3 No, I prefer bread and jam.
4 Mojca and Luka like cereal for breakfast.
5 What do you like most for lunch?
6 Peter loves Maja.

Language point

Favorite activities

The expression **rad** can be used with other verbs in the present tense to say that one enjoys doing something. The position of **rad** does not change like it does with **imeti**. Make sure that **rad** agrees in number and gender with the subject. For example:

Anže rad igra računalniške *i*grice.
Anže likes to play computer games.

V prostem času mama in oče rada hodita v hribe.
In their spare time, my mom and dad like to hike.

Kadar imam čas, rada kolesarim in plavam.
When I have time, I [f.] like to bike and swim.

Tina rada spi.
Tina likes to sleep.

Exercise 4

Say in full sentences who likes to do each activity.

		Andrej	Tina	Marko	Sonja
1	hike	✔		✔	✔
2	swim		✔		
3	bike			✔	
4	play tennis		✔		✔
5	ski	✔	✔	✔	✔
6	golf	✔		✔	

 Dialogue 2

 A si vegetarijanec? Are you a vegetarian? (Audio 1:74)

Nejc calls Lara about their lunch date. They need to agree on a restaurant. What food preferences do they have?

LARA   Halọ?
NEJC   Žịvjo, Lara, Nejc tụkaj. A si še za kosịlo?
LARA   Sevẹda, jụtri. Kam pa grẹva?
NEJC   Ne vẹm. Kaj rada jẹš: pịco, solato, kitajsko, mẹhiško, . . .
LARA   Kitajske in mẹhiške hrane nịmam rada. Ne maram preveč
          začịnjene hrane. Kaj pa tị?
NEJC   Zadnje čase jẹm zelọ malo mesạ.
LARA   A si vegetarijanec?
NEJC   Nịsẹm, ampak raje imam jedị brez mesa, ker so bolj zdrave.
          A poznaš kakšno dobro vegetarijansko restavracijo?
LARA   Tụ blịzu našega faksa je nova špageterịja. Imajo razne
          testenịne, pịce in solate. Vse imaš lahkọ brez mesa.
          Pọrcije so velịke in pocẹni.
NEJC   Super. Dobịva se pred faksom ob enih.
LARA   V rẹdu. Čao.

LARA   *Hello?*

NEJC   *Hi, Lara, this is Nejc. Do you still want to go for lunch?*

LARA   *Of course, tomorrow. Where are we going?*

NEJC   *I don't know. What do you like to eat: pizza, salad, Chinese, Mexican . . . ?*

LARA   *I don't like Chinese or Mexican food. I don't like overly spicy food. What about you?*

NEJC   *Lately I have been eating very little meat.*

LARA   *Are you a vegetarian?*

NEJC   *I am not, but I prefer dishes without meat because they are healthier. Do you know of a good vegetarian restaurant?*

LARA   *There is a new pasta place close to our school. They have different kinds of pasta, pizza, and salads. You can have everything without meat. Portions are large and cheap.*

NEJC   *Super. Let's meet in front of school at one.*

LARA   *OK. Bye.*

Vocabulary

blizu (+G)	near		**poznati**	to know, be familiar with
bolj	more (higher degree)			
brez (+G)	without		**preveč**	too (much)
dobiti se	to meet up		**preveč začinjen**	too spicy
hrana	food		**razni** (pl.)	various
ker	because		**solata**	salad
kitajski	Chinese		**testenine** (pl.)	pasta
mehiški	Mexican		**vegetarijanec**	vegetarian (m.)
meso	meat		**vegetarijanski**	vegetarian (adj.)
pica	pizza		**vse**	everything
poceni	cheap		**zdrav**	healthy
porcija	portion		**bolj zdrav**	healthier

Language points

Expressing dislikes

To say that you don't care for something or somebody, you negate the verb in the expression **imęti rad**. With the negated verb, the direct object must be in the genitive case:

Lara níma rada kitajske in męhiške hrane.
Lara doesn't like Chinese and Mexican food.

Similarly, this can be done with the negated verb **marati**. For example:

Ne maram špinače.   I don't like spinach.

You would express more intense dislike with **ne prenesem** 'I can't stand' and the genitive, as in **Ne prenesem kalamarov** 'I can't stand squid.'

Brez 'without' **with the genitive**

The preposition **brez** 'without' is one of several prepositions that take the genitive case. An example from the dialogue:

Raje imam jedí brez mesa.   I prefer dishes without meat.

Some examples from the food-advertising industry:

kava brez kofeína	coffee without caffeine
sǫk brez (dodanega) sladkǫrja	juice without (added) sugar
pívo brez alkohǫla	beer without alcohol
mlęko brez maščǫb	non-fat milk
hrana brez konzervansov	food without preservatives
ǫlje brez holesterǫla	cholesterol-free oil

Masculine nouns ending in -r

Note that the genitive of **sladkor** 'sugar' is **sladkǫrja**. Most masculine nouns with more than one syllable and ending in a vowel (except schwa) + **r** add **j** to the stem before adding any ending, not just the genitive singular, e.g., **denar** 'money' **denarja**, **krompir** 'potato' **krompirja**, **kuhar** 'cook (m.)' **kuharja**. There is a fairly large number of exceptions to this rule, which you will have to memorize. Note that the genitive plural of the nouns that extend their stem with **j** ends in **-ev**, e.g., **kuharjev**, **krompirjev**.

Exercise 5

Ask your friend if she likes the following things and provide negative answers.

1 tea without sugar
2 coffee without caffeine
3 lunch without meat
4 beer without alcohol
5 cereal without milk

Language points

Vocabulary building

Obroki **'meals'**

zajtrk	breakfast	**kosilo**	lunch
malica	snack	**večerja**	dinner

The main meal of the day is **kosilo**. When not constrained by work schedules, people in Slovenia typically eat lunch in the early afternoon, between 1 and 3 P.M. A full main meal includes **juha** 'soup', some kind of **meso** 'meat', **priloga** 'side dish', **solata** 'salad', and **sladica** 'dessert'. **Večerja** is usually a light meal, often consisting of bread and cold cuts, a milk product or a salad, typically consumed between 7 and 9 P.M. Dining out, in a **restavracija** or **gostilna** 'restaurant', is for special occasions and in that case people will eat a more substantial meal in the evening.

Jedi **'dishes'**

Following are some typical dishes for each course of the main meal that you will find on a Slovene **jedilnik** 'menu':

juhe 'soups'
  goveja/zelenjavna juha beef/vegetable soup
mesne jedi meat dishes
  telęčja pečenka veal roast **svinjska pečenka** pork roast
  ocvrt piščanęc fried chicken **puranji zręzęk** turkey cutlet
  gǫlaž gulash
prilǫge side dishes
  krompir potatoes **riž** rice **ręzanci** noodles **testenine** (pl.)
  pasta **kuhana zelenjava** boiled (steamed) vegetables
solate salads
  zelena/męšana/paradižnikova solata green/mixed [usually of
  greens and beans]/tomato salad
sladice desserts
  zavitęk strudel **potica** nut roll **tǫrta** layer cake **palačinke**
  crêpes **sladolęd** ice cream

Potica

 Offering food (Audio 1:76)

Notice how Alenka suggests something for breakfast:

A bi mogǫče ocvrto ali mehko kuhano jajce za zajtrk?
Would you perhaps like a fried or a soft-boiled egg for
breakfast?

The word **radi** is left out, but implied; therefore, the thing that is offered is still a direct object (accusative); **bi** stays unchanged regardless of formality.
Here are some more examples:

A bi juho? — Would you like (some) soup?
Janez, a bi mešano solato? — Janez, would you like (some) mixed salad?

It is customary for Slovenes and considered proper hospitality to offer food to guests repeatedly, so you will most likely hear your host say:

A bi še (juho/solato/zavitek . . .)?
Would you like some more (soup/salad/strudel . . .)?

More formal:

Izvoli(te) še (juho/solato/zavitek . . .).
Here you go, some more (soup/salad/strudel . . .).

Complimenting the host, politely declining food, toasting

In accepting seconds, you might include a compliment to the host (**gostitelj**). For example:

Ja, prosim, juha je zelo okusna.
Yes, please. The soup is very tasty.

Ja, prosim, zavitek je res odličen.
Yes, please. The strudel is really excellent.

Here are some examples of politely declining food:

Ne, hvala. Zavitek je odličen, ampak jaz sem sit(a).
No, thank you. The strudel is excellent, but I am full.

Zelo je okusno, ampak nisem več lačen/lačna.
It is very tasty, but I am not hungry any more.

Zelo je dobro, ampak žal ne morem več.
It is very good, but, unfortunately, I can't (eat) any more.

Before starting a meal, the host (or anyone from a group when there is no host) will say **dober tęk** 'bon appétit'; the answer to that is **hvala enako** 'thank you, the same to you'. To toast, you say **na zdravje** 'to (your) health'.

Exercise 6

The dishes on the menu are all mixed up. Arrange them by categories.

For example: **juhe: zelenjavna juha . . .**

torta, goveja juha, palačinke, testenine, puranji zrezek, krompir, sladoled, ocvrt piščanec, mešana solata, riž, kuhana zelenjava, potica, svinjska pečenka, zelena solata, zelenjavna juha, golaž

Exercise 7

Do the following things in Slovene.

1 Offer your guest more salad.
2 Politely decline what is offered, say you are full.
3 Say that the soup is very tasty.
4 Ask if your guest would like dessert.
5 Find out if your friend [m.] is a vegetarian.
6 Find out from your guests if they like spicy food.

Reading

Moja najljubša (favorite) **hrana** (Audio 1:77)

When school children were asked about their food preferences, here is what some of them said:

Sara (10 let): Ne maram zelenjave, čeprav ['even if'] je zdrava. Jem samo zelenjavno juho in zeleno solato. Tudi sadja ['fruit'] ne maram preveč. Rada imam sladkarije ['sweets'].

Blaž (12 let): Najraje imam dunajski zrezek ['Wiener schnitzel'] in pomfri ['French fries']. Rad imam ocvrto hrano. Vem, da to ni zdravo. Na srečo ['fortunately'] ocvrto hrano jem samo včasih in ne vsak dan.

Eva (8 let): Moja najljubša hrana je sladoled. Drugih sladkarij ne jem, ker niso dobre za zobe ['teeth'].

Polona (11 let): Brez zelenjave ni zdravega kosila. Obožujem ['adore'] solate. Samo špinače ne prenesem, ker nima dobrega okusa.

Žiga (13 let): Najraje jem ribe ['fish'] in kalamare, obožujem vso hrano iz ['from'] morja.

Exercise 8

a Based on the information from the survey, write down what the children's favorite and least favorite foods are.
b Which children express awareness of what food is good for them?

Unit Eight
Še o sorodnikih
More about relatives

In this unit you will learn about:

- More about family
- The locative case
- Particles **še** and **že**
- Verbs with **se/si**
- Verbal pairs

Dialogue 1

Kję živijo vaši starši? Where do your parents live?
(Audio 1:79)

Andrej and Ben are talking some more about their families. How many siblings do they have? Are they married? Do they have any children? What do Andrej's parents do?

ANDREJ   A imate vi brata ali sestro?

BEN   Imam mlajšega brata, imę mu je Chris. V New Yorku študira medicino.

ANDREJ   Je poročen?

BEN   Ni, ampak ima punco. Hodita že dvę lęti. Drugo lęto se nameravata poročiti.

ANDREJ   Tudi jaz imam majhno družino: samo mamo, očęta in sestro.

BEN   Je sestra mlajša ali starejša kot vi?
ANDREJ Precej mlajša je, a je že poročena. Ima trilẹtno punčko in
        jesẹni pričakuje drugega otroka.
BEN   A so starši žẹ upokọjeni?
ANDREJ Ja, žẹ nẹkaj lẹt. Živijo v Kamniku, v isti hiši kot sestra.
        Varujejo malo nečakinjo, kadar sta sestra in svak v službi.
        Kjẹ pa živijo vaši starši?
BEN   V majhnem kraju v Pensilvaniji. Tam je rojena mama, oče
        pa v Clevelandu, a pravi, da je doma v Slovẹniji. Ima
        sorọdnike nekjẹ pri Ribnici* in zelọ dobro se počuti na
        Dolẹnjskem.

Kapela na Malem gradu v Kamniku

ANDREJ   *Do you have a brother or sister?*

BEN   *I have a younger brother. His name is Chris. He studies medicine in New York.*

ANDREJ   *Is he married?*

BEN   *No, he is not, but he has a girlfriend. They have been together for two years. Next year they are planning to get married.*

ANDREJ   *I also have a small family: just my mom, my dad, and my sister.*

BEN   *Is your sister younger or older than you?*

ANDREJ   *She is considerably younger, but she is already married. She has a three-year-old girl and she is expecting her second child in the fall.*

BEN   *Are your parents retired yet?*

ANDREJ   *Yes, for several years already. They live in Kamnik, in the same house as my sister. They baby-sit my little niece while my sister and brother-in-law are at work. Where do your parents live?*

BEN   *In a small town in Pennsylvania. My mom was born there, my dad [was born] in Cleveland, but he says that his home is in Slovenia. He has relatives somewhere near Ribnica and he feels very well in Lower Carniola.*

---

* **Ríbnica**: a small town in Lower Carniola (**Dolęnjska**), a region south of Ljubljana.

Vocabulary

drugi	second (adj.)	**medicína**	medicine (as a field)
drugo lęto	next year		
hǫdita	they are dating	**mlajši**	younger
ísti	the same	**najbǫlje**	best (adv.)
jesęni	in fall	**nameravati**	to intend
kadar	whenever (conj.)	**nečakinja**	niece
kot	than	**nękaj**	a few
kraj	town	**nekję**	somewhere
lęto	year	**otrok**, pl. **otroci**	child

počut*i***ti se**	to feel		**pun***č***ka**	little girl
poro*č***en**	married		**sestra**	sister
poro*č***iti se**	to get married		**sor***o***dnik**	relative
precej	fair amount		**starejši**	older
pri (+L)	near, by		**tr***i***let***e***n**	three-year-old
pri*č***ak|ov***a***ti**	to expect		**upok***o***jen**	retired
-*u***jem**			**var|ov***a***ti -***u***jem**	to take care

Language point

The locative case

In the dialogue you have several prepositional phrases indicating the location of verbal action. For example:

Živ*i***ta *v Kamniku*, v is***t***i hiši kot sestra.**
They live in Kamnik, in the same house as my sister.

Zel*o* **dobro se poč***u***ti *na Dol***e***njskem*.**
He feels very well in Lower Carniola.

Im*a* **sor***o***dnike nekj***e* *pri Ribnici*.**
He has relatives somewhere near Ribnica.

The case used with the prepositions **v** and **na** this time is locative. Refer back to Unit 6 for the rules about using **v** vs. **na**. Although these prepositions are familiar to you, as you have been using them to say 'to' with the accusative, e.g., **Gr***e***m v Ljubljan***o**, remember that you need to use the locative case with them to say 'in', 'on', or 'at'. Other prepositions commonly used with the locative:

pri 'by, near' a place, e.g., **pri R***i***bnici** 'near Ribnica';
ob 'next to' an object, e.g., **ob h***i***ši** 'next to the house';
o 'about', e.g., **govor***i***m o Slov***e***niji** 'I am talking about
    Slovenia'.

Pri is also used with nouns denoting people to say 'at that person's [place]', e.g., **pri Marku** 'at Marko's [place]'. The locative case is always used with a preposition.

Locative singular of nouns and adjectives

The locative singular endings are **-u** for masculine and neuter nouns (**Kamniku, Clevelandu, mestu**), and **-i** for feminine nouns and adjectives (*isti h*/**ši, Sloveniji**). The masculine/neuter ending for adjectives is **-em** (**majhnem**).

Locative plural and dual of nouns and adjectives

You have been using these forms with the preposition **ob** for temporal expressions like **ob petkih, ob sobotah**. The locative plural and dual endings are the same. Most masculine and neuter nouns end in -**ih**, e.g., **(ob) petkih, (o) sorodnikih, (v) k**/**oskih, mestih**. The majority of feminine nouns end in -**ah**, e.g., **(ob) sobotah, (v) h**/**šah**. The ending for all three genders of adjectives in dual and plural is the same, i.e., you need to memorize only the ending -**ih** (remember **ob petih**), e.g., **(v) vel**/**kih k**/**oskih/bankah/jezerih**.

Here is an overview of basic locative endings for nouns and adjectives.

	m./n.		f.	
	adj.	noun	adj.	noun
sg.	velikem	k/osku jezeru	veliki	banki
pl. du.	velikih	k/oskih jezerih	velikih	bankah

Exercise 1

Say in complete sentences where the following people live.

1 sestra – univerzitetno mesto
2 starši – stara hiša
3 profesor – lepa soseska ('neighborhood')
4 teta – majhen kraj
5 bratranec – velik blok ('apartment building')
6 prijatelj – novo stanovanje

Exercise 2

Now say the same thing with the nouns and adjectives in the plural.

Exercise 3

Use the nouns in parentheses in the accusative or locative, as appropriate.

1 V _____ ima poslovne ('business') partnerje. – Pogosto potuje
   v _____. (Pariz)
2 A tečeš v _____? – Ja, v _____ moram biti že ob pol osmih.
   (šola)
3 Sestra študira na _____, brat pa hodi še v _____. (fakulteta,
   srednja šola)
4 V _____ se vozim z vlakom. – Danes imam v _____ že zgodaj
   sestanek. (služba)
5 Luka vsak teden leti v _____. – V _____ je ponavadi samo
   nekaj ur. (Rim)
6 A pogosto hodite v _____? – Samo na dopustu ('vacation') jemo
   v _____. (restavracija, pl.)

Language points

The noun oče and personal names ending in -e

The noun **oče**, as well as Slovene male personal names ending in **-e**,
like **Anže, Jure, France**, add **-t-** before adding any ending; therefore,
their genitive (and accusative) singular is **očęta, Anžęta, Juręta, Francęta**.
In everyday spoken language, Slovene male names ending in other
vowels, like **Marko, Jani**, are treated the same way (G sg. **Markota,
Janita**), but this is not acceptable in standard written language.

To say `already', `yet' and `still', `not yet'

Notice two particles that are very similar in appearance, but not at
all in meaning: **žę** for 'already, yet' and **še** for 'still, not yet'.

Sestra je žę poročena.   (My) sister is already married.
A so starši žę upokojeni?   Are (your) parents retired yet?

Oče še ni upokojen. My father is not retired yet.
Za alkohol je še prezgodaj. It is still too early for alcohol.

Note that they appear in front of the word or phrase in focus, not at the end of the sentence as 'yet' and 'already' often do.

Exercise 4

Find the most appropriate Slovene equivalent to each English sentence.

1 Is Marko married yet?
   (a) A Marko še ni poročen? (b) A je Marko že poročen? (c) A je Marko še poročen?
2 My sister has a child already.
   (a) Sestra ima že otroka. (b) Sestra ima še otroka. (c) Sestra ima otroka že.
3 My parents are not retired yet.
   (a) Starši še niso upokojeni. (b) Starši že niso upokojeni. (c) Starši so še upokojeni.
4 Is Ana still married?
   (a) A Ana še ni poročena? (b) A je Ana že poročena? (c) A je Ana še poročena?

Language points

Verbs with se/si

You might have noticed that some verbs come with **se**, as in:

Nameravata se poročiti drugo leto.
Next year they are planning to get married.

Zelo dobro se počuti na Dolenjskem.
He feels very well in Dolenjsko.

Kako se pišeš? What is your last name?
Kava se vedno priléže. Coffee always tastes good.

Some Slovene verbs always have **se** or (less commonly) **si**, respectively, like **smejati se smejim se** 'to laugh', **bati se bojim se** 'to be afraid', **zapomniti si** 'to memorize'. Others come with or without **se/si**, but the two verbs of the pair have a different meaning. Compare these verbs:

pisati **p/šem** to write	**p/šem se** ... my last name
	is ...
prile̦|či -žem to lie down next	**prile̦či se** to do (feel)
to someone	good
poroč/ti to marry	**poroč/ti se** to get married
predstavljati to introduce,	**predstavljati si** to imagine
represent	

Further in the book we will talk about other uses of **se/si** (meaning 'oneself', for example). Be aware that verbs need to be learned and used with **se/si** for specific meanings when listed as such in glossaries. **Se/si** is a clitic and has a fixed (second) position in a clause. Since the verb itself does not, there might be other words between the two, as in the sentence **Oče se zel̦o dobro poču̦ti na Dole̦njskem.**

Adversative conjunctions

Clauses that contrast in meaning are connected with **pa** 'while; on the other hand', positioned after a fully stressed word (or phrasal unit). For exampe:

Mama je rojena v Pensilvaniji, oče pa [je rojen] v Clevelandu.
My mother was born in Pennsylvania, while my father was born in Cleveland.

Clauses with an opposing meaning are connected with **a** or **ampak** 'but' (in formal speech and writing the prepositions **vendar** and **toda** are also used). For example:

Sestra je precej mlajša, a je že̦ poročena.
My sister is considerably younger, but she is already married.

Zel̦o je oku̦sno, ampak jaz nise̦m več lačna.
It is very tasty, but I am not hungry any more.

Vocabulary building: kinship terms

Here are some more kinship terms (in addition to the ones you have learned so far) that will come in handy when talking about **druž/na** 'family' and **sorǫdniki** 'relatives'. Note that there is no term for 'sibling'; rather, the words **brat** 'brother' and/or **sestra** 'sister' are used to express the concept.

Družina
oči or **ati** Daddy **mami(ca)** Mommy **ǫčim** stepfather **mačeha** stepmother

Sorǫdniki
babica or **stara mama** grandmother **dędek** or **stari oče/ata** grandfather **teta** aunt **bratranec** male cousin **sestrična** female cousin **nečak(inja)** nephew/niece **svakinja** sister-in-law **vnuk(inja)** grandson/granddaughter **snaha** daughter-in-law **zet** son-in-law **tast** father-in-law **tašča** mother-in-law

The prefix ne-

Many interrogative pronouns and adverbs have indefinite pairs, formed with the prefix **ne-**. Examples:

Pronouns:

ne- + **kaj** → **nękaj**	something; some (indefinite quantity)
+ **kdǫ** → **nekdǫ**	someone
+ **kakšen** → **nekakšen**	some kind
+ **katęri** → **nekatęri**	some (of)

Adverbs:

ne- + **kję** → **nekję**	somewhere (indefinite location)
+ **kam** → **nękam**	somewhere (indefinite destination)
+ **kakǫ** → **nekako**	somehow

Exercise 5

Correct the statements so that they will correspond to the information in Dialogue 1.

1 Benov starejši brat je še študent.
2 Chris je poročen.
3 Andrejevi starši imajo dva sina in hčerko.
4 Andrejeva družina je velika.

5 Andrejeva sestra ima enega otroka in poleti pričakuje drugega.
6 Andrejeva mama je še v službi.
7 Dedek in babica varujeta vnuka.

Reading

Pismo domov   A letter home (Audio 1:84)

Ben writes an email about his day to his wife, Špela.

Draga Špęla,
    danes je nedęlja, zatǫ ne gręm ne v knjižnico
ne na inštitut. Vstanem pozno, Alęnka skuha
kavo in pripravi zajtrk. Počasi zajtrkujemo,
beremo časopis in se pogovarjamo. Lepǫ je,
nikamor se ne mudi. Ko pozajtrkujem, preberem
ę-pǫšto, se stuširam in oblęčem. Potęm gręva
Andrej in jaz na kratęk sprehod ob ręki, Alęnka
in Anita pa kuhata kosilo. Kasneje tudi midva
pomagava. Andrej ima v četrtek rojstni dan,
a praznuje danes. Na kosilo so povabljeni vsi
bližnji sorǫdniki. Pridejo Andrejevi starši,
sestra, svak in nečakinja. Tu so tudi Alęnkini
starši in Anitin fant. Kosilo imamo ob enih,
ogromno je, kǫsimo skoraj do tręh. Po kosilu
Andrej razręže tǫrto, mi pa zapojemo Kǫl'kor
kapljic tol'ko lęt . . .* Alęnka prinese tudi
potico in kavo. Ob potici in odličnem primorskem vinu potęm sedimo na vrtu, pojemo in
klepetamo skoraj do večęra.
    Škǫda, da ti in Simon nista tukaj. Upam, da
je doma vse v rędu.
    Lępe pozdrave in poljube pošiljam za oba,

Ben

* **Kǫl'kor kapljic tǫl'ko lęt**: a traditional toasting song with wishes for as many
years of life as there are drops of wine.

Majolka

Vocabulary

bl*i*žnji	close (adj.)	**ogrom*e*n**	enormous
br*a*ti berem ipf.	to read	**p*e*ti p*o*jem** ipf./	to sing
prebr*a*ti pf.		**zap*e*ti** pf.	
fant	boy (friend)	**po (kos*i*lu)**	after (lunch)
klepet*a*ti ipf.	to chat	**pogov*a*rjati se** ipf.	to converse
ko	when (conj.)	**polj*u*b**	kiss
k*o*siti ipf.	to have lunch	**pom*a*gati** pf./ipf.	to help
ob*a*	both	**poš*i*ljati** ipf.	
obl*e*|či -čem	to get	**posl*a*ti p*o*šljem**	to send
se pf.	dressed	**pf.**	

povabljen	invited	**rojstni dan**	birthday
prazn|ovati	to celebrate	**sprehod**	stroll
-*u*jem ipf.		**stuš*i*rati se** pf.	to take a
prim*o*rski	from the		shower
	Littoral	**tuš*i*rati se** ipf.	
	region	**šk*o*da**	a pity
pripr*a*viti pf.	to prepare	**trajati** ipf.	to last
pripr*a*vljati ipf.		**upati** ipf.	to hope
razre|zati	to cut up	**vs*i*** pl.	all, everybody
-**žem** pf.		**zajtrk|ovati**	to eat
r*e*zati ipf.		-*u*jem ipf.	breakfast
r*e*ka	river	**pozajtrkovati** pf.	

Language point

Verbal pairs

Look at the verbs in these pairs of sentences:

Po*č*asi *zajtrkujemo* in *beremo* časopis.
We are leisurely eating breakfast and reading the newspaper.

Ko *pozajtrkujem*, *preberem* e-p*o*što.
When I finish eating breakfast, I read (my) email.

Al*e*nka in An*i*ta *pripravljata* kos*i*lo.
Alenka and Anita are making lunch.

Al*e*nka *pripravi* zajtrk.
Alenka makes breakfast.

Vstanem pozno.
I get up late.

Ob d*e*lavnikih *vstajam* zg*o*daj.
On weekdays I get up early.

You notice pairs of verbs that have the same root but differ either by
an extra part at the beginning (called a prefix), or in the part just
before the ending (the suffix). For example:

zajtrkujem	I am eating breakfast	**pozajtrkujem**	I finish eating breakfast
kuhata	they are cooking	**sku**hata	they make (by cooking)
berem	I am reading	**preberem**	I read through
vstajam	I get up [repeatedly]	**vstanem**	I get up
pripravlja	she is preparing	**pripravi**	she prepares (until it's done)

The verbs in the left column denote actions that are either incomplete, in progress, or repetitive, while the verbs in the right column denote actions that are completed or instantaneous, e.g., the process of eating breakfast (taking up a certain amount of time) vs. finishing breakfast (at a certain point in time), or the process of cooking vs. producing something cooked. The verbs expressing completed actions are called *perfective* and the ones expressing incomplete or repetitive actions are called *imperfective*, while the category itself is called *verbal aspect*. Most Slovene verbs come in pairs like this. When learning a verb, you should also learn whether it is perfective (pf.) or imperfective (ipf.), which is marked from this point on in the vocabulary lists.

There is no simple way to determine whether the verb is perfective or imperfective. The majority of simple (non-prefixed) verbs are imperfective. These verbs become perfective when they get a prefix, e.g., **ku**hati ipf.→ **sku**hati pf.; **br**ati ipf.→ **prebr**ati pf. However, a prefix might also change or add a more specific meaning, not just perfectivize the verb, e.g., **preku**hati 'to overcook'. Certain suffixes also help you recognize the aspect: verbs in -**ovati/-evati** -**ujem** are imperfective and most verbs in -**niti** -**nem** are perfective. Some verbs are perfective and imperfective, e.g., **telefon***i*rati 'to phone', **pom***a*gati 'to help'.

Exercise 6

When you are thoroughly familiar with Ben's letter, fill in the missing verbs. Then put the actions in order according to Ben's account of his Sunday.

1 Andrej in Ben _____ na sprehod.
2 Mlakarjevi _____ in _____ na vrtu skoraj do večera.
3 Alenka _____ kavo in _____ zajtrk.

4 _____ Andrejevi starši, sestra, svak in nečakinja.
5 Potem počasi skupaj _____.
6 Ob enih _____ Mlakarjevi kosilo.
7 Alenka _____ tudi potico in kavo.
8 Ko _____, Ben _____ e-pošto.
9 Alenka in Anita _____ kosilo.
10 Po kosilu Andrej _____ torte.
11 V nedeljo Ben pozno _____.

Exercise 7

Complete the sentences with the verbs **pogovarjati se, pisati se, stu-širati se, počutiti se, poročiti se, obleči se** in the appropriate form.

1 Alenka _____ Mlakar.
2 Zjutraj _____ najprej _____, potem _____. (1sg)
3 Moja sestra ima fanta in drugo leto _____ nameravata _____.
4 Ben in Špela _____ vsak dan _____ na Skypeu.
5 Oče _____ zelo dobro _____ v Sloveniji.

Language point

Sentence building: noun ('that') and temporal ('when') clauses

Notice these dependent clauses and the conjunctions that introduce them:

Ko pozajtrkujem, preberem e-pošto.
When I finish breakfast, I read my email.

Škoda, da ti in Simon nista tukaj.
It's a shame that you and Simon are not here.

Upam, da je doma vse v redu.
I hope that everything is OK at home.

Ko introduces the temporal clause, **da** the noun clause that is a statement. Notice that **da** translates the conjunction 'that' only to introduce a noun clause, but not to introduce a relative (adjective) clause, as in 'I don't like the food that they serve.'

The nominal clause normally follows the main clause, while the temporal clause can precede or follow it. Instead of **Ko pozajtrkujem, preberem e-pošto** you can say **Preberem e-pošto, ko pozajtrkujem.** There is a subtle difference in meaning: in the first case the emphasis is on your reading of the email, in the second it is on the time of your reading. Whether it comes first or second, the dependent clause is always separated from the main clause by a comma. Unlike in English, where you could say 'It's a shame you and Simon are not here', in Slovene you cannot leave the subordinating conjunction out. If there are clitics in the subordinate clause, they will come directly after the conjunction, for example, in this causal clause, introduced by the conjunction **ker** 'because':

> **Raje imam jedi brez mesa, ker so bolj zdrave.**
> I prefer dishes without meat, because they are healthier.

 ## Exercise 8

Answer the following questions about Ben's letter.

1 Zakaj ('why') Ben danes pozno vstane?
2 Kdo skuha kavo in pripravi zajtrk?
3 Kaj dela Ben, ko pozajtrkuje?
4 Ali gresta Anita in Alenka na sprehod?
5 Zakaj so vsi bližnji sorodniki povabljeni na kosilo?
6 Kaj imajo za sladico?
7 Ali Andrejevi sorodniki po kosilu odidejo ('leave')?

Unit Nine
Z avtom ali vlakom?

By car or by train?

In this unit you will learn about:

- Transportation
- The past tense
- The instrumental case
- The verbs **vẹdeti** and **povẹdati**
- Prepositions corresponding to 'from'

Dialogue 1

Kakọ ste potovali? How was your trip? **(Audio 1:87)**

Andrej and Alenka pick up Ben at Ljubljana train station after his trip
to Maribor. They are asking questions about his trip.

ALENKA	Kakọ ste potovali, Bẹn?
BEN	Odlično. Potovanje z vlakom je udọbno. Lani sẹm šẹl v Maribor z avtom. Bịl sẹm utrujen in še zamudil sẹm, ker nịsẹm takoj našel fakultẹte.
ANDREJ	Ste šlị s postaje na fakultẹto z avtobusom?
BEN	Nịsẹm, kolẹgica Jana je čakala na postaji in me z avtom peljala na fakultẹto. Vlak je v Maribor pripeljal z zamudo, a sva bila vseeno na fakultẹti žẹ ob pol enajstih.
ANDREJ	A ste imẹli kaj časa za ogled mẹsta?

BEN   Ja, predaval sem do dvanajstih in po predavanju sem se
         še pol ure pogovarjal s študenti. Potem sem šel z Jano
         in njeno prijateljico na kosilo v gostilno Pri treh ribnikih.
ALENKA   To je zelo dobra gostilna v čudovitem mestnem parku.
BEN   Ja, res. Po kosilu smo si ogledali stari del z Lentom.
ALENKA   Ste videli Staro trto in Vodni stolp?
BEN   Smo. V vinoteki sem kupil tole vino za Andreja, ker ima
         danes rojstni dan. Vse najboljše, Andrej.
ANDREJ   O, traminec je moje najljubše vino. Hvala lepa.

Štiristoletna trta

Vocabulary

čakati ipf.	to wait (for)	**me**	me (A of **jaz**)
čudovit	wonderful	**mestni**	city (adj.)
del	part	**naj|ti -dem** pf.	to find
kaj	any	**odlično**	excellently
kolegica	colleague (f.)	**ogled**	viewing
lani	last year	**ogledati si** pf.	to view

pogovarjati se ipf.	to converse	**takoj**	right away
potovanje	travel, trip	**traminec**	variety of white wine
pot|ovati -ujem ipf.	to travel		
		udoben	comfortable
predavati ipf.	to lecture	**vid|eti -im** ipf./pf.	to see
prip|eljati se	to arrive by	**vinoteka**	wine cellar
-eljem se pf.	driving or riding	**vseeno**	nevertheless
		zamuditi pf.	to be late

Vocabulary notes

Lent: the oldest, waterfront, district of Maribor;
Vodni stolp: 'The Water Tower', a 16th-century fortress that protected the city from the south-east (water) side, now a wine cellar;
Stara trta: the world's oldest (over 400 years old) grapevine, in Lent;
Vse najboljše: 'all the best' is how you say 'happy birthday'.

Language points

Expressing actions in the past tense

Note how past actions are expressed in the following sentences:

Predaval sem **do dvanajstih.**   I lectured until noon.
Kolegica Jana *je čakala* **Bena na postaji.**
[His] colleague, Jana, waited for Ben at the station.
Videli smo **Staro trto.**   We saw the Old Vine.

The italicized words are the past tense forms of the verbs **predavati** 'to lecture', **čakati** 'to wait', **videti** 'to see'. Slovene past tense translates as English simple past (e.g., 'I lectured'), present perfect (e.g., 'I have lectured'), past continuous (e.g., 'I was lecturing'), or past perfect continuous (e.g., 'I had been lecturing'); without a context, it is translated as the English simple past tense. It is constructed of two parts: the present tense of the auxiliary **biti** 'to be' and the -l-participle of the verb you want to use in the past tense. Both parts agree with the subject, i.e., in number and person (auxiliary) or number and gender (participle), respectively. To negate a verb in the past tense, use the negative form of the auxiliary. For example:

Ben ni šel z avtobusom na fakulteto.
Ben did not go by bus to the university.

Formation of the -l-participle

The -l-participle is formed from the infinitive.

1 In most cases when the verb ends in -**ti** preceded by a vowel, this is very straightforward: replace the -**ti** with -**l**, e.g., **predavati** → **predaval**, **čakati** → **čakal**, **videti** → **videl**. This is the m. sg. form; for other genders and numbers add the endings as in the chart:

	m.	f.	n.
Sg.	delal	delala	delalo
Du.	delala	delali	delali
Pl.	delali	delale	delala

2 Infinitives ending in -**sti**: replace the -**ti** with -**el**, e.g., **nesti** 'to carry' → **nesel nesla**. Most often the **s** before -**ti** becomes **t**, **d**, or **z** in the participle, e.g., **jesti** 'to eat' → **jedel jedla**; **lesti** 'to crawl' → **lezel lezla**; usually the underlying consonant also appears in the present tense, but not always.

3 Infinitives ending in -**či**: after removing -**či** add **k** or **g** + -**el**, e.g., **peči** 'to bake' → **pekel pekla**; **streči** 'to serve' → **stregel stregla**. Most often you can determine whether the consonant in the participle is **k** or **g** by the present tense: **k** when the verb has -**č**- before the present-tense ending (**peče**), **g** when it has -**ž**- (**streže**).

4 The -l-participle of the verb *iti* 'to go' is **šel šla**; similarly in prefixed verbs from *iti*: **priti** 'to arrive', **prišel**; **oditi** 'to leave', **odšel**.

Note that the past tense of the auxiliary **biti** is constructed the same way as any other verb, e.g., **sem bil, bila** . . . 'I was', **si bil, bila** . . . 'you were'. The -l-participles of **biti** and **iti** are end-stressed.

Exercise 1

Form -l-participles of the following verbs for masculine singular and plural:

1 potovati   4 videti   7 jesti
2 misliti   5 iti   8 piti
3 imeti   6 peljati   9 prinesti

Language point

Word order

If there is no explicit subject or an adverbial to occupy the first position in a simple declarative sentence, the -l-participle will, which means that the auxiliary can follow the participle, as in **Predaval sem do dvanajstih**, or precede it, as in **Kolegica Jana je čakala na postaji.** Other words may come in between, for example:

Kolegica Jana je celo uro čakala na postaji.
My colleague, Jana, waited at the train station for a whole hour.

Se or **si** directly follows any present-tense auxiliary except **je**. For example:

Po kosilu *smo si* ogledali stari del.   After lunch, we viewed the old part.
Ben *se je* peljal z vlakom v Maribor.   Ben went to Maribor by train.

In questions, the auxiliary follows the question word, for example:

Kako ste potovali?   How was your trip?
A ste imeli kaj časa za ogled mesta?   Did you have any time for sightseeing?

In yes/no questions, the question word **a** (or **ali**) can be omitted, and in that case the auxiliary will occupy the first position, for example:

Ste videli Staro trto in Vodni stolp?
Did you see the Old Vine and the Water Tower?

Lent: Vodni stolp z vinoteko

In a short answer to a yes/no question you use the auxiliary alone:

Ste šli s postaje na fakulteto z avtobusom?
(Ja,) sem./(Ne,) nisem.
Did you go from the train station to the university by bus?
    Yes, I did./No, I did not.

Exercise 2

Rewrite the following part of Ben's account of his Sunday in the past
tense.

Pridejo Andrejevi starši, sestra, svak in nečakinja. Tu so tudi Alenkini starši in Anitin fant. Kosilo imamo ob enih, ogromno je, kosimo skoraj do treh. Po kosilu Andrej razreže torto, mi pa zapojemo Kol'kor kapljic tol'ko let . . . Alenka prinese tudi potico in kavo. Ob potici in odličnem primorskem vinu potem sedimo na vrtu, pojemo in klepetamo skoraj do večera.

Exercise 3

These are some things that the Mlakar family planned for Thursday. Only the activities with checkmarks were carried out. Ask questions and give short answers on whether or not the people did each activity, as is shown in the example.

1 Ben predava v Mariboru. ✔ <u>A je Ben predaval v Mariboru? – Ja, je.</u>
2 Alenka pelje Bena na železniško postajo. ✔
3 Anita ima izpit iz ekonomije.
4 Andrej praznuje rojstni dan v službi. ✔
5 Anita in Alenka povabita Andreja na kosilo. ✔
6 Benov vlak pripelje v Ljubljano ob 7h.
7 Alenka in Andrej čakata Bena na ljubljanski postaji. ✔

Dialogue 2

S katerim avtobusom? Which bus to take?
(Audio 1:90)

On the way to lunch with Nejc, Lara is stopped by a tourist who does not know which city bus to take to get to the zoo.

TURIST	Oprost*i*te, gospod*i*čna, a mi lahk*o* pov*e*ste, kat*e*ri *a*vtobus v*o*zi do žival*s*kega v*r*ta?
LARA	M*i*slim, da od gl*a*vne postaje v*o*zi *a*vtobus štev*i*lka tr*i*indvajset. Do postaje se p*e*ljete z dev*e*tko, pot*e*m pa s tr*i*indvajsetko do konca.
TURIST	A lahk*o* plačam z gotov*i*no?
LARA	N*e*, plačate lahk*o* sam*o* z m*e*stno k*a*rtico. K*a*rtico k*u*pite v k*i*osku ali na avtom*a*tu.
TURIST	A mog*o*če v*e*ste, kak*o* pog*o*sto v*o*zi dev*e*tka?
LARA	Ne v*e*m, *a*mpak lahk*o* pogl*e*dava na v*o*zni r*e*d na t*a*bli.

Vocabulary

avtom*a*t	vending machine	**kon*e*c**	end
dev*e*tka	(bus) number 9	**od**	from (a source)
do	(up) to	**pov*e*|dati -m** pf.	to tell
gl*a*vni	main	**t*a*bla**	(display) board
gotov*i*na	cash	**tr*i*indvajsetka**	(bus) number 23
k*a*rtica	card, pass	**v*o*zni r*e*d**	timetable
kat*e*ri	which	**žival*s*ki v*r*t**	zoo

Language point

The instrumental case

The instrumental case is another case, besides the locative, that is always used with a preposition. One of its uses is with the preposition **z** 'by; with' (or **s** in front of a voiceless consonant) to express:

1 the means or instrument of carrying out an action:

Lani s*e*m šel z avtom.	Last year I went by car.
A lahko plačam z gotovino?	May I pay with cash?
Manca riše s svinčnikom po zidu.	Manca is drawing with pencil on the wall.

2 the accompaniment, combination:

> **Bẹn je šel z Jano in njeno prijateljico na kosilo.**
> Ben went for lunch with Jana and her friend.

> **Želite kavo s sladkorjem ali z mlekom?**
> Would you like coffee with sugar or with milk?

Instrumental singular of nouns

The instrumental singular ending of masculine and neuter nouns is -om (-em if following a 'soft' consonant), e.g., **(z) vlakom, letalom** 'airplane', **(s) študentom**. It differs from the adjectival ending, which will be discussed later.

The instrumental singular ending of feminine nouns and adjectives is -o, like in **(z) ladjo** 'ship', **mẹstno kartico** 'city pass' (lit. 'city card'), **njẹno prijateljico** 'her friend'.

Instrumental plural and dual of nouns

The instrumental plural and dual endings of nouns differ, but at least they are the same for masculine and neuter. The plural ending for most masculine and neuter nouns is -i, e.g., **(z) vlaki, letali, (s) študenti**, and for feminine -ami, e.g., **(z) ladjami, (s) prijateljicami**. The dual endings for masculine and neuter are -oma/-ema, e.g., **(z) vlakoma, letaloma, (s) študentoma**, while for feminine it is -ama, e.g., **(z) ladjama, (s) prijateljicama**.

Here is an overview of the instrumental endings for nouns:

	Masculine	Feminine	Neuter
I sg.	vlakom	ladjo	letalom
I pl.	vlaki	ladjami	letali
I du.	vlakoma	ladjama	letaloma

	m./n.	f.
sg.	-om*	-o
pl.	-i	-ami
du.	-oma*	-ama

* -em(a) before **c, č, j, š, ž**

Exercise 4

Complete the sentences using the nouns in parentheses in the instrumental case with the preposition **z** or **s**.

1 Iz Ljubljane v New York danes potujemo _____. (letalo)
2 Moja babica je potovala v Ameriko _____. (ladja)
3 Ben je šel lani v Maribor _____. (avto)
4 Letos ('this year') se je raje peljal _____. (vlak)
5 Na mestnem avtobusu ne morete plačati _____. (gotovina)
6 Želite kavo _____ ali brez sladkorja? (sladkor)
7 Od postaje do živalskega vrta se lahko peljete _____. (avtobus)
8 Marko se v šolo vozi _____. (motor 'motorcycle')

Language point

The verbs vẹdeti 'to know' and povẹdati 'to tell'

These two verbs end up with the same root and conjugation in the present tense, i.e., **vẹdeti vẹm**, **povẹdati povẹm**. Make sure not to confuse them. Examples from the text:

A mogọče vẹste, kakọ pogọsto vọzi devẹtka?
Do you perhaps know how frequently bus number 9 runs?

A mi lahkọ povẹste, katẹri avtobus vọzi do živalskega vrta?
Can you tell me which bus goes to the zoo?

Vẹm and **povẹm** conjugate like **jẹm** and **grẹm**, i.e., they have endings **-ste/-sta** instead of **-te/-ta** in the second-person plural and second- and third-person dual.

Vẹdeti vs. poznati and znati

The verb **vẹdeti** only partially corresponds to the verb 'to know'. It refers to knowing facts, so it is more often used with subordinate clauses than nouns as direct objects.

A vẹš, kjẹ stanuje Sọnja?   Do you know where Sonja lives?
A vẹš Sọnjin naslov?   Do you know Sonja's address?

If talking about being familiar with people or things, you need to use the verb **poznati**. For example:

Poznam Janeza in Tanjo.   I know Janez and Tanja.
Lara dobro pozna Ljubljano.   Lara knows Ljubljana well.

You already know the verb **znati**, which is used for knowing things through active pursuit of knowledge (studying, practice) and skills.

Ben zna dobro slovensko. Ben knows Slovene well.
Slabo znam slovnico. I know grammar poorly.
A znaš plavati? Do you know how to swim?

Note that to say 'to know how to' **znati** with the infinitive is used; do not try to translate 'how'.

Exercise 5

Decide whether you need the verb **vedeti**, **znati**, or **poznati** and use it in the present tense to fill in the blanks.

1 Marjana _____ italijansko.
2 A vi _____, kdaj je odprt fitnes?
3 Marko _____ mojo sestro.
4 Moj sin _____ matematiko veliko bolje ('better') kot jaz.
5 Ne _____ (3du), kdaj imata vlak za Ljubljano.
6 Zdaj že dobro _____ (1sg) Ameriko.
7 Moj prijatelj gre na rafting, a ne _____ plavati.
8 A _____ (2pl), kje stanuje Lucija?

Language points

Prepositions corresponding to 'from'

Several prepositions express the meaning 'from', as in the following sentences:

Ste šli s postaje na fakulteto z avtobusom?
Did you go *from* the station to the university by bus?

Ben se je vrnil *iz* Maribora ob osmih.
Ben returned *from* Maribor at 8.

***Od* glavne postaje vozi avtobus številka triindvajset.**
Bus number 23 runs *from* the main station.

When expressing the place one is moving out of or away from, use the preposition **iz** or **z/s** with the genitive.
   Use **iz** to say 'from' when you would use **v** to say 'to'. Example:

Grem v Maribor. → **Grem iz Maribora.**

Use **z/s** (depending on the voicing of the following sound) to say 'from' when you would use **na** to say 'to'. Example:

Grem na postajo. → **Grem s postaje.**

Make sure to differentiate between **z/s**, meaning 'from' (which takes the genitive), and **z/s**, meaning 'by; with' (which takes the instrumental).

When you want to indicate that the place is the starting point of movement, use **od** with the genitive; it is often used in a pair with **do** 'to; as far as' + G, e.g., **od postaje do živalskega vrta, od Ljubljane do Maribora**; in both cases we are talking about the distance or route between the two points. Also, use **od** (not **iz** or **z/s**) when indicating movement away from a person or an object (not from the inside or the top of it):

Prišla je od Janeza.	She came from Janez's (house).
Odselila sta se od staršev.	They moved away from their parents.
Stopil je od okna.	He stepped away from the window.

 ## Vocabulary building (Audio 1:93)

Javni prevoz 'public transportation'

Slovenia has a well-developed **javni prevoz**. You can get around larger cities, like Ljubljana or Maribor, on the **mestni avtobus** 'city bus', and between cities on **medkrajevni avtobus** 'inter-city bus' or **lokalni vlak** 'commuter train' (as opposed to **mednarodni vlak** 'international train'). The lines (**proge, linije**) of **mestni avtobusi** are numbered, e.g., **avtobus številka devet**, but nouns derived from numerals are often used for short. For example:

Kako pogosto vozi devetka [< avtobus številka devet]?

To ride the **mestni avtobus** in Ljubljana, you need a **mestna kartica (Urbana)**, bought from kiosks or vending machines.

Vozovnica or **vozna karta** '(bus) ticket' for the **medkrajevni avtobus** can be bought at the **avtobusna postaja** 'bus station' or on a bus and for the **vlak** at **železniška postaja**. Here are some examples of expressions a **potnik** 'passenger' might say at the **blagajna** 'ticket counter':

Eno karto do Maribora, prǫsim.
One (train) ticket for Maribor, please.

Prvi/drugi razred, prǫsim.
First/second class, please.

Kǫliko stane povratna karta do Zagreba?
How much does a round-trip ticket to Zagreb cost?

A potrebujem rezervacijo?
Do I need a reservation?

At the information counter (**informacije**):

Na katęrem perǫnu stoji vlak za Maribor?
At what platform is the train for Maribor standing?

Kdaj imam vlak za Celje?
When is my train for Celje?

Kdaj ima prihod/odhod vlak za Dunaj?
When does the train for Vienna arrive/leave?

Vozovnica za vlak in mestna kartica

A vlak/avtobus ustavi v Lit/ji?
Does the train/bus stop in Litija?

Exercise 6

Based on Dialogue 1, determine whether the following statements are true (T), false (F), or there is not enough information (NI) in the text to decide.

1 Ben rad potuje z vlakom.
2 Ben se je od postaje do fakultete peljal s taksijem.
3 Ben je skoraj zamudil na predavanje, ker je imel vlak zamudo.
4 Jana, njena prijateljica in Ben so šli peš na kosilo.
5 Benu je bila gostilna Pri treh ribnikih všeč.*
6 Po kosilu so si ogledali stari del mesta.
7 Ben je za Alenko in Andreja kupil vino.
8 Andrej ima rad traminca.

* **biti všeč** 'to appeal (to somebody)'

Reading

Dobri stari časi (Audio 1:94)

Andrej se spominja potovanja iz mladosti:

»Dobro se spominjam potovanja, ko sva šla z Alenko prvič skupaj na počitnice z avtom. Bila sva še študenta in Alenka je imela starega rumenega fička.* Najina končna destinacija je bil Solun ['Thessaloniki'] v Grčiji ['Greece'] – predaleč za starega fička. Zato sva v Ljubljani fička naložila na vlak in vsi trije smo se peljali do Beograda ['Belgrade']. Ko sva si ogledala Beograd, sva fička spet naložila na vlak in peljali smo se do zadnje postaje v Makedoniji ['Macedonia']. Od tam potem ni bilo več daleč do Soluna.«

* **fičko**: a very small Fiat, a ubiquitous car in the former Yugoslavia.

But in certain instances (e.g., the pronoun is emphasized, in focus, contrasted, or with a preposition) a full form needs to be used. In the first- and second-persons dual and plural, that form is identical to the clitic form plus the stress (e.g., **naju, vaju**); all others are clitic forms extended by the part given in parentheses plus the stress (e.g., **njega, nj/ju**). At this point we are focusing on the clitic forms, but you should be aware of the difference. The genitive forms are identical to the accusative, except for the genitive of **ona**, which is **(n)je**, as in the sentence:

Alenka *je* še n*i* videla.   Alenka has not seen it yet.

If a clitic cluster consists of the present-tense auxiliary and the pronominal accusative, the accusative (or genitive) follows the auxiliary except when the auxiliary is **je**. For example:

Spoznal si ga.   You met him.
Spoznala ga je.   She met him.

Exercise 1

Fill in the accusative or genitive form of the pronoun in parentheses.

1 Prijateljica Jana _____ je peljala na fakulteto. (jaz)
2 Ben _____ ne pozna. (ona)
3 Ustavila sta _____ na postaji. (mi)
4 A _____ je Alenka že videla? (vi)
5 Anita _____ ni povabila na kosilo. (midva)
6 Kdaj _____ je včeraj poklical Borut? (ti)

Exercise 2

Answer the following questions positively as in the example. Replace the italicized words with a pronoun in your answers.

1 A Ben pozna *Ireno in Petra*?   <u>Ja, pozna ju.</u>
2 A sta Irena in Peter prodala *stanovanje*?
3 A sta Peter in Irena ustavila *Mlakarjeve* na postaji?
4 A je Peter poklical *Andreja*?
5 A Peter vidi *planine* iz dnevne sobe?
6 A so zgradili *novo hišo*?
7 A je Andrej naredil *načrt*?

Language points

Verbs in -ovati/-evati

All verbs ending in **-ovati/-evati** (all imperfective), e.g., **stanovati** 'to reside', **oboževati** 'to adore', **pričakovati** 'to expect', **zajtrkovati** 'to have breakfast', **praznovati** 'to celebrate', **potovati** 'to travel', **potrebovati** 'to need', form the present tense by replacing the suffix **-ova-/-eva-** with **-uje-** before adding the present-tense endings. For example:

> **stanovati** → **stanujem, stanuješ, stanuje, stanujeva**, . . .
> **oboževati** → **obožujem, obožuješ, obožuje, obožujeva**, . . .

Temporal adverbials accompanying the past tense

Here are some temporal adverbials that oblige you to use the past tense:

včeraj	yesterday
sinǫči	last night
predvčerajšnjim	the day before yesterday
prejšnji teden/mesec	last week/month
lani	last year
predlanskim	two years ago
pred + I (e.g., **trẹmi lẹti**)	(three years) ago

Exercise 3

Complete the sentences using the verbs **stanovati, potovati, zajtrkovati, potrebovati, pričakovati** in the present or past tense, as appropriate.

1 Običajno _____ (1sg) ob sedmih, ampak včeraj _____ že ob šestih.
2 Kje _____ Peter? Ne vem, kje zdaj _____, lani _____ v študentskem domu.
3 Kdaj nas _____ Novakovi? _____ nas že pred dvema urama.
4 A vidva res _____ novo stanovanje? Ne, _____ ga pred tremi meseci.
5 A Nada pogosto _____ v Ameriko? Zdaj ne, zadnjič _____ predlanskim.

Dialogue 2

Jan potrebuje cimra   Jan needs a roommate
(Audio 2:4)

At lunch, Nejc mentions that he is looking for a place to live. Lara has an idea. What does she suggest?

LARA   A še vedno stanuješ v študentskem domu?

NEJC   Ja, samo še letos. Hočem se preseliti. Iščem stanovanje ali sobo.

LARA   Lahko telefoniraš Janu. Živi v dvosobnem stanovanju in potrebuje novega cimra. Njegov se je prejšnji teden preselil nazaj k staršem.

NEJC   Kakšno je to stanovanje?

LARA   Ni veliko, a je udobno, svetlo in mirno. Ima eno spalnico, dnevno sobo, majhno kuhinjo, kopalnico in WC. Opremljeno je in pohištvo je še precej novo. Ima tudi pralni stroj in internet.

NEJC   In kje je stanovanje?

LARA   V eni hiši na Viču, blizu faksa in postaje mestnega avtobusa.

NEJC   A veš, koliko je najemnina?

LARA   Ne vem natančno, a mislim, da ni draga. Lahko pošljem Janu SMS in ga vprašam.

Vocabulary

cimer	roommate	**pohištvo**	furniture
drag	expensive	**pralni stroj**	washing machine
hoteti hočem ipf.	to want	**SMS [es-em-es]**	text message
iskati iščem ipf.	to look for	**spalnica**	bedroom
kopalnica	bathroom	**svetel**	bright
kuhinja	kitchen	**študentski dom**	student dorm, hall of
letos	this year		residence
miren	peaceful	**telefonirati**	to call (on the phone)
najemnina	rent	pf./ipf.	
nazaj	back to	**vprašati** pf.	to ask (a question)
		WC [ve-ce]	restroom, toilet

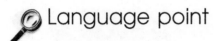

Language point

The dative case

In this unit, we will look at two typical uses of the dative case.

The first use is for the indirect object, meaning the one to whom or for whom the action is done. For example:

Lahkọ telefoniraš Janu.   You can call [phone] Jan.
Sinọči sẹm poslal Irẹni e-pošto. I sent Irena an email last night.

Lara je predlagala Nejcu stanovanje na Viču.
Lara suggested to Nejc an apartment in Vič.

The ending alone (no preposition) marks the recipient of the action. The verbs taking the indirect object often contain the meaning of giving or communicating (something) to someone. Here are some that are familiar to you:

dati dam*	to give	**re|či -čem**	to say
poslati pọšljem	to send	**povẹ|dati -m**	to tell
pomagati	to help	**govoriti**	to speak
(pri)nes|ti -em	to bring	**telefonirati**	to phone
podariti	to give as a gift	**odgovoriti**	to answer
plačati	to pay	**pisati pišem**	to write
kupiti kupim	to buy	**predstaviti**	to introduce
		predlagati	to suggest

* conjugates like **jẹm**

The second use is with the preposition **k** (**h** before **g** or **k**) when indicating movement towards an object or when the destination of movement is a person. For example:

Popoldne grẹmo na obisk k Pẹtru.
In the afternoon, we are going for a visit to Peter's house.

Moj cimer se je preselil k staršem.
My roommate moved to his parents' house.

Grẹm k frizerju/zdravniku/advokatu.
I am going to the hairdresser's/doctor's/lawyer's.

Note that to say 'to someone's place', neither the possessive nor the noun denoting that place (house, apartment, office) is included. Slovene does not distinguish between saying 'I am going to Peter' and 'I am going to Peter's house', as both are rendered **Grem k Petru**. If there is any doubt that we mean going to Peter's residence, we can add the adverb **domov** '[to] home', e.g., **Gremo k Petru domov.**

Make sure to know the difference between the adverbs **domov**, which answers the question **Kam?** (destination of motion), and **doma**, answering the question **Kje?** (location), since English in both cases uses 'home'. For example:

Peter je šel pred eno uro domov in zdaj je doma.
Peter went home an hour ago and now he is home.

Dative singular of nouns

For nouns, the dative endings are identical to the locative ones: **-u** for masculine and neuter (**Petru, mestu**) and **-i** for feminine (**Ireni**).

Dative plural and dual of nouns

Most of these endings will remind you of the instrumental endings you just learned. In the dual, they are actually identical to the instrumental dual: **-oma/-ema** for masculine and neuter (**študentoma, prijateljema, mestoma**) and **-ama** for feminine (**študentkama**). Plural endings are **-om/-em** for masculine and neuter (**študentom, prijateljem, mestom**) and **-am** for feminine (**študentkam**).

Here is an overview of the basic dative endings for nouns.

	m./n	f.
D sg.	**študentu** **mestu**	**študentki**
D pl.	**študentom** **mestom**	**študentkam**
D du.	**študentoma** **mestoma**	**študentkama**

	m./n.	f.
sg.	-u	-i
pl.	-om*	-am
du.	-oma*	-ama

* -em(a) before **c, č, j, š, ž**

Exercise 4

Compose yes/no questions in the past tense from the given words.

1 Andrej/telefonirati/Irena
2 Lara/poslati/Jan/SMS
3 vi/dati/študent (pl.)/naloga
4 Alenka/kupiti/prijatelj (du.)/darilo ('present')
5 ti/prinesti/Andrej/vino za rojstni dan
6 Ben/pisati/Špela

Exercise 5

Give short answers to the questions using the information in parentheses.

1 Kam se je preselil Boris? (starši, Maribor)
2 Kam ste šli sinoči? (prijatelji, Ljubljana)
3 Kam pelješ otroka? (babica, mesto)
4 Kam potujejo Mlakarjevi? (sorodniki, morje)
5 Kam hodiš ob nedeljah? (brat, Gorenjsko)
6 Kam ste šli včeraj na obisk? (gospod Kovač, bolnica)

Language point

Vocabulary building

Types of housing: (**pritlična** 'one-story'/**enonadstropna** 'two-story', **vrstna** 'attached') **hiša** 'house', **blok** 'apartment building', (**eno-** 'one-'/**dvo-** 'two-'/**trosobno** 'three-room') **stanovanje** 'apartment', **garsonjera** 'studio', **mansarda** 'loft'.

Prostor 'room'	**Pohištvo** 'furniture' and items typically in the room:
A kopalnica	**1 tuš**; **2 umivalnik**; **WC školjka** toilet; **ogledalo** mirror; **brisača** towel
B predsoba	**omara za plašče** coat closet
C kuhinja	**3 štedilnik**; **4 pomivalno korito**; **hladilnik** fridge; **posoda** dishes
D jedilnica	**5 miza**; **6 stol**

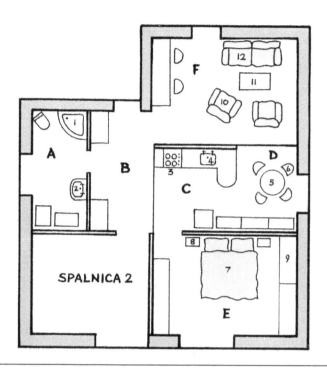

Načrt trosobnega stanovanja

E spalnica	**7 postelja; 8 nočna omarica; 9 omara; posteljnina** linens; **odeja** blanket; **blazina** pillow
F dnevna soba	**10 fotelj; 11 klubska mizica; 12 kavč; televizor** TV; **regal** entertainment center; **preproga** rug; **zavesa** curtain
pisarna office	**pisalna miza** desk; **(namizna) svetilka** (table) lamp; **police** shelves

Remember that **prvo nadstropje** 'first floor' is the floor above the ground floor (**pritličje**). The living room is included in the number of rooms; therefore, **dvosobno stanovanje** will most likely have one bedroom and a living room, **trosobno** two bedrooms. The unit of measurement for housing is **kvadratni meter** (m²), 'square meter', colloquially also **kvadrat**, which approximately equals 10 ft². **Oglasi** 'ads' will list the **cena** 'price (of rent)' per month, usually not including **stroški** 'utilities'.

Stanovanja - Oddam

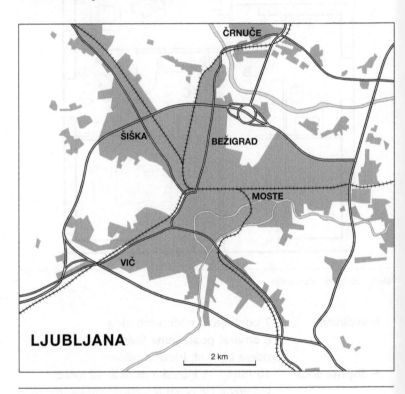

Ljubljana

A	Enosobno stanovanje v **CENTRU** blizu železniške postaje, delno opremljeno, vseljivo takoj, oddam mirnemu paru, cena 350 evrov + stroški. Tel. 062/834-570
B	V **ČRNUČAH** oddamo prostorno, svetlo stanovanje v stolpnici, 66 m² – spalnica, velika dnevna soba, kuhinja, kopalnica in predsoba, dvigalo, bližina mestnega avtobusa, mirna lokacija. Tel. 061/444-372
C	Trosobno stanovanje v **MOSTAH**, prenovljeno l. 2005, pritličje, možnost parkiranja, vsi priključki, opremljeno, oddamo. 600 evrov + stroški (okrog 100 evr./mesec). Tel. 043/555-387
D	V **ŠIŠKI**, blizu Tivolija, oddam garsonjero, 30 m², popolnoma opremljeno, z ločeno kuhinjo, v 1. nadstropju, nizek blok, vsi priključki, bližina infrastrukture, oddam samski osebi ali paru brez otrok. Cena: 370 evrov. Tel. 062/271-431
E	Iščemo cimro za sobo v hiši za **BEŽIGRADOM** blizu ekonomske fakultete. V hiši živimo samo študentke. Souporaba kuhinje, kopalnice, hodnika in balkona. Internet, parking. Cena: 120 evrov. Tel. 061/040-219

Vocabulary

oddajati ipf./**oddati** pf.	to rent out
priključek	hook-up (like Internet, cable)
samska oseba	single person
souporaba	joint use
vseljiv	ready to move in

Exercise 6

From the ads above choose the apartment that best satisfies each person's needs.

1 An old lady needs a spacious apartment in a quiet area; she cannot walk upstairs.
2 A student needs a room in a house shared with other students.
3 A young professional is looking for a small furnished apartment.

4 A family with two children and a car is looking for an apartment.
5 A young couple needs a small apartment in the city center immediately.

Dialogue 3

Enopọsteljna ali dvopọsteljna soba?   Single or double room? **(Audio 2:7)**

Katja saw the ad for a room in Bežigrad. It is not clear whether she will have the room to herself or will have to share, so she decides to call. What does she find out? Do you think she will take the room?

ŽENSKI GLAS	Halọ?
KATJA	Dober dan. Kli̇čem zaradi oglasa. A še oddajate sobo?
ŽG	Ja, še. Kaj te pa zani̇ma?
KATJA	Kakọ veli̇ka je in a je enopọsteljna ali dvopọsteljna?
ŽG	Kar veli̇ka je, okrọg dvajset kvadratov, dvopọsteljna.
KATJA	A so strọški vključeni v cẹno?
ŽG	Ne, posẹbej so. Ponavadi so okrog tri̇deset ẹvrov na mẹsec.
KATJA	Hvala, na svi̇denje.
ŽG	Na svi̇denje.

Vocabulary

posẹbej	separately
vključen	included
zani̇mati (ipf.) **kọga**	to interest someone
zaradi (+G)	because of

Exercise 7

The furniture store **Dom pohištva** has the following **oddelki** 'departments':

1 **Kopalnica**
2 **Kuhinja**
3 **Dnevna soba**

4 **Spalnica**
5 **Pisarna**
6 **Tekstil**

Here is the list of things you need to buy. Sort them by the departments where they would be located:

kavč, kuhinjske omare, postelja, kopalna kad, pisalna miza, regal, odeje, pomivalno korito, klubska miza, garderobna omara, umivalnik, štedilnik, posteljnina, police, preproga

Exercise 8

Answer the following questions about Dialogue 2.

1 Kje stanuje Nejc in kje Jan?
2 Zakaj Jan potrebuje novega cimra?
3 Kakšno stanovanje ima?
4 Katere prostore ima njegovo stanovanje?
5 Kako je opremljeno?
6 Kakšno lokacijo ima stanovanje?

Unit Eleven
Načrti za vikend
Weekend plans

In this unit you will learn about:

- The weather
- Seasons, months
- Shopping for food
- The future tense
- The genitive of adjectives
- Nouns with numerals and other quantifiers

 Dialogue 1

 Kakšno bo jutri vreme? What will the weather be like tomorrow? **(Audio 2:9)**

It has been raining a lot. The Mlakar family wants to make plans for the weekend, but they depend on the weather. What is the weekend forecast like and what do they decide to do?

BEN   A je junija v Sloveniji vędno takǫ hladnǫ in dežẹvno?

ANDREJ   Ne, ponavadi je junija prijętno toplǫ. Včasih je tudi vrǫče s popoldanskimi plohami in nevihtami. Lętos imamo zelǫ čudno vreme.

ALENKA   Ampak konęc tędna bo sǫnčno in tudi ogrẹlo se bo. Vremẹnska napoved pravi, da bo jutri pętindvajset stopinj.

ANDREJ	Končno bomo lahko imeli piknik na našem vikendu. Sedeli bomo v senci in pekli meso in zelenjavo na žaru.
ALENKA	Že nocoj bom spekla jabolčni zavitek. Povabila bom tudi Anito in njenega Boruta. Onadva bosta najbrž pripeljala še kakšnega prijatelja in bo veselo.
BEN	Bomo v vikendu tudi prenočili?
ANDREJ	Ne, naš vikend je zelo majhen in nima dovolj postelj za vse.
BEN	In kako zgodaj bomo krenili na pot?
ALENKA	Ne zelo zgodaj, verjetno okrog desetih. Do vikenda je samo pol ure vožnje. Jaz bom zjutraj še malo pospravila, Andrej bo šel pa v trgovino. Vi boste lahko spali vsaj do devetih.
BEN	Ne bom, raje bom šel z Andrejem v trgovino.

Vocabulary

čuden	strange	**prenočiti** pf.	to overnight
deževen	rainy	**prip|eljati**	to bring
hladen	cool, chilly	**-eljem** pf.	
junij	June	**sončen**	sunny
končno	finally	**spati spim** ipf.	to sleep
kreniti krenem pf.	to set out	**spe|či -čem** pf.	to bake
napoved	forecast	**stopinja**	degree
nevihta	storm	**topel**	warm
ogre|ti -jem se pf.	to get warm	**verjetno**	probably
		vesel	merry
piknik	picnic	**vožnja**	drive
ploha	shower (rain)	**vreme**	weather
popoldanski	afternoon (adj.)	**vremenski** adj.	
pospraviti pf.	to clean up	**vroč**	hot
pov|abiti -abim pf.	to invite	**vsaj**	at least

Vocabulary notes

vikend: besides 'end of the week', as in the title of the dialogue, the word also means 'house for weekend retreat'. Many Slovenes own a

Vikend. Photograph by Miran Hladnik

vikend, which is often a modest cottage either in the mountains or at least close to nature.

 # Language point

The future tense

The future tense is constructed from the unstressed simple future tense of **biti** 'to be' and the -l-participle of the verb you want to use in the future tense. The rules of agreement are the same as with the past tense. Here is the future-tense conjugation of **biti** (like **vęm** or **gręm**):

	sg.	du.	pl.
1	**bom**	**bova**	**bomo**
2	**boš**	**bosta**	**boste**
3	**bo**	**bosta**	**bodo/bojo**

This is the only future-tense form of **biti**, i.e., it is not constructed of two parts like the future tense of other verbs. For example:

Konec tędna *bo* sǫnčno.	It will be sunny this weekend.
Nocǫj *bom* spekla	I will bake an apple strudel
jabolčni zavitek.	tonight.
Andrej *bo* šę̆l v trgovino.	Andrej will go to the market.

The same word-order rules apply as you learned with the past tense if the future auxiliary is the only clitic. If there are other clitics, then it takes the same place as **je**. For example:

Ogrę̆lo se bo.	It will warm up.
Ogrę̆lo se je.	It warmed up.

To negate the verb in the future tense, use **ne** in front of the future auxiliary. The negated auxiliary will normally precede the participle, i.e., both together may appear at the beginning of the sentence. For example:

Bęn *ne bo* spal do devetih.	Ben will not sleep until nine.
***Ne bo* se ogrę̆lo.**	It won't warm up.

Exercise 1

Based on the information from Dialogue 1, complete the sentences with the appropriate verbs in the future tense.

1 Konec tedna _____ sončno.
2 Mlakarjevi _____ piknik.
3 _____ v senci in _____ (3pl., m.) meso na žaru.
4 Alenka _____ že nocoj _____ jabolčni zavitek.
5 Andrej: »Alenka, a _____ na piknik _____ tudi Anito in njenega fanta?«
6 Andrej: »V vikendu ne _____, ker tam ni dovolj postelj za vse.«
7 Zjutraj _____ Alenka malo _____, Andrej pa _____ v trgovino.
8 Ben: »A _____ zgodaj na pot?«

Language points

Vreme 'weather'

The noun **vreme** is neuter singular, which is apparent from the adjectives modifying it, e.g., **lepo/slabo/čudno vreme**. It is extended by **-n-** in the oblique cases, then regular endings are added, e.g., **vremena, vremenu**... (note the shift in stress). To describe the weather, i.e., to answer the question **Kakšno je vreme?** 'What is the weather like?', as in English, commonly 'impersonal' sentences (no subject) are used. The impersonal 'it', which appears in the subject position in such sentences in English, does not have an equivalent in Slovene.

Danes je... Today it's...

lepo	nice	**suho**	dry	**deževno**	rainy
sončno	sunny	**soparno**	humid	**megleno**	foggy
jasno	clear	**oblačno**	cloudy	**vetrovno**	windy
toplo	warm	**hladno**	chilly		
vroče	hot	**mraz**	cold		

Dežuje.	It's raining.
Sneži.	It's snowing.
Sonce sije.	The sun is shining.
Veter piha.	The wind is blowing.
Jutri bo dež ali sneg.	There will be rain or snow tomorrow.

Popoldne bodo plohe in nevihte.
There will be showers and thunderstorms in the afternoon.

The gender and number of verbs without a subject is neuter singular. For example:

Jutri bo snežilo.	It will snow tomorrow.
Včeraj je bilo sončno.	It was sunny yesterday.

Temperatura 'temperature' is measured in **stopinje Celzija** 'degrees Celsius'. For a very approximate conversion to Fahrenheit degrees double the number in Celsius and add 32.

Lętni časi 'seasons'

Note the difference between nouns (answering the question **Kaj?** 'what') and adverbs (answering the question **Kdaj?** 'when').

Kaj?	**Kdaj?**
Pomlad* **je običajno dežęvna.**	*Spomladi* **kolesarimo.**
The spring is usually rainy.	We bike in the spring.
Polętje **je vrǫče in suho.**	*Polęti* **hǫdimo v hrỉbe.**
The summer is hot and dry.	We hike in the summer.
Jesęn* **je meglęna.**	*Jesęni* **nabỉramo gǫbe.**
The fall is foggy.	We pick mushrooms in the fall.
Zima **je mrzla.**	*Pozimi* **smučamo.**
The winter is cold.	We ski in the winter.

* The nouns **pomlad** and **jesęn** belong to a minority group of feminine nouns that end in a consonant rather than **-a**. The adjective indicates feminine. This group of nouns has its own declension paradigm (see Unit 16).

Adjectives derived from the nouns for seasons: **pomladni** (e.g., **pomladna temperatura** 'spring temperature'), **polętni** (e.g., **polętni urnik** 'summer schedule'), **jesęnski** (e.g., **jesęnsko vreme** 'fall weather'), **zimski** (e.g., **zimski špǫrt** winter sports).

Męseci 'months'

januar	aprỉl	julij	oktǫber
fębruar	maj	avgust	november
marec	junij	september	december

Names of months are not capitalized in Slovene. To say 'in a particular month', use the name of the month in the genitive case, but no preposition. For example:

Septembra bom diplomỉral.	I will graduate in September.
Anỉta bo fębruarja potovala v Kanado.	Anita will travel to Canada in February.

Note that **januar** and **februar** lengthen with -j- before adding endings; the months with a fleeting schwa drop it before adding endings, e.g., **marca, novembra**. If not in focus (the most important or new information), a temporal adverbial e.g., **jutri, spomladi, februarja**, is not placed at the end of the sentence, but rather at the beginning (*not* offset by a comma) if there is no explicit subject, or following the subject if there is one.

Exercise 2

Here are some things Ben is planning for next year. Imagine you are Ben talking about his plans in Slovene.

1 May   sell the house
2 June   move to Chicago
3 July   Chris gets married
4 August   travel to Slovenia with the family
5 September   begin (**začeti začnem**) a new job

Exercise 3

Translate the following sentences.

1 Marko likes dry and hot summers.
2 My sister will graduate in spring.
3 What is fall like in Slovenia?
4 Does the library now have a summer schedule?
5 This year we had fall weather already in July.
6 Peter bikes in the summer and skis in winter.

Dialogue 2

Nakupovanje za piknik Shopping for a picnic
(Audio 2:13)

On Saturday morning, Andrej and Ben are going to the supermarket. Since they have several things to buy, they divide the job. What is each of them going to get?

ANDREJ Ben, vi boste poiskali kruh, zelenjavo in pijačo. Potrebujemo hlebec črnega kruha, dve kili paradižnika, eno kilo solate, štiri kumare, pol kile mlade čebule pa nekaj piva in ledenega čaja.

BEN Koliko piva in ledenega čaja želite?

ANDREJ Lahko vzamete deset steklenic temnega piva in štiri plastenke ledenega čaja. Jaz bom medtem kupil meso, sir in pršut. Dobiva se pri blagajni.

BEN Mislim, da potrebujem voziček, vi lahko vzamete košaro.

At the meat counter . . .

MESAR Želite, prosim?

ANDREJ Rad bi pol kile mlete svinjine, sedemdeset dek mlete govedine in kilo puranjega mesa.

MESAR Puranjega mesa danes žal nimam. Imam pa čisto sveže piščance.

ANDREJ Potem pa dva piščanca, šest svinjskih zrezkov in tri klobase, prosim.

MESAR Izvolite. Še kaj?

ANDREJ Ne, to bo vse.

MESAR Hvala, na svidenje.

Vocabulary

blagajna	cash register	**mleto meso**	ground meat, mince
čebula	onion	**nekaj**	some
čisto	entirely	**paradižnik**	tomato
deka	decagram	**plastenka**	plastic bottle
govedina	beef	**po|iskati**	to find
hlebec	(round) loaf	-iščem pf.	
kila	kilogram	**pršut**	prosciutto
klobasa	sausage	**steklenica**	bottle
košara	basket	**svinjina**	pork
kumara	cucumber	**voziček**	cart
medtem	meanwhile	**vzeti vzamem** pf.	to take

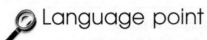 Language point

Expressing quantities

...by counting

The numerals 1–4 distinguish gender (1 all three, 2–4 masculine vs. feminine and neuter) and agree with the counted nouns in gender, number, and case. In the nominative the agreement looks like this:

	m.	f.	n.
Tu je...	en zrezek	ena hruška	eno jabolko
Tu sta...	dva zrezka	dve hruški	dve jabolki
Tu so...	trije zrezki	tri hruške	tri jabolka
Tu so...	štirje zrezki	štiri hruške	štiri jabolka

You already know which accusative forms differ from the nominative:

Imam...

m. sg. (animate)	enega	brata
f. sg.	eno	hruško
m. pl.	tri/štiri	zrezke

The numerals 5–100 do not distinguish gender. In the nominative and accusative they take the genitive plural of the quantified nouns (and adjectives). For example:

Tu je .../ Imam...   pet zrezkov   pet hrušk   pet jabolk

An indefinite number of things is expressed by quantifying adverbs, such as **nekaj** 'a few', **malo** 'few', or **veliko** 'many', which also take the genitive plural, e.g., **nekaj hrušk** 'a few pears', **veliko jabolk** 'many apples'; similarly **koliko** 'how many' (**zrezkov, hrušk, jabolk**). For example:

Koliko bratov ima Ben?
How many brothers does Ben have?

Samo enega.
Only one.

Koliko stopinj bo jutri?
How many degrees will it be tomorrow?

Petindvajset.
Twenty-five.

Exercise 4

Following is a list of items that Vesna needs to buy, with the number of each of the items in parentheses.

banane (5), jajca (10), zrezki (2), piščanec (1), kotleti (4), klobase (7), jabolka (3)

Imagine you are a **prodajalka** asking how many of each item Vesna wants. Write out your questions and Vesna's answers.

Example:

P: Koliko *banan* želite?   **V: *Pẹt banan*, prosim.**

. . . by measuring

When things are measured rather than counted, the amounts may be expressed with measurement (metric) units, e.g., **kilogram** [abbr. **kg**, coll. **kila**], **dekagram** [abbr. **dkg**, coll. **dẹka**], **lit̲e̲r** [abbr. **l**], **decilit̲e̲r** [abbr. **dl**, coll. **dẹci**]; containers or shapes as units, e.g., **steklen̲i̲ca** 'bottle', **plastẹnka** 'plastic bottle', **zav̲i̲tek** 'package', **kozarẹc** 'glass', **skodẹlica** 'cup', **hlẹbẹc (kruha)** 'round (of bread)'; or quantifying adverbs, such as **nẹkaj** 'some', **malo** 'a little bit', or **vel̲i̲ko** 'a lot', **pol** 'half', **četrt** 'a quarter'. All of these quantifiers take the quantified noun (and adjective) in the genitive, i.e., singular if the quantified noun is a mass (uncountable) noun, and plural if it is countable; therefore, **steklen̲i̲ca p̲i̲va, hlẹbec kruha, k̲i̲la mesa, k̲i̲la solate**. With fruit and vegetables, countability often differs from English, as it depends on whether they are seen as a collection of items or as an unbounded mass. In the latter case, the singular is used when talking about a vegetable as a type (e.g., **parad̲i̲žnik** 'tomatoes', **čebula** 'onions', **krompir** 'potatoes', **fižol** 'beans') or the quantity of this vegetable (**k̲i̲la parad̲i̲žnika** 'a kilo of tomatoes', **l̲i̲ter fižọla** 'a liter of beans'). You have to put rules for both counted and measured things together, as most often the amounts will be multiple units or containers of things. For example:

Prọsim. . . .	**tr̲i̲ k̲i̲le hrušk.**	3 kilograms of pears
	dvajset dẹk šunke.	20 decagrams of ham
	pẹt l̲i̲trov v̲i̲na.	5 liters of wine
	eno k̲i̲lo solate.	1 kilogram of lettuce
	dvẹ škatli piškọtov.	2 boxes of cookies

Exercise 5

Write out the amounts in words with the quantified nouns in the correct form.

1 60/dkg/govedina
2 4/steklenica/pivo
3 25/dkg/sir

4 2/kg/paradižnik
5 0,5/kg/salama
6 5/kg/krompir

Exercise 6

Write out Andrej's shopping list. Include the quantities as they appear in the dialogue; use numerals and standard abbreviations for metric units.

Language point

Adjectival genitive endings

By now, you have had some practice with nouns in the genitive and you already know several uses for the genitive case. To be able to use adjectives with nouns in the genitive, you need to learn adjectival endings, which, with the exception of f. sg., differ from the nominal endings. Some examples:

deset steklenic *temnega* piva   ten bottles of dark beer
štiri plastenke *ledenega* čaja   four [plastic] bottles of iced tea
pol kile *mlade* čebule   half a kilo of green onions
šest *svinjskih* zrezkov   six pork cutlets

There is a considerable overlap and only two endings to memorize, i.e., **-ega** for masculine and neuter singular and **-ih** for all genders in the plural and dual. Remember that **-ega** is also the adjectival ending in the *accusative* m. sg. if the adjective modifies an *animate* masculine noun (accusative = genitive). For example:

Alenka bo povabila   Alenka will invite Anita's boyfriend.
Anitinega fanta.
Ben ima mlajšega brata.   Ben has a younger brother.

Exercise 7

Fill in the correct forms of the adjectives and nouns in parentheses.

1 A imate _____? – Žal _____ danes nimamo. (puranji, meso)
2 Kupila boš _____. – Koliko _____ naj ('should') kupim? (temen, pivo)
3 A so to _____? Prosim kilo _____. (svinjski, kotlet [pl.])
4 Tu imam _____ za Alenko. – Alenka ne mara _____. (mrzel, limonada)
5 Prinesel boš pol kile _____. Samo _____ so dobre. (svež, riba [pl.])
6 Alenka je naredila _____. Brez _____ ni piknika. (jabolčni, zavitek)

Dialogue 3

Koliko je star Žiga?   How old is Žiga? **(Audio 2:17)**

Anita calls up Borut to invite him to the picnic. Will he be able to come? Why does Anita ask about Žiga's age?

ANITA	Naši bodo jutri imeli piknik na vikendu. Tudi midva sva povabljena. A boš prišel?
BORUT	Jutri pa res ne morem. Moj bratranec Žiga ima rojstni dan in pripravlja veliko zabavo v očetovi koči na Pokljuki. Mislim, da bo dobra družba. Obljubil sem, da bom peljal njega in še tri prijatelje.
ANITA	Koliko je pa star?
BORUT	Pojutrišnjem bo star osemnajst let. Prihodnji teden bo dobil vozniško dovoljenje in potem bo lahko sam vozil.
ANITA	Dobro, če si že Žigu obljubil . . . Boš pa drugič prišel na piknik. Dobro se imej na zabavi.
BORUT	Ti tudi na pikniku.

Vocabulary

dovoljenje	licence	**mọrem (mọči)** ipf.	I am able to
vozni̇́ško d.	driver's licence	**obljubi̇́ti** pf.	to promise
drugič	another time	**prihọdnji**	next, future
družba	company	**vozi̇́ti** ipf.	to drive
kọča	cottage	**zabava**	party

Vocabulary notes

Pokljuka: a forested plateau in northwestern Slovenia, in the Triglav National Park; **naši**: 'our family'; similarly **tvoji bodo prišli** 'your family will come'; you already know about using the possessive adjectives from family names like that, e.g., **Novakovi** 'the Novak family'.

Language point

Asking and saying...

...how old one is

The question word **kọliko** is used to ask about one's age. In answering the question, the word **lẹto** 'year' is normally included, its form depending on the preceding number. Examples:

Kọliko si stara?
How old are you [f. sg.]?

(Stara sẹm) ọsem lẹt.
I'm eight (years old).

Kọliko je star Žiga?
How old is Žiga?

(Žiga je star) sẹdẹmnajst lẹt.
Žiga is seventeen (years old).

Pojutrijšnjem bo star ọsẹmnajst lẹt.
The day after tomorrow he will be eighteen (years old).

Kọliko sta stara dvọjčka?
How old are the twins?

Januarja bosta stara tri lẹta.
They will be three (years old) in January.

...what kind of time one is having

The verb **imęti se** + adverbial (**dobro, fíno** [coll.], **super, odlíčno, slabǫ**) are used to express what kind of time one is having.

Kakǫ ste se imęli na Žigovi zabavi?
How was it at Žiga's party?

Imęli smo se super.
We had a great time.

The question **Kakǫ se imaš/imate?** can also mean nothing more than **Kakǫ si/ste?** 'How are you?' To wish someone a good time, the imperative of **imęti se** is used, i.e., **Dobro se imej(te)** 'Have a good time.'

Reading

Letni horoskop (Audio 2:19)

DEVICA (24. 8.–22. 9.)

ZIMA

Novo leto se bo začelo po starem, tudi v ljubezni bo mirno. Februarja boste bolj družabni, a imeli boste težave s partnerjem in v karieri. Marec bo zelo delaven. Ne boste imeli časa za zabavo in romantiko.

POMLAD

Želeli si boste avanture, flirtali boste bolj kot običajno. Nekaj časa boste sedeli na dveh stolih, kar se bo slabo končalo – na koncu boste obsedeli na tleh ['floor']. Junija boste šli na potovanje s prijateljem. Predali ['surrender'] se boste gurmanskim užitkom in naravi.

POLETJE

Poletje bo zelo dinamično. V službi bo vroče, a ne samo zaradi poletnih temperatur. Na žalost poletne vročine ne boste preživljali ['spend'] na plaži, ampak v pisarni. Julija vas bo presenetil obisk družinskega člana. Avgusta priložnost za renoviranje stanovanja.

JESEN

Jesen boste začeli utrujeni, a trdo delo v poletni vročini bo obrodilo sadove. Imeli boste več časa za ljubezensko življenje in tokrat bo šlo brez problemov. Našli boste pravo ljubezen, a za skupne načrte je pred koncem leta še prezgodaj. Leto boste končali polni energije in optimizma.

Vocabulary

član	member	**poln**	full
končati (se) pf.	to end	**pravi**	real, true
lętni	yearly	**presenętiti** pf.	to surprise
ljubęzen f.	love	**prilǫžnost** f.	opportunity
ljubęzenski adj.		**trd**	hard
narava	nature	**užîtek**	pleasure
obrodíti sadove	to bear fruit	**življenje**	life
plaža	beach		

Exercise 8

Nina is reading her yearly horoscope. According to its prediction, what part of the year (month or season) will she . . .

1 . . . take a trip
2 . . . be very busy
3 . . . not get along with her boyfriend
4 . . . be very tired
5 . . . have a happy love life
6 . . . get a visitor
7 . . . have two love interests

Unit Twelve
Po Ljubljani

Around Ljubljana

In this unit you will learn about:

- Ljubljana
- Asking for and giving directions
- Checking into a hotel
- More spatial prepositions
- The instrumental of adjectives
- Real conditions

Dialogue 1

Od Uniona na Grad From the Union Hotel to the castle (**Audio 2:20**)

Ben's friends from Chicago, David and Monica, are passing through Ljubljana. Ben is planning to spend a day showing them around. What ideas do Andrej and Alenka have for their tour?

BEN   *En* dan bom vod*ič* po Ljubljani. Moja prijatelja David in Monica sta v Nemčiji naj*e*la *a*vto in zdaj pot*u*jeta proti m*o*rju. J*u*tri se bosta ustavila v Ljubljani. V četrtek ju bom peljal po m*e*stu, a ne v*e*m, kaj lahk*o* pokažem v enem dn*e*vu.

ANDREJ Predlagam Grad in Staro Ljubljano. Grad zaradi razgleda
in Staro Ljubljano zaradi čudovite baročne arhitekture.

ALENKA Kje bosta vaša prijatelja stanovala?

BEN Sobo sem rezerviral v hotelu Union.

ALENKA To je čisto v centru in blizu Prešernovega trga. Na drugi
strani Ljubljanice je Stara Ljubljana. S Prešernovega
trga greste lahko peš čez Tromostovje in naravnost po
Stritarjevi ulici do Mestnega trga. Pred mestno hišo boste
videli znameniti Robbov vodnjak.

ANDREJ Misliš – kopijo Robbovega vodnjaka. Original si lahko
ogledate v Narodni galeriji. – Če greste od Robbovega
vodnjaka naprej po Mestnem trgu, pridete na Stari trg.
Po poti boste videli veliko butikov, trgovin s spominki,
starinarnic in prijetnih lokalov.

Hotel Union

ALENKA Če pa takoj za Tromostovjem zavijete levo, pridete
na tržnico. Tudi če tam ne boste kupovali, se splača
sprehoditi med prepolnimi stojnicami in pisanimi dežniki.
Za ljubitelje arhitekture pa so na tržnici tudi Plečnikove
arkade.

BEN In kako se pride na Ljubljanski grad? Vidva sta me zadnjič
peljala z avtom.

ANDREJ Že od hotela ga boste videli na hribu nad starim delom
mesta. Če bo lepo vreme, greste na Grad lahko peš s
Starega trga. Pot je precej strma, ampak razgled na rdeče
strehe starega mesta je res slikovit. Lahko pa se peljete
tudi z mestno vzpenjačo. Spodnja postaja je nasproti
tržnice.

Vocabulary

arhitektura	architecture		**pisan**	colorful
čez (+A)	across		**po** (+L)	along, around
čisto v centru	right in the center		**poka|zati**	to show
dežnik	umbrella		**-žem** pf.	
drugi	the other		**pot** f.	path, way
kopija	copy		**pred** (+I)	in front of
kup|ovati -ujem	to shop		**prepoln**	too full
ljubitelj	admirer		**proti** (+L)	towards
lokal	bar or restaurant		**rezervirati** pf.	to reserve
med (+I)	between		**slikovit**	picturesque
mestna hiša	city/town hall		**splača se**	it's worthwhile
nad (+I)	above		**spodnji**	lower
naj|eti	to rent		**spominek**	souvenir
-amem pf.			**spreh|oditi**	to take a
naprej	forward		**-odim se** pf.	walk
naravnost	straight		**starinarnica**	antique shop
narodni	national		**stojnica**	stand, stall
nasproti (+G)	across from		**stran** f.	side
peš	on foot		**streha**	roof

st**r**m	steep	vzpenja**č**a	funicular
t**r**g	square	za (+I)	behind
tr**ž**nica	marketplace	za**d**njič	the other day
vod**i**č	guide	zavi|ti -jem pf.	to turn
vodnj**a**k	fountain	znamen**i**t	renowned

Vocabulary notes

Grad: short for **Ljubljanski grad**, referring to the castle as well as to the hill on which it is located (therefore: *na* **Grad** 'to the castle');
Ljubljanica: river running through Ljubljana;
Trọmostovje: 'the Three Bridges', designed by the Slovene architect Jože Plečnik;
Plẹčnikove arkade: riverside colonnade at the **tržnica**, also by Plečnik.

Language point

Giving directions: prepositional phrases

To explain where things are located and how to get to them, it is essential that you have a good grasp of prepositions, i.e., both of their meaning and the cases they require. You are already familiar with several prepositional phrases denoting the location and motion towards, from, or between points.

		Location: **kje**? where
v, na + L	**Trgov**i**na se nahaja** The store is located **Vodnjak stoj**i The fountain stands	**v Str**i**tarjevi ulici.** in Stritarjeva Street. **na M**ẹ**stnem t**r**gu.** in the town square.
pri + L	**Pla**č**ate** You pay **Marko stan**u**je** Marko lives	**pri blaga**j**ni.** at the cash register. **pri str**i**cu.** at his uncle's.
blizu* + G	**Zgrad**i**li so novo h**i**šo** They built a new house	**bl**i**zu Kra**n**ja.** near Kranj.

* similarly **nasproti** 'across from', **zraven** 'next to'

		Motion towards: **kam?** where to
v, na + A	**Gremo** We are going **Vodič pelje turiste** The tour guide is taking tourists	**v Stritarjevo ulico.** to Stritarjeva Street. **na Mestni trg.** to the town square.
k + D	**Andrej nese košaro** Andrej is taking a basket **Marko se je preselil** Marko moved	**k blagajni.** to the cash register. **k stricu.** to his uncle's.

These prepositions, taking the genitive, express the origin or beginning (**iz**, **z/s**, **od**) and end point (**do**):

iz, z/s + G   **Prijatelja potujeta/sta iz Nemčije.**
Friends travel/are from Germany.

od, do + G   **Devetka vozi od postaje do živalskega vrta.**
Bus number nine runs from the station to the zoo.

Exercise 1

Complete the sentences as indicated in the parentheses.

1 Monica in David sta prijatelja _____. (from America)
2 Zdaj potujeta _____. (from Germany)
3 Za par dni se bosta ustavila _____. (in Ljubljana)
4 Ben jih bo peljal _____. (to the Old [part of] Ljubljana)
5 Hotel Union je _____. (close to Prešeren Square)
6 Lahko greste peš _____. (to Ljubljana castle)
7 _____ (from hotel) _____ (to the Three Bridges) ni daleč.
8 _____ (at the marketplace) boste videli Plečnikove arkade.

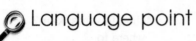 Language point

Prepositions of spatial orientation

The following group of prepositions, taking the instrumental case, denotes orientation of objects relative to other objects in three-dimensional space:

nad above	**Stanujem nad trgovino.** I live above the store.
pod under, below	**Stara Ljubljana je pod Gradom.** The old city of Ljubljana is below the castle.
med between	**Sprehajamo se med stojnicami.** We are strolling between the stands.
pred in front of	**Turisti stojijo pred vodnjakom.** The tourists are standing in front of the fountain.
za behind, after	**Zavili boste levo za mostom.** You turn left after the bridge.

To express motion into these positions, the same prepositions are used with the accusative. For example:

Turisti so prišli pred vodnjak.
The tourists came in front of the fountain.

Two other prepositions are used in Dialogue 1 to express motion or location:

proti towards or in the direction of something + dative
Prijatelja potujeta proti morju.   [My] friends are traveling
towards the sea.

po on the surface, along, or all over something + locative
Po Mestnem trgu pridete do Starega trga.
You get to the Old Square [walking] along the City Square.

Exercise 2

Say it in Slovene.

1 We [two] will meet in front of the theater.
2 Parking is in the marketplace.
3 The tour guide speaks to tourists in front of the fountain.
4 There are apartments above the stores.
5 The gallery is located between the park and the opera.
6 I will wait in front of the station.

Language point

Adjectival instrumental endings

With the exception of f. sg., adjectival endings differ from nominal endings in the instrumental case. Some examples:

Singular: **pred** *novim* **delom/***glavno* **pošto/***starim* **mestom**
Plural: **med** *prepolnimi* **stojnicami/***pisanimi* **dežniki/***zelenimi*
   polji
Dual: **za** *velikima* **hoteloma/***visokima* **hišama/***praznima*
   parkirišcema

You need to memorize three new endings: **-im** for masculine and neuter singular, **-imi** for all genders plural, and **-ima** for all genders dual.

Exercise 3

Expand the sentences from Exercise 2 by using the following adjectives in the prepositional phrases:

1 narodni
2 glavni
3 baročni

4 zanimiv
5 mestni, državni ('state, national')
6 železniški

Language point

Inflection of street and square names

The three most common nouns in Slovene street addresses are **ulica** 'street', **cęsta** 'road', and **trg** 'square'. Their name is usually an adjective, i.e., most often possessive, as in **Stritarjeva ulica**, **Vǫdnikov trg**, but sometimes not, as in **Stari trg**, **Celovška cęsta**. The nouns **ulica** and **cęsta** are commonly omitted, but not the noun **trg**. For example:

> **Mi** stanujemo na **Celovški [cęsti]**, **Bǫris** pa stanuje na **Krękovem trgu**.
> **Preselili** so se v **Jakčevo [ulico]**.

The agreement of the adjective is with the noun, even if it is just implied. You should also note that to say 'to' or 'at', **na** is used with **cęsta** and **trg**, and **v** with **ulica**. You use prepositions **iz** or **z/s** accordingly to say 'from': **iz Jakčeve**, but **s Krękovega trga**. When the name is a right attribute (rather than an adjective) to **ulica**, **cęsta**, or **trg**, only these nouns will decline depending on their syntactic role, but the attribute will stay unchanged. For example:

> **Tǫ je Trg republike. Parkirali smo na Trgu republike.**
> This is Republic Square. We parked on Republic Square.

 Exercise 4

Say in what **ulica**, **cesta**, or **trg** the institutions from the left column are located, as in the example.

	Naslov	
Filozofska fakulteta	**Aškerčeva cesta 2**	Filozofska fakulteta je na Aškerčevi.
1 **Mestna knjižnica**	**Kersnikova ulica 2**	
2 **Univerza**	**Kongresni trg 12**	
3 **Narodni muzej**	**Prešernova cesta 20**	
4 **Pošta**	**Čopova ulica 11**	
5 **Blagovnica* Maxi**	**Trg republike 1**	

* department store

Language point

Cardinal directions

Although people will generally not direct you in terms of cardinal directions, but rather will point you **naravnost, levo, desno**, or in the direction of something recognizable on the way (**križišče** 'intersection', **vogal** 'corner', **semafor** 'traffic light', **benc/nska črpalka** 'gas/petrol station', or a building), they are nevertheless used in descriptions of location. Note that unlike in English where the same word, e.g., north or south, fulfills the role of a noun, adjective, and adverb, in Slovene the adjective and the adverb are derived from the noun.

Noun	Adjective	Adverb
sever -a north	**severni** -a -o	**severno**
jug -a south	**južni** -a -o	**južno**
vzhod -a east	**vzhodni** -a -o	**vzhodno**
zahod -a west	**zahodni** -a -o	**zahodno**

A veš kje je sever? Do you know where north is?
Danes piha severni veter. The north wind is blowing today.

Živim dvajset kilometrov severno od Ljubljane.
I live twenty kilometers north of Ljubljana.

Exercise 5

Complete the sentences as indicated in parentheses.

1 _____ soseda Slovenije je Italija. (west)
2 _____ in _____ od Slovenije je Hrvaška. (south, east)
3 Zdaj gledate proti _____. (north)
4 Jeseni ptice ('birds') odletijo na _____. (south)
5 V _____ Sloveniji bo deževalo. (west)

Language point

Expressing real conditions

Notice how Alenka and Andrej talk about possibilities:

Če takoj za Tromostovjem zavijete levo, pridete na tržnico.
If you turn left immediately after the Three Bridges, you get to
the marketplace.

Če bo lepo vreme, greste na Grad lahko peš.
If the weather is nice, you can go to the castle on foot.

The conditions, which all have the potential of being realized, are
introduced with **če** 'if'. What tense to use in the conditional clause
depends on the time of realization of the condition, i.e., the present
tense if the condition can be fulfilled now or any time, as in **če
zavijete levo**, and the future tense if in the future, as in **če bo lepo
vreme**. Clitics directly follow **če**, and they go at the beginning of
the main clause if that clause is preceded by the **če**-clause. For
example:

Če boste na tržnici kupovali, se splača priti zgodaj.
If you are going to shop at the marketplace, it is worthwhile
coming early.

Splača se priti zgodaj, če boste na tržnici kupovali.
It is worthwhile coming early if you are going to shop at the
marketplace.

 Dialogue 2

 Kako se pride do Tivolija? How do you get
to Tivoli? **(Audio 2:23)**

Nejc is approached by a tourist at the **Kongresni trg**.

TURIST   Oprostite, prosim, a mi lahko poveste, kako se pride do
Tivolija?

Križišče Prešernove in Šubičeve

NEJC Vidite tisto cesto na koncu trga? To je Slovenska. Na vogalu prečkate Slovensko in greste naravnost po Šubičevi do Prešernove. Prečkate Prešernovo in zavijete desno. Potem greste mimo ameriške ambasade in Moderne galerije. Za galerijo zavijete levo in videli boste podhod pod cesto in železnico. Greste skozi podhod in že ste v Tivoliju.

TURIST A je to daleč?

NEJC Ne, samo kakšnih deset minut.

TURIST Hvala.

NEJC Ni za kaj. Srečno.

Vocabulary

ambasada	embassy
mimo (+G)	past
podhod	underpass
prečkati ipf./pf.	to cross
skozi (+A)	through
srečno	good luck
Tivoli	main city park
železnica	railway

Exercise 6

(a) Ask a passer-by . . .

1 . . . where the Old Square is
2 . . . where the main marketplace is
3 . . . how one gets to the Three Bridges
4 . . . how one gets to the train station

(b) Tell a passer-by:

5 . . . to go straight along Čopova to Slovenska, then turn right
6 . . . to go to the traffic light and cross the street there
7 . . . that the Three Bridges are close to the Prešeren Square
8 . . . to turn behind the gallery and go through the underpass

Exercise 7

Answer the questions about Dialogue 1.

1 Zakaj Andrej pravi, da bo vodič po Ljubljani?
2 Kje bosta stanovala njegova prijatelja?
3 Kaj za ogled predlaga Andrej?
4 Kam se pride od Tromostovja po Stritarjevi ulici?
5 A je pred mestno hišo pravi ('real') Robbov vodnjak?
6 Kam bodo obiskovalci prišli, če za Tromostovjem zavijejo levo?
7 Kaj bodo tam videli ljubitelji arhitekture?
8 Zakaj se splača iti na Ljubljanski grad?
9 Kako se pride na Grad?

 Dialogue 3

 V hotẹlski recẹpciji   At the reception desk **(Audio 2:25)**

Mr. and Mrs. Sitar, Slovene Americans from Cleveland, are checking
into a hotel for a short stay.

G.* SITAR	Dobẹr dan. Imava rezervacijo za dvopọsteljno sobo.
RECEPTOR	Na katẹro imẹ in za kọliko časa?
G. SITAR:	Rezervacija je na imẹ Sịtar za dva dnị.

RECEPTOR	Aha, žę imam. Tǫ bo soba 204 v drugem nadstrǫpju. Samǫ še podpis potrebujem in osębna dokumenta, prǫsim.
G. SITAR	Izvǫlite najina pǫtna lista. – In kję lahkǫ parkirava?
RECEPTOR	V garaži. Vhod v garažo je za hotęlom iz Lęvstikove ulice. Tu je ključ od sobe. Ko izstǫpite iz dvigala, zavijete lęvo in gręste po hodniku do konca. Soba 204 je na dęsni strani. Če boste šli po stopnicah, pa mǫrate v drugem nadstrǫpju zaviti dęsno.
G. SITAR	Kdaj stręžete zajtrk?
RECEPTOR	Samopostręžni zajtrk je od šestih do desetih v restavraciji in na terasi.

* G.: **Gospod**

Vocabulary

dvigalo	elevator
hodnik	corridor
izst|opiti -ǫpim pf.	to exit
ključ	key
osęben	personal
podpis	signature
pǫtni list	passport
samopostręžni	self-serve
stopnice pl.	stairs
vhod	entrance

Language point

To take the elevator or the stairs

Notice the difference in phrasing compared to English and between the two Slovene expressions: **gręm z dvigalom** 'I am going by elevator' vs. **gręm po stopnicah** 'I am going by the stairs.' The preposition **v**, rather than **na**, is used with the noun **nadstrǫpje** 'floor'. For example:

Vaša soba je v tretjem nadstropju.	Your room is on the third floor.
V tretje nadstropje gremo z dvigalom.	We are taking the elevator to the third floor.

Exercise 8

Say it in Slovene.

1 I need a double room.
2 Your room is on the second floor.
3 Where can I park?
4 The entrance to the garage is behind the hotel.
5 When do you serve breakfast?
6 Will we go to the second floor by elevator or by the stairs?

Reading

(Audio 2:27)

Ljubljana – znamenitosti

Tromostovje

Srednji most današnjega Tromostovja je bil zgrajen na mestu 'in place of' starega lesenega mostu* čez Ljubljanico l. 1842. Temu mostu, ki je postal preozek za ves promet, je arhitekt Jože Plečnik okrog l. 1930 dodal še dva mostova samo za pešce. Tromostovje je eden† od simbolov slovenskega glavnega mesta. Maketa Prešernovega trga s Tromostovjem predstavlja Slovenijo v bruseljskem parku Mini Evropa.

---

* The genitive sg. of **most** is **mostu** rather than **mosta**; certain monosyllabic masculine nouns have the ending **-u** (stressed) in the genitive instead of **-a**, e.g. **gradu**, **ledu**, **zidu** 'wall', **glasu** 'sound'. Most of these nouns also lengthen with **-ov-** in du. and pl. before adding the endings, e.g., **mostova**, **mostovom** . . . , but they do not add another **-ov** in G du./pl. (**mostov**).

† **eden**: long form of **en** when used without a noun.

Tromostovje in Plečnikove arkade

Robbov vodnjak

Znameniti ljubljanski vodnjak je l. 1751 izdelal baročni kipar Francesco Robba. Vodnjak se imenuje tudi Vodnjak treh kranjskih* rek, ker tri skulpture iz belega marmorja predstavljajo slovenske reke Savo, Krko in Ljubljanico. Vodnjak je do l. 2006 stal pred ljubljansko mestno hišo, kjer je zdaj kopija, original pa je razstavljen v Narodni galeriji.

* **kranjski** 'Carniolan'; Carniola (**Kranjska**), which included most of today's western Slovenia, was a historical region of the Habsburg Empire.

Vocabulary

dodati pf.	to add	**pešec**	pedestrian
eden od	one of	**posta|ti**	to become
glavno mesto	capital (city)	**-nem** pf.	
imen|ovati se	to be called	**predstavljati**	to represent
-uje se ipf.		ipf.	
izdelati pf.	to create	**promet**	traffic
ki	which (conj.)	**razstavljen**	displayed
kipar	sculptor	**srednji**	middle
lesen	wooden	**ves vsa vse**	all
maketa	diorama	**zgrajen**	built
marmor	marble	**znamen|tost** f.	landmark

Unit Thirteen
Kultura in zabava
Culture and entertainment

In this unit you will learn about:

- Cultural events
- Dates
- Biographies
- Numbers above 100
- Ordinal numerals
- The conditional
- Expressing possession

Dialogue 1

Kaj je na sporedu? What's on the program?
(Audio 2:28)

Andrej and Alenka are discussing the summer cultural offerings in Ljubljana. What would Alenka like to see? Can Ben attend any performances at the Ljubljana summer festival? What do they decide to see together?

ANDREJ   Alenka, a bova šla letos na kakšno predstavo na ljubljanskem poletnem festivalu? Vstopnice bi lahko kupila že zdaj.

ALENKA   Jaz imam rada opero in balet, ampak letošnjega programa še nisem videla.

ANDREJ   M/slim, da sta lętos na sporędu *Carmen* in *Pikova dama*.
         Takǫj ti bom povędal kdaj ... *Carmen* bo v izvędbi
         Hrvaškega narodnega gledal/šča na sporędu osmega julija,
         Pikova dama pa v izvędbi mariborske opere
         dvaindvajsetega julija.

ALENKA   Dvaindvajsetega julija bova na morju, takǫ da *Pikova dama*
         ne pr/de v poštev. Vsekakor bi rada v/dela *Carmen*. Je
         morda v prvi polov/ci julija na sporędu tudi kakšen balęt?

ANDREJ   Je. Št/rinajstega julija bo v Cankarjevem domu balęt A*na
         Karęnina*. Takrat bova še doma. Zamud/la boš opero
         Čajkovskega, lahkǫ pa boš v/dela vsaj balęt z njegovo
         glasbo. Kar takǫj bom na /nternetu kupil vstǫpnice.

BEN   Škǫda, da se festival začne šelę julija, ko ne bom več v
         Ljubljani. V/dim, da bo kar nękaj dobrih koncertov. Paco
         de Luc/a bo nastǫpil avgusta. Zelǫ rad bi ga sl/šal.

ALENKA   Ampak Ljubljana ima tudi junija zelǫ bogato kulturno
         ponudbo. Žę od št/rinajstega junija potęka na
         Prešęrnovem trgu prired/tev̲ Junij v Ljubljani. Vsak dan
         so tam brezplačne glasbene, gledal/ške in plęsne
         predstave z znanimi slovęnskimi umętniki.

BEN   Ja, z Monico in Davidom smo včęraj tam poslušali nastop
         enega zbora.

ALENKA   Lahkǫ bi šl/ tudi nocǫj, če vas zan/ma slovęnska drama.
         Nastop/lo bo Męstno gledal/šče ljubljansko.

BEN   Z veseljem.

 Vocabulary

bi	would	**kultΜrna** **ponudba**	cultural offerings
bogat	rich		
glasba	music	**lętošnji**	this year's
glasben adj.		**nastop**	performance
gledal/šče	theater	**nast|op/ti**	to appear
gledal/ški adj.		-**opim** pf.	(in a show)
izvędba	rendition	***Pikova dama***	*The Queen of Spades*
kultura	culture	**plęsni**	dance (adj.)

polov*i***ca**	half	**veselje**	pleasure
poslu*š***ati** ipf.	to listen to	**vsekakor**	by all means
pot*ę***kati** ipf.	to run (event, show)	**vst***ǫ***pnica**	ticket
		zabava	entertainment
predstava	show	**zamud***i***ti** pf.	to miss
sl*i***š|ati -im** ipf./pf.	to hear	**zbor**	choir
spored	program	**znan**	well-known
tak*ǫ* **da**	therefore (conj.)		

Vocabulary notes

Cankarjev d*ǫ***m**: Ljubljana cultural and congress center;
k*a***r**: intensifier, e.g., **k***a***r tak***ǫ***j** 'right away'; **k***a***r precej** 'quite a few';
ne pr*i***de v p***ǫ***štev**: it's not an option;
M*ę***stno gledal***i***šče ljubljansko**: the name of one of Ljubljana's main theaters.

Language point

Ordinal numerals

You will have to memorize the ordinal numerals 1st–4th: **p***r***vi** 'first', **dr***u***gi** 'second', **tr***ę***tji** 'third', **čet***r***ti** 'fourth'. The rest you can derive from the ordinal numerals by adding **-i** (or **-a**, **-o**, **-e** . . . , depending on the gender and number, as ordinal numerals are adjectives, agreeing with the nouns they precede). The stressed vowels **e** and **o** in the numerals **peti**, **šesti**, **sedmi**, **osmi**, **deveti**, **deseti**, and **stoti** are open (as opposed to closed in 5–10 and 100); the schwa in **s***ę***d***ę***m** and **ǫs***ę***m** is dropped before the ending is added. When ordinal numerals are written with numbers, a dot added to a number makes it ordinal. For example:

25. [p*ę***tindvajseti] avg***u***st**	25th of August
4. [čet*r***ta] v***r***sta**	row 4
II. [druga] svetovna vojna	Second World War
5. [peto] nadstropje	5th floor

The context indicates how to read the ordinal numeral written with a number. For example:

Želim sedež v 4. [četrti] vrsti.   I want a seat in row 4.
Peljemo se v 5. [peto]   We are riding an elevator to
nadstropje.   the fifth floor.
Moja hči je v 7. [sedmem]   My daughter is in seventh
razredu.   grade.

Exercise 1

Write out the numerals.

1 3. razred	4 10. nadstropje	7 2. potovanje
2 17. vrsta	5 4. knjiga	8 9. predstava
3 35. rojstni dan	6 11. leto	9 26. junij

Exercise 2

Complete the sentences using phrases 1–5 from Exercise 1 in the appropriate case.

1 Njen sin hodi v _____.
2 Želimo vstopnice za _____.
3 Andrej je praznoval _____.
4 Moja pisarna je v _____.
5 Nisem še prebrala njegove _____.

Language points

Cardinal numerals above 100

The hundreds are compounds consisting of cardinals 2–9 and **sto**; for 2–4 feminine forms are used:

200	**dvesto**		600	**šeststo**
300	**tristo**		700	**sedemsto**
400	**štiristo**		800	**osemsto**
500	**petsto**		900	**devetsto**

Tisoč '1000' is a noun that does not change when quantified. The thousands separator, if used, is not a comma, but a dot. Examples:

2000	**dva tisoč**	5000	**pet tisoč**
3000	**tri tisoč**	10.000	**deset tisoč**
4000	**štiri tisoč**	500.000	**petsto tisoč**

Milijon 'million' and **milijarda** 'billion' decline like ordinary nouns and follow the same rules for quantification as other nouns. Slovene **bilijon** is a false cognate, as it means 'trillion'.

Dates

A Slovene **datum** 'date' consists of an ordinal numeral representing the day, the name of the month or the ordinal numeral representing the month and a cardinal numeral for the year. When just saying what date a particular day is, they are used in the nominative. For example:

> **Danes je šestindvajseti junij dva tisoč deset.**
> Today is the 26th of June, 2010.

> **Kateri dan je dvanajsti osmi? Ponedeljek.**
> What day is the 12th of August [the eighth month]? (It's) Monday.

Note that masculine forms of ordinal numerals are used to agree with the implied nouns **dan** 'day' and **mesec** 'month'.

When the date is the adverbial of time, i.e., expressing **kdaj** 'when' something takes place, the day and month need to be used in the genitive case. For example:

> **Kdaj imaš rojstni dan? – Prvega februarja.**
> When is your birthday? – On Febuary 1.

> **Kdaj se bo Ben vrnil v Ameriko? – Tretjega julija.**
> When will Ben return to America? – On July third.

> **Kdaj ste rojeni? – 17. [sedemnajstega] 9. [devetega] 1973**
> **[tisoč devetsto triinsedemdeset].**
> When were you born? – On September 17, 1973.

Exercise 3

Following are some names of performers with the times of their appearance at the festival **Poletje v Stari Ljubljani**. Say when each artist or ensemble will perform (use the verb **nastopiti**); use names of the months.

1 Kvartet Bartók: 4. 6. ob 20.00
2 Moški komorni zbor Bolgarija: 15. 7. ob 21.00
3 Kvartet Orfeo: 25. 7. ob 21.00
4 Ljubljanski trio violončel: 2. 8. ob 20.30
5 Nikola Matošič trio: 6. 8. ob 21.00

 Language points

The forms and use of the conditional

The conditional form of a verb consists of the auxiliary **bi** (for all persons and numbers) and the -l-participle of the verb, which marks the gender and number, e.g., **ględati** 'to watch' → **jaz bi ględal(a)** 'I (m./f.) would watch', **vi bi ględali** 'you (m./formal) would watch', **one bi ględale** 'they (f.) would watch', etc. To negate the conditional, use **ne** in front of **bi**, e.g., **one ne bi ględale** 'they would not watch'.

In Dialogue 1, the conditional forms are used:

1 With **rad** to say 'would like to . . .'. For example:

Alęnka bi rada videla Carmen.   Alenka would like to see *Carmen*.

Rad bi rezerviral vstopnice za ǫpero Carmen.
I would like to reserve tickets for the opera *Carmen*.

As you learned in Unit 5, the position of **rad** before or after **bi** depends on whether or not there is another fully stressed word or phrasal unit available to occupy the initial position in the sentence. **Bi** appears in second position except when something is omitted, like the question word **a/ali** in:

Bi radi rezervírali karte?   Would you like to reserve the tickets?

2 With **lahko**, to express a possibility of doing something—to say 'could . . .'. For example:

Vstǫpnice bi lahkǫ kupíla   We could buy the tickets now.
že zdaj.

Lahkǫ bi šlí na predstavo   We could also go to a
tudi nocǫj.   performance tonight.

The possibility is expressed more mildly than if you use the present tense with **lahkǫ**, e.g., **vstǫpnice lahkǫ kupiva že zdaj** 'we can buy the tickets now'.

Hearing and seeing vs. listening and watching

Make sure you know the difference between these verbs of perception:

sl/šati sl/šim (ipf./pf.)	to hear
v/deti v/dim (ipf./pf.)	to see
poslu/šati (ipf.)	to listen to
gl/edati (ipf.)	to watch, to look at

Exercise 4

Say in full sentences what the people would like to do.

1 Andrej/buy tickets for *Carmen*
2 Marko and Mira/hear Bob Dylan
3 my friends/see the ballet *Anna Karenina*
4 we/watch a Slovene drama
5 Ben/take his friends to Old Ljubljana

Exercise 5

Answer the questions about Dialogue 1.

1 Katere predstave bi na ljubljanskem festivalu rada videla Alenka?
2 Katera predstava je na sporedu prej: *Carmen* ali *Pikova dama*?
3 Zakaj Alenka ne bo mogla videti *Pikove dame*?
4 Kaj bo lahko videla od Čajkovskega?
5 A bo Ben lahko obiskal kakšne predstave? Zakaj?
6 Kateri izvajalec ('performer') ga zanima?
7 Kakšna je junijska kulturna ponudba v Ljubljani?
8 Kaj se dogaja ('is going on') na Prešernovem trgu?

Dialogue 2

Plečnikove mojstrov/ne Plečnik's masterpieces
(Audio 2:32)

Ben's friends are fascinated by the work of the famous Slovene architect, Jože Plečnik. Ben would like some advice from Andrej on what else to show them.

BEN	Monici in Davidu sem pokazal nekaj Plečnikovih del v središču mesta in bila sta očarana. Kaj bi še morala videti?
ANDREJ	Ste ju peljali mimo Narodne in univerzitetne knjižnice?
BEN	Nisem. Hodili smo po Stari Ljubljani in ob Ljubljanici, šli smo tudi na Grad.
ANDREJ	NUK je eno Plečnikovih glavnih del v Sloveniji. Načrt za knjižnico je naredil leta 1931, dogradili pa so jo deset let kasneje. Že od daleč boste prepoznali mogočno štirinadstropno stavbo s slikovito fasado iz rdeče opeke in sivega kamna.
BEN	Mislim, da smo jo videli z Gradu.
ANDREJ	Vredno si je ogledati tudi notranjost z impozantnim stopniščem v črnem marmorju in čitalnico. Slavni arhitekt pa je uredil tudi prostor okrog knjižnice: Trg francoske revolucije, Vegovo ulico in Križanke. V Križankah si morate vsekakor ogledati znamenito dvorišče. Tu je tudi poletno gledališče – glavno prizorišče prireditev poletnega festivala.

Narodna in univerzitetna knjižnica

Vocabulary

čitalnica	reading room	očaran	fascinated
dęlo	work	okrǫg (+G)	around
dogradíti pf.	to finish building	opęka	brick
dvoríšče	courtyard	prepoznati pf.	to recognize
kamęn	stone	prizoríšče	scene, stage
marmor	marble	prostor	space
mogǫčen	impressive	stopníšče	stairway
mǫrala bi	they (two) should	uredíti	arrange
notranjost f.	interior	vrędęn	worthwhile

Vocabulary notes

Narodna in univerzitętna knjížnica (NUK): National and University Library; **Krížanke:** formerly a monastery, now the main venue for the events of the Ljubljana summer festival.

Language point

Expressing possession

From singular nouns denoting people, possessive adjectives are formed with the suffix **-ov/-ev** if the noun is masculine (e.g., **Plęčnikov, Markov, Míhov, prijateljev**) and **-in** if the noun is feminine (e.g., **Alenkin, mamin**). The ending comes off before adding the suffix (e.g., **Alęnka + -in → Alęnkin**). Changes that normally happen before adding an ending, e.g., dropping a schwa or adding a consonant, as well as **c** changing to **č**, occur before these suffixes are added (e.g., **stríc → stríčev, bratranęc → bratrančev, Tǫne → Tǫnetov, babica → babičin**).

When the owner is denoted by a phrase rather than a single noun, the possessive genitive is used instead, like saying 'of that person'. For example:

načrti Jožeta Plečnika	Jože Plečnik's plans
hiša stare tete	an old aunt's house
avto prijatelja Andreja	[my] friend Andrej's car
opera Čajkovskega	Tchaikovsky's opera

Čajkovski (like **slovenski**) has adjectival, not nominal, inflection and therefore no possessive adjective can be derived from it. In everyday spoken language people will often use the possessive genitive even when the derivation is possible; they will also use the possessive genitive with the preposition **od**, e.g., **hiša od brata** '[my] brother's house', **načrti od Plečnika** 'Plečnik's plans'; **sodelavec od prijateljice Alenke** '[my] friend Alenka's co-worker'. This is substandard and not appropriate in writing.

Remember that the possessive adjective agrees with the noun it modifies (you have been using them in street names), but when possession is expressed with the possessive genitive, only the head noun will be governed by the verb or preposition and change the case accordingly. For example:

Peljali smo se z *bratovim* avtom.	We rode in [my] brother's car.
Videli so *Plečnikovo* Tromostovje.	They saw Plečnik's Three Bridges.
Bil sem na koncertu	I was at the Slovenski oktet
***Slovenskega* okteta.**	concert.
Gledali smo dramo *Dušana*	We watched Dušan Jovanovič's
***Jovanoviča*.**	play.

Exercise 6

Complete the sentences with the appropriate expressions for possession, derived from the words in parentheses.

1 Borut bo šel na _____ zabavo. (Irena)
2 Piknik bomo imeli na _____ vikendu. (Andrej)
3 Alenka bo zamudila opero _____. (Čajkovski)
4 Peljali se bomo s _____ avtom. (prijatelj)
5 V Narodni galeriji smo videli sliko _____. (Ivana Kobilica)
6 Tudi NUK je delo _____. (slavni arhitekt)

Exercise 7

Complete the sentences according to the information from Dialogue 2.

1 Ben je prijateljema pokazal Plečnikova dela v _____ _____.
2 Plečnik je _____ _____ za NUK leta 1931.
3 Fasada knjižnice je iz _____ _____ in _____ _____.
4 Plečnik je _____ _____ okrog knjižnice.
5 V _____ _____ v Križankah so prireditve poletnega festivala.

Dialogue 3

Na blagajni za vstopnice At the box office
(Audio 2:34)

Lara is at the box office, buying tickets for herself and two friends
for the concert of Vlado Kreslin, a popular Slovene folk rock musician.

LARA	Dober dan. Rada bi tri karte za koncert Vlada Kreslina 20. avgusta.
PRODAJALKA	Kje bi pa radi sedeli?
LARA	Na balkonu, če je še kaj prosto.
PRODAJALKA	Na žalost je na balkonu že vse razprodano.
LARA	Potem pa v parterju, bolj spredaj na sredini.
PRODAJALKA	V parterju imam tri sedeže skupaj na sredini samo še v zadnjih vrstah, bolj spredaj pa v parterju desno ali levo.
LARA	Potem bom vzela tri v parterju desno. In kakšna je cena?
PRODAJALKA	Redna cena je devetindvajset evrov, študenti imajo desetodstotni popust.
LARA	Tu je moja študentska izkaznica.
PRODAJALKA	Hvala. Vse skupaj bo oseminsedemdeset evrov in trideset centov.

Vocabulary

desętodstǫtęn	10 percent	prost	unoccupied
izkaznica	ID	razprodan	sold out
karta = vstopnica		rędęn	regular
na žalost	unfortunately	sędež	seat
parter	orchestra (seating)	sprędaj	in front
		vrsta	row
popust	discount	zadnji	back, last

Exercise 8

Say it in Slovene.

1 I would like two tickets for Bob Dylan's concert.
2 Where would you (pl.) like to sit?
3 In the orchestra, the fifth or sixth row.
4 Unfortunately, the fifth and sixth rows are already sold out.
5 Where do you have seats available?
6 I have two seats available in the tenth row.
7 Do students have a discount?

Reading

Kratka biografija (Audio 2:36)

Jože Plečnik (Ljubljana, 23.1.1872–7.1.1957), slovenski arhitekt in urbanist.

Rojen je bil v družini mizarja. Na državni obrtni šoli v Gradcu se je izučil za umetnostnega mizarja in načrtovalca pohištva. Arhitekturo je študiral na Dunaju pri Ottu Wagnerju. Za odlično diplomsko delo je dobil štipendijo, s katero je šel za nekaj mesecev na študijsko potovanje po Italiji in Franciji. Leta 1901 je odprl arhitekturni atelje na Dunaju. Tu je na novo zgradil in preuredil več stavb. Od l. 1911 je predaval na šoli za umetno obrt v Pragi. Leta 1920 se je vrnil v Ljubljano in postal profesor arhitekture na novi ljubljanski univerzi. V tem času je tudi začel preurejati praški grad Hradčani. To delo je trajalo do l. 1935 in Pragi vtisnilo neizbrisen pečat. V petnajstih letih pred 2. svetovno vojno je ustvaril večino arhitekturnih in urbanističnih projektov v svojem rojstnem mestu, ki so danes znani kot Plečnikova Ljubljana, npr. Tromostovje, tržnice, NUK, ureditev nabrežja Ljubljanice, Kongresnega trga, Tivolija. Ljubljano je iz provincialnega mesta spremenil v nacionalno prestolnico.

Vocabulary

atelje m.	studio	**preurediti** pf.	
mizar	carpenter	**rojstni**	birth (adj.)
neizbrisen	indelible	**spremeniti** pf.	to change
obrtna šola	trade school	**umetnostni**	art (adj.)
odprļeti -em pf.	to open	**urediti** pf.	to arrange
pečat	seal, imprint	**ustvariti** pf.	to create
prestolnica	capital (city)	**večina**	majority
preurejati ipf.	to redesign	**vtisɭniti -nem** pf.	to imprint

Vocabulary notes

npr. = **na primer** 'for example';
Gradec, **Praga**: Graz (Austria), Prague.

Exercise 9

What is the significance of the following years in Plečnik's life?

1	1901	3	1920
2	1911	4	1935

Unit Fourteen
Obleka naredi človeka
Clothes make the man

In this unit you will learn about:

- Clothing
- Shopping for clothes
- The dative of pronouns
- The reflexive possessive pronoun **svoj**
- Another way to express likes and dislikes
- Reflexive verbs

 Dialogue 1

 Kje je moj svetlosivi suknjič? Where is my light gray blazer? **(Audio 2:37)**

Ben can't find his light gray blazer. Where does he think he left it and what does Alenka suggest they do?

BEN   Alenka, ste morda videli moj svetlosivi suknjič? Že celo dopoldne ga iščem. Preiskal sem že celo hišo, pogledal sem tudi v avtu, a vse zastonj.

ALENKA   Ne, danes ga nisem videla, ampak včeraj ste ga še nosili na inštitutu. Morda ste ga pozabili tam.

BEN   Ne, imel sem ga še zvečer, ko smo bili na večerji v gostilni Pri dveh lipah. Oblekel sem ga, ker je bilo zunaj hladno, ampak potęm smo sedęli znǫtraj. Najbrž mi je bilǫ vrǫče in sęm ga slękęl. Ne spomnim se, če sęm ga imęl, ko smo prišli iz gostilne.

ALENKA Gotovo ste ga pozabili v gostilni. Takǫj jih bom poklicala.

A little later . . .

ALENKA Na žalost Pri dvęh lipah niso našli vašega suknjiča. Morda ga boste še našli, medtęm pa vam Andrej lahkǫ posǫdi kakšen svǫj suknjič.

BEN Andrejev mi bo premajhęn. Če bo zvečęr hladnǫ, imam še špǫrtno jakno in pulover. Suknjič potrebujem za na inštitut. Če ga do jutri ne najdem, bom mǫral kupiti novega.

ALENKA Jutri je sobǫta. Lahkǫ vas dopoldne pęljem v męsto in poględava v kakšni veleblagǫvnici. Če gręva popoldne, pa je bǫlje iti v nakupovalni cęnter. Tam je veliko trgovin s konfękcijo in tudi ob sobǫtah so odprte do večęra.

BEN Hvala za pomǫč. Zelǫ nerad kupujem oblęko.

ALENKA Ni problęm, rada vam pomagam. Tudi Andrej ne mara nakupovanja in vędno hǫče, da mu svetujem pri oblęki.

Vocabulary

gotovo	most likely	**oblę|či -čem** pf.	to put on
iskati iščem ipf.	to search	**oblęka**	clothing
preiskati pf.	to s. through	**pomǫč** f.	help
jakna	jacket	**pozabiti** pf.	to forget
konfękcija	apparel	**pulover**	sweater
lipa	linden	**suknjič**	blazer
najti najdem pf.	to find	**svet|ovati -ujem** ipf.	to advise
nakupovalni cęnter	shopping mall	**veleblagovnica**	department store
nerad	reluctantly	**zastǫnj**	to no avail
nositi nǫsim ipf.	to wear	**znǫtraj**	inside

 Language points

Personal pronouns: the dative case

Notice the dative forms of pronouns in the dialogue. For example:

Andrejev suknjič *mi* bo premajh<u>e</u>n. Andrej's blazer will be too small for me.

Z veseljem *vam* pomagam. I'm glad to help you.

The chart provides short and full dative forms. The rules for their use are the same as with the accusative and genitive.

	N (kd<u>o</u>?)	D (k<u>o</u>mu?)
sg.	j*a*z	**mi**/meni
	t*i*	**ti**/tebi
	on, ono	**mu**/njemu
	ona	**ji**/njej
du.	m*i*dva, m<u>e</u>dve	n*a*ma
	v*i*dva, v<u>e</u>dve	v*a*ma
	onadva, onidve	**jima**/nj*i*ma
pl.	m*i*, m<u>e</u>	nam
	v*i*, v<u>e</u>	vam
	oni, one, ona	**jim**/nj*i*m

More uses of the dative case

Besides the familiar use of the dative as the indirect object with the verbs **pos<u>o</u>diti** 'to lend', **pom<u>a</u>gati** 'to help', **svet<u>o</u>v<u>a</u>ti** 'to advise', notice two other uses of the dative in Dialogue 1:

1 As the logical subject in impersonal sentences expressing how one feels, as in the sentences:

Bilọ *mi* je vrọče.	I was hot.
Marku je slabọ.	Marko feels nauseous.
Sonji je nerọdno.	Sonja feels awkward.
Žal *mi* je.	I am sorry.

Note the clitic order. However, a negated auxiliary is not a clitic. For example:

N*i* mu bilọ vrọče.
N*i* mi žal.

2 To say how something fits:

| **T*i*sti klobuk je Bẹn*u* prevelik.** | That hat is too large for Ben. |
| **Tvoja oblẹka *ji* je prav.** | Your dress will fit her. |

Tọ kr*i*lo *ti* je predolgo (prekratko/prešroko/preọzko).
This skirt is too long (too short/too wide/too tight) for you.

Definite form of adjectives

You already know about the definite form of adjectives in the nominative singular masculine, as in **mọj svẹtlos*i*vi suknjič**. Some more examples:

| **S*i*vi plašč je v avtu.** | The gray coat is in the car. |
| **T*i*sti s*i*vi plašč je že star.** | That gray coat is already old. |

In standard (written) language the nominative (and the same accusative) singular masculine is the only form that marks definiteness; there is no difference in other forms of adjectives. In everyday spoken language this is done by putting the particle **ta** (unchanging and unstressed, hence *not* the same as the demonstrative **ta** 'this') in front of the adjective, e.g., **ta črn pulover** 'sweater', **njẹna ta črna oblẹka**, which makes an expression of definiteness possible in any form. For example:

| **M*i*ran ni našel ta črnega** | Miran did not find the black |
| **puloverja.** | sweater. |

The verbs iskati 'to look for' **and** najti 'to find'

The perfective pair to the imperfective verb **iskati** *iščem* is **poiskati** 'to find (as a result of searching)'. Another prefix, **pre-**, also makes **iskati** perfective, but **preiskati** means 'to search through', i.e., besides completion the prefix adds the meaning of thoroughness. The perfective verb **najti** (**najdem, našel**) means 'to find', which can be unintentional or a result of searching. Examples:

Alęnka in Bęn bosta v nakupovalnem cęntru poiskala nov suknjič.
Alenka and Ben will find a new blazer at the shopping mall.

V gost/lni n/so našli Bęnovega suknjiča.
They did not find Ben's blazer in the restaurant.

Exercise 1

(a) Say how the clothing item given in parentheses fits each person, as in the example.

1 Marko (red sweater – too large)   **Rdeči pulover je Marku prevelik.**
2 I (gray blazer – too short)
3 Anka (red skirt – too tight)
4 you [sg.] (black coat – fits well)
5 Breda, Vesna (blue dress – too wide)
6 you [pl.] (brown hat – too small)

(b) Rewrite the sentences 1, 3, and 5 using pronouns instead of names.

Exercise 2

(a) Say it in Slovene.

1 We are sorry.
2 The two of us felt awkward.
3 Are you [pl.] hot?
4 They felt nauseous.
5 The two of them were hot.

(b) Negate the sentences you compiled.

Language point

The reflexive possessive pronoun svoj
`one's own'

When talking about the subject's possession, the pronoun **svoj** 'one's own' is used for any possessor. For example:

Včeraj ste še nosili svoj suknjič.
You were still wearing your [own] blazer yesterday.

Andrej vam lahko posodi kakšen svoj suknjič.
Andrej can lend you one of his blazers.

As you can see, the determining factor in using the reflexive **svoj** instead of **vaš** or **njegov** is the fact that the possession is the subject's: in the first sentence the possessor is the second-person plural and in the second it is Andrej. Note that **svoj** does not necessarily correspond to a possessive pronoun + 'own' in English. Like other possessive pronouns, **svoj** declines like an adjective. Since it refers to the subject's possession, it will not appear in the subject and only rarely in the nominative, as in **On je svoj človek** 'He is his own man.'

Exercise 3

Fill in the blanks using a regular or reflexive possessive pronoun, as appropriate.

1 Ben je izgubil _____ suknjič. Alenka je videla _____ suknjič na inštitu. (his)
2 Andrej je naredil načrt za _____ hišo. A so se že preselili v _____ hišo? (their)
3 A boste šli na morje z/s _____ avtom? Mislim, da je _____ avto prestar. (your, pl.)
4 Mojca bi ti rada posodila _____ bleko. Žal ti bo _____ obleka prevelika. (her)
5 To je _____ stanovanje. V _____ stanovanje smo se preselili lani. (our)

Exercise 4

Andrej is trying to figure out where Ben left his blazer. So he is asking him some questions. Provide Ben's answers.

1 Kakšne barve je bil suknjič?
2 Kje ste ga nazadnje nosili?
3 A ste ga imeli, ko ste prišli iz gostilne?
4 A ste telefonirali v gostilno?
5 Kaj ste izvedeli ('find out')?
6 Kaj boste naredili, če ne najdete suknjiča?
7 A vam lahko jaz posodim svoj suknjič?

Dialogue 2

Na oddelku z moško konfekcijo   In the men's department (Audio 2:40)

Ben and Alenka are looking for a new blazer for Ben. A sales clerk is trying to be helpful. Which blazer does Ben choose and why? What else do they buy?

PRODAJALKA	Dober dan. A vam lahko kaj pomagam?
BEN	Iščem suknjič v svetli barvi. Všeč mi je tale svetlorjavi, a je premajhen.
PRODAJALKA	Katero številko nosite običajno?
BEN	Ne vem, prihajam iz Amerike in ameriške velikosti so drugačne od slovenskih.
ALENKA	Andrej nosi številko petdeset in njegov suknjič vam je malo premajhen. Najbrž potrebujete dvainpetdeset.
PRODAJALKA	Potem lahko pomerite tega sivega ali pa tistega modrega.
ALENKA	Oba vam zelo lepo pristajata. Samo modri bo morda prevroč za poletje.
PRODAJALKA	Sivi je zelo lahek, iz svile in volne. Tudi cena je ugodna, ker je na razprodaji.
BEN	Dobro, vzel bom sivega. Rad bi tudi par srajc s kratkimi rokavi.

PRODAJALKA	Srajce so tamle. Imamo jih v različnih barvah, kar izvolite pogledati.
BEN	Niso drage. Vzel bom eno belo in eno svetlomodro.
ALENKA	Tudi jaz bom kupila eno za Andreja. Všeč so mu temne barve. Mislim, da mu bo všeč tale temnosiva.

V I. nadstropju blagovnice VELE

-ženska konfekcija
-moška konfekcija
-perilo
-kopalke
-spalni program
-nogavice
-modni dodatki

Vocabulary

drugačen	different		**rokav**	sleeve
nositi nosim ipf.	to wear		**srajca**	shirt
pomeriti pf.	to try on		**svila**	silk
pristajati ipf.	to look good on someone		**ugodna cena**	good price
			velikost f.	size
različen	various		**volna**	wool
razprodaja	sale			

Language points

A masculine adjective without a noun as direct object

When the direct object is a masculine adjective without an accompanying noun, that adjective appears as animate accusative (the same as genitive) even if the omitted noun is inanimate. For example:

> **Če Ben do jutri ne najde suknjiča, bo moral kupiti *novega*.**
> If Ben doesn't find the blazer by tomorrow, he will have to buy a new one.

> **Lahko pomerite *tega sivega* ali pa *tistega modrega*.**
> You can try this gray one on or that blue one.

> **Vzel bom *sivega*.**
> I will take the gray one.

The italicized adjectives refer to **suknjič**, which is omitted to avoid repetition since it is mentioned in the preceding sentence(s). In English you would use an adjective + 'one' in this case.

Another way to express likes and dislikes

You already know how to express likes and dislikes with **rad imeti**. It expresses liking or, more precisely, fondness for something; when referring to a person, it means 'to love'. When expressing liking that means 'appealing to one's taste', the predicate construction **biti všeč** with the logical subject in the dative is used. **Všeč** does not change. For example:

> **Andreju so všeč temne barve.**
> Andrej likes dark colors. [Literally: Dark colors appeal to Andrej.]

> **Oba suknjiča sta mi všeč.**   I like both blazers.
> **Janu je všeč Lara.**   Jan likes Lara.

The word order depends on what is in focus, i.e., the new information is put last. In the first sentence that is the colors Andrej likes, in the second it is the appeal of both blazers. In questions, the clitics follow the question word or come first:

(A) mu je všeč Lara?
Does he like Lara?

Zakaj vam je bila všeč Ljubljana?
Why did you like Ljubljana?

To express a dislike, the auxiliary is negated. For example:

Rdeča srajca mu ni bila všeč. He did not like the red shirt.
Benu niso všeč temne barve. Ben does not like dark colors.

This construction does not work to express the appeal of actions (unless they are expressed with nouns); that should still be done with **rad**. To say that one does not like to do something you can either negate the verb or add the prefix **ne-** to **rad**. Examples:

Marko ne pomaga rad očetu.
Marko does not like to help his father.

Ben nerad kupuje obleko.
Ben does not like to shop for clothes.

Exercise 5

Alenka is asking Ben some questions. Translate her questions and Ben's affirmative answers into Slovene.

1 Do you like Ljubljana?
2 Does Simon like Slovenia?
3 Did Monica and David like the Union Hotel?
4 Did they [two] like Plečnik's architecture?
5 Does Špela like large cities?
6 Do you like Slovene food?

Language point

Vocabulary building

Obleka **'clothing'**

... za moške	men	... za moške in **ženske**	
srajca	shirt	hlače (pl.)	pants, slacks,
suknjič	blazer		trousers
obleka	two-piece suit	kratke hlače	shorts
kravata	tie	pulover	sweater
... za ženske	women	jopica	cardigan
krilo	skirt	majica	T-shirt
obleka	dress	jakna	jacket
bluza	blouse	plašč	coat
kostim	two-piece suit	klobuk	hat
		kapa	cap
		šal	scarf
		kopalke (pl.)	swimsuit
		spodnje perilo	underwear
		nogavice	socks
		pižama	pyjamas

With items that are worn by both sexes, the adjectives **moški** or **ženski** are used to specify 'men's' or 'women's'; the same goes for footwear.

Obutev **'footwear'**

čevlji	shoes	**natikači**	flip-flops
sandale/sandali	sandals	**copate/copati**	slippers
škornji	boots		

All footwear items are listed in the plural. Even if they come in pairs, the plural is used, unless talking specifically about two pieces. For example:

Kje imaš čevlje?	Where do you have [your] shoes?
Izgubil je oba čevlja.	He lost both shoes.

Verbs related to clothing

		Transitive	
		ipf.	pf.
to put on	clothes	**oblačiti**	**oblę|či -čem**
	shoes	**obuvati**	**obu|ti -jem**
to take off	clothes	**slačiti**	**slę|či -čem**
	shoes	**sezuvati**	**sezu|ti -jem**

nositi (ipf.) — to wear   **pristajati** (ipf.) — to fit well
prati perem (ipf.) — to wash   **likati** (ipf.) — to iron
pakirati (ipf.) — to pack

Reflexive verbs: se as a direct object

The verbs in the table above can have clothing or footwear as a direct object, as in:

Oblękla je pulover.   She put on a sweater.

When the direct object is a person rather than clothing or footwear, then they mean 'to (un)dress someone', as in:

Marko je oblękel sina.   Marko dressed his son.

In this case, these verbs can be reflexive, i.e., the reflexive pronoun **se** 'self' can be used in place of a direct object, indicating that the action is directed towards the subject. For example:

Marko se je oblękel.   Marko got dressed.
Vędno se sezujem v   I always take my shoes off in
predsobi.   the hall.

Some other examples of reflexive verbs with **se** 'self':

umivati se ipf.   to wash oneself
kǫpati se ipf.   to bathe oneself
česati čęšem se ipf.   to comb one's own hair
ględati se ipf.   to look at oneself
učíti se ipf.   to teach oneself

Exercise 6

From the list of clothing choose seven items that Peter must pack for a business trip.

Kaj mora Peter spakirati za poslovno potovanje?
Answer in a full sentence.

kratke hlače	krilo	pižama
bluza	srajca	hlače
majica	spodnje perilo	jakna
nogavice	kopalke	klobuk
suknjič	kostim	kravata

Exercise 7

Translate this dialogue between Vesna and a **prodajalka** into Slovene.

PRODAJALKA	May I help you?
VESNA	I am looking for a coat.
PRODAJALKA	What color do you like and what size do you usually wear?
VESNA	I like light colors. I wear size 40.
PRODAJALKA	You can try this (**tega**) light brown one.
VESNA	This one is a little too large for me.

PRODAJALKA   You probably need size 38. You can try this light blue one.

VESNA   This one fits me. And I like the color, too. OK, I will take the light blue one.

Reading

Slovenci in copate (Audio 2:42)

Ko boste šli prvič na obisk v slovensko hišo ali stanovanje, boste najbrž začudeni, če vam bo gostitelj takoj pri vratih ponudil copate. Veliko Slovencev ima namreč navado, da takoj, ko stopijo v domače stanovanje, sezujejo čevlje in obujejo copate, to pa običajno pričakujejo tudi od gostov. Copate morda res lahko rešijo zadrego, ko gost ne ve, ali bi se sezul ali vstopil v čevljih. Vendar pa pri tujcih, ki nimajo te navade, lahko povzročijo nove zadrege. Takole pripoveduje Slovenka Irena Blatnik, ki že 25 let živi v ZDA:

»Doma smo se vedno sezuvali in po hiši nosili copate in to navado sem prinesla tudi v naš ameriški dom. Tu, kjer živim, ljudje* nimajo kakšnega trdnega pravila glede čevljev v stanovanju: nekateri se sezuvajo, drugi hodijo v čevljih. Če se sezuvajo, hodijo po hiši v nogavicah ali bosi in le redko v copatah, a nikoli ne bi copat ponudili obiskovalcu. Zdaj razumem, zakaj so me gledali tako začudeno, ko sem prva leta gostom kar avtomatično ponudila copate, če so se sezuli. Ampak po kratkem oklevanju so jih vedno obuli. Dokončno me je te navade odvadila znanka, ki sem ji ponudila copate, ko je sezula snežene in mokre škornje. Brez oklevanja je zavrnila ponujene copate: »No, thank you. Can I have a clean pair of socks?«

* **ljudje** 'people', pl. of **človek** 'man, person'

Vocabulary

bọs	barefoot	**pričakovati** ipf.	to expect
dokončno	ultimately	**pripovedovati** ipf.	to narrate
dọm	home	**rẹšiti** pf.	to solve
glẹdẹ (+G)	regarding	**snežẹn**	snowy
gostitelj	host	**stopiti stọpim** pf.	to step
mọkẹr	wet	**trdno pravilo**	strict rule
namrеč	namely	**tujẹc**	foreigner
navada	habit, custom	**vst|opiti**	to enter
obiskovalẹc	visitor	**-ọpim** pf.	
odvaditi	to break a habit	**začudẹn**	surprised
oklẹvanje	hesitation	**zadrẹga**	embarrassment
pon|udıti	to offer	**zav|rniti**	to refuse
-udim pf.		**-rnem** pf.	
ponujen	offered		

Exercise 8

Based on the article, determine whether the following statements are true (T), false (F), or there is not enough information (NI) in the text to decide.

1 The article talks about the Slovene custom of wearing slippers.
2 The author shows that offering slippers to the guest is a good idea.
3 Irena Blatnik is a Slovene living in America.
4 Irena and her family always wear slippers in her house.
5 She used to offer slippers to her American guests.
6 Her American guests thought that was an interesting custom.
7 Only one woman refused to wear the slippers Irena offered.

Unit Fifteen
Telo in zdravje
The body and health

In this unit you will learn about:

- The body
- Health
- Personal appearance
- The dative of adjectives
- Commands and prohibitions
- Expressing how you feel

Dialogue 1

Vse me boli Everything hurts (Audio 2:42)

Ben is not feeling well. What are his symptoms? What does Alenka want him to do? Why can't Andrej call his doctor? Whom do they end up calling and will Ben get help?

ALENKA Ben, čisto bledi ste. Je morda kaj narobe? Upam, da niste bolni.

BEN Res se ne počutim dobro. Vse me boli. Že sinoči me je bolela glava, danes me pa bolijo tudi roke, noge in grlo. Tudi slabo mi je.

ALENKA Takoj bom prinesla toplomer, da boste izmerili vročino.

After Alenka has taken Ben's temperature. . . .

ALENKA   Osemintrideset dve. Vročino imate, morali boste k
         zdravniku. Lahko bi šli kar k Andrejevemu, ker je tu
         blizu. . . . Andrej, prosim, pokliči v zdravstveni dom in
         vprašaj, kdaj dela doktor Peklaj.
ANDREJ   Doktor Peklaj je ta teden na dopustu.
ALENKA   Dobro, bom pa jaz telefonirala svoji zdravnici. A lahko
         poiščeš njeno telefonsko številko v imeniku? Ali pa poglej
         na internet.
ANDREJ   Že imam. Doktor Bavčarjeva danes dela dopoldne. Kar
         takoj pokliči v ambulanto in se naroči. Zgodaj je še, morda
         še nima vse zasedeno.

After Alenka's phone call to the doctor. . . .

ALENKA   Ben, imeli ste srečo, prišli ste takoj na vrsto. Naročeni ste
         za ob enajstih. Moja zdravnica ima ordinacijo v Ljubljani,
         od doma bova šla okrog pol enajstih. Medtem pa počivajte
         in veliko pijte – tu imate vodo, lahko vam skuham tudi čaj.
         Ste morda lačni?
BEN   Ne, jesti ne morem, gre mi na bruhanje. Tudi čaja ne bom,
         samo vodo, prosim.

Vocabulary

bled	pale (adj.)	**počut|iti**	to feel
bolan bolna	sick	**(-im) se** ipf.	
boleti bol*i* ipf.	to hurt	**roka**	arm, hand
glava	head	**toplomer**	thermometer
grlo	throat	**vročina**	fever
izmeriti pf.	to measure	**zaseden**	taken, occupied
narobe	wrong	**zdravn|ik, -ica**	physician
noga	leg, foot	**zdravstveni**	health center
počivati ipf.	to rest	**dom**	

Vocabulary notes

naročíti se pf. **(pri zdravniku/pri frizerju/kozmetičarki)** 'to make an
   appointment (at the doctor's/hairdresser's/beautician's)';
bíti naročen 'to have an appointment';
príti na vrsto 'to get your turn'; **bíti na vrsti** 'to be one's turn';
od dọma 'from home'; **šla bova od dọma** 'we will leave home';
ọsẹmintrídeset dvẹ = 38.2°C;
(telefọnski) imeník 'phone book'

Language point

The imperative

Notice how Andrej and Alenka are telling each other and Ben to do
things:

Pokliči **v ambulanto.**	Call the clinic.
Poglej **na** *internet.*	Look on the Internet.
Počivajte **in velíko** *pijte.*	Rest and drink as much as possible.

The italicized forms are imperatives, which are specifically used for
commands, requests, or orders. So far you have been using other means
to express these, for example, **mọrati** + infinitive. The imperative
is derived from the present tense. After removing the present-tense
ending and the preceding vowel add the suffix as shown in the chart
below to form the second-person singular imperative.

Present tense		Imperative (2 sg.)	
-am	čak~~am~~	-aj	čakaj
-em -im	piš~~em~~ kup~~im~~	-i	píši kupi
-(V)j-em*	píj~~em~~	—	píj

* verbs having a vowel + **j** before **-em**

Note: the verbs in **-či** ending in **-čem** and **-žem** in the present change
-č- to **-c-** and **-ž-** to **-z-** in the imperative, e.g., **peci** 'bake', **strízi**
'cut'.

Memorize the irregular imperatives of these verbs:

	imp. 2 sg.
*i*ti (gr**ę**m)	p**ǫ**jdi
b*i*ti (s**ę**m)	b**ǫ**di
v**ę**deti (v**ę**m)	v**ę**di
j**ę**sti (j**ę**m)	jej
pov**ę**dati (pov**ę**m)	povej
im**ę**ti (imam)	imej
gl**ę**dati (gl**ę**dam)	glej

The imperative is conjugated. The first-person dual or plural imperative is for appealing to or exhorting a group that includes the speaker, i.e., equal to 'let's' + verb. The following personal endings are added to the basic, second-person singular form for other persons and numbers:

	Dual		Plural	
1	-va	čakajva	-mo	čakajmo
2	-ta	čakajta	-te*	čakajte

* 2 pl. used for giving commands to more than two people or to one (formal)

To say what you want the third person to do, use **naj** + the present tense. Examples:

Katja naj pom*i*je posǫ**do.**	Katja should wash the dishes.
Pacienti naj po*č*akajo v čakalnici.	Patients should wait in the waiting room.

Exercise 1

Each of your friend's problems is followed by some advice. Complete the responses with the appropriate verbs from the list below in the imperative.

pogledati, iti, počivati, poklicati, naročiti, vprašati, piti, preseliti se, kupiti, počakati

1 Zelo sem žejna. – _____ liter mineralne vode.
2 Ne vem, kako se gre do postaje. – _____ prodajalca v kiosku.

3 Imam visoko vročino. – _____ k zdravniku.
4 Ne vem, kdaj dela doktor Miklavc. – _____ v ambulanto.
5 Prehlajena sem. – _____ in _____ veliko čaja.
6 Zamudila sem vlak ob 4h. – _____ na drug vlak.
7 Ne vem, kakšno vreme bo jutri. – _____ v časopis.
8 To stanovanje mi ni všeč. – _____ v drugo stanovanje.
9 Izgubil sem suknjič. – _____ novega.

Exercise 2

Rewrite the following directions using the imperative (2 pl.) instead of the future tense.

Peljali se boste do zdravstvenega doma in parkirali zadaj na parkirišču. Po stopnicah boste šli v drugo nadstropje. Zavili boste desno in šli naravnost do čakalnice ('waiting room') na koncu hodnika. Poiskali boste ordinacijo doktorja Zajca. Potrkali* boste in počakali na sestro ('nurse'). Ko pride sestra, boste oddali* zdravstveno kartico. Potem boste počakali, da pridete na vrsto.

* **potrkati (potrkam)** 'to knock'; **oddati (oddam)** 'to hand in'

Language point

Adjectival dative endings

With the exception of f. sg., adjectival endings differ from nominal endings in the dative case. Some examples:

Singular: ***Andrejevemu** prijatelju/**Alenkini** prijateljici/ **glavnemu** mestu;*
Plural: ***Andrejevim** prijateljem/**Alenkinim** prijateljicam/ **glavnim** mestom;*
Dual: ***Andrejevima** prijateljema/**Alenkinima** prijateljicama/ **glavnima** mestoma.*

You need to memorize three endings: -**emu** for masculine and neuter singular, -**im** for all genders plural, and -**ima** for all genders dual.

You now know all the adjectival endings. Refer to the charts in the Grammar summary for review. The same endings apply to the adjectival pronouns, i.e., the ones that behave like adjectives, with the exception of **ta** 'this' and **vẹs** 'all' (see the Grammar summary). For example:

Telefoniral bom *svojemu* **zdravniku.**	I will call my doctor.
Pri *tistem* **semaforju zavijete levo.**	You turn left at that traffic light.

K *čigavi* **zdravnici bo šel Bẹn? K** *tvoji.*
To whose doctor will Ben go? To yours.

Exercise 3

Use the phrases given in parentheses in the appropriate form.

1 Šli smo na obisk k _____. (Andrejevi starši)
2 A je bil _____ všeč hotel Union? (Benov prijatelj)
3 Vodič je _____ pokazal Križanke. (angleški turisti)
4 _____ bo to krilo gotovo prav. (tvoja hčerka)
5 Aleš, a lahko telefoniraš _____? (moj oče)
6 Te obleke lepo pristajajo _____. (visoke ženske)

Language point

Saying how one feels

The answer to the question **Kakọ se počutiš/počutite?** 'How are you feeling?' can be similar to the answer to the question **Kakọ ste?**, i.e., some sort of adverb(ial), like **dobro** 'well', **slabọ** 'bad, not well', **odlično** 'excellent'. There is a difference between **slabọ se počutim** 'I don't feel well' and **slabọ mi je** 'I feel nauseous.'

A predicate adjective with the auxiliary can also indicate how one feels, as in **Bolan (bolna) sẹm** 'I am sick.' Some other useful adjectives:

zaspan	sleepy	**utrujẹn**	tired
žejẹn	thirsty	**lačẹn**	hungry
prehlajen	having a cold	**zdrav**	healthy
žalostẹn	sad	**vesẹl**	merry, happy
srẹčẹn	(profoundly) happy	**jẹzẹn**	angry

Here are some patterns of expressions for giving a more specific account of your health:

1 Saying what hurts: the verb **bolęti boli** 'to hurt' with the owner of the hurting part in the accusative (no possessive!). For example:

Boli me glava/roka/srcę.
My head/hand (arm)/heart hurts.

Bolęlo ga je grlo/kolęno.
His throat/knee hurt.

Bolęle so jih noge.
Their legs (feet) hurt.

Mętko so bolęle ledvice/oči.
Metka's kidneys/eyes hurt.

2 Saying what ailment or symptom one has:

Imam glavobol/vročino/nahod/prehlad/gripo/alergijo.
I have a headache/a fever/sniffles/a cold/flu/an allergy.

3 Using verbs as symptoms:

Kašljam/kiham/težkǫ diham/potim se/bruham.
I am coughing/sneezing/having a hard time breathing/
sweating/vomiting.

Reševalno vozilo

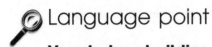

Language point

Vocabulary building

Telo 'body'

gl*a*va	head	**r*o*ka**	arm, hand
lasjẹ (m. pl.)	hair	**p*r*st**	finger, toe
obr*a*z	face	**n*o*ga**	leg, foot
nọs	nose	**kolẹno**	knee
oč*i* (f. pl.)	eyes	**p*e*ta**	heel
ušẹsa (n. pl.)	ears	**h*r*bet**	back
***u*sta** (n. pl.)	mouth	**želọdec**	stomach
zobjẹ (m. pl.)	teeth	**plj*u*ča** (n. pl.)	lungs
g*r*lo	throat	**jẹtra** (n. pl.)	liver
		srcẹ	heart
		ledv*i*ce	kidneys

Several names for body parts are plural only, e.g., ***u*sta**, **plj*u*ča**, **jẹtra** (all neuter). Some others are listed in the plural because you will mostly use them in the plural, although they also have a singular form. **Zobjẹ** and **lasjẹ** are plural forms of the nouns **zọb** and **l*a*s**; note that the N pl. has an exceptional ending, stressed **-jẹ** (similarly **možjẹ**). Parts that come in pairs, e.g., **ledv*i*ce**, **ušẹsa**, **oč*i***, are also normally used in the plural, unless we are talking about one **ledv*i*ca**, **uhọ**, or **okọ** or **obẹ** 'both' **ledv*i*ci**, **ušẹsi**, **očẹsi**. The noun **uhọ** has the stem **ušẹs-** in all oblique cases, but the endings are regular neuter. The noun **okọ** is neuter, but **oč*i*** is feminine. Therefore, **rj*a*ve oč*i*** 'brown eyes'; **oč*i* so me bolẹle** 'my eyes were hurting'.

Common vocabulary related to . . .

. . . zdrav -a 'healthy'

zdr*a*vje	health
(po)zdr*a*viti (+A)	to cure
(po)zdr*a*viti se	to recuperate
zdravn|*i*k -*i*ca	physician
zobozdravn|*i*k -*i*ca	dentist
zdrav*i*lo	medication
zdravil*i*šče	health resort

zdravstveni dọm	health center
zdravstvena kartica	(health) insurance card
zdravstveno zavarovanje	health insurance

. . . bolạn bolna 'sick' and **bolẹti** 'to hurt'

boln|ik -*ica*	patient
bọlnica	hospital
bolečịna	pain
bolẹzẹn f.	illness
zbolẹti	to get sick

Personal appearance

tẹža	weight	**tẹhtati**	to weigh
viš*i*na	height	**visok(a)**	tall
postạva	figure		

Visok sẹm 183 centimẹtrov.	I am 183 cm (6 ft) tall.
Tẹhtam 82 kilogramov.	I weigh 82 kg (180 lb).
Sẹm svetlolasa/temnolasa.	I am blond/dark-haired.
Imạm tẹmne lasẹ in rjave očị.	I have dark hair and brown eyes.
Sẹm n*i*zke/v*i*tke/srẹdnje postạve.	I am [of] short/slim/average [build].

Exercise 4

(a) Say what hurts. People affected are indicated in parentheses.

1 throat (Ben)
2 eyes (we)
3 knee (she)
4 legs (two of you)

5 tooth (I)
6 ears (Irena)
7 stomach (he)
8 heart (you, sg.)

(b) Rewrite your sentences in the past tense.

Exercise 5

These are the symptoms Tom has. Write down what he needs to say to the doctor to convey his problems.

1 fever
2 headache

3 sore throat
4 nausea

5 sweating   7 very tired
6 coughing   8 always sleepy

Dialogue 2

Pri zdravniku   At the doctor's **(Audio 2:46)**

After Ben has explained his problems, the doctor examines him and
instructs him on what to do.

ZDRAVNICA	Koliko časa se že slabo počutite?
BEN	Glava in grlo sta me začela boleti včeraj, vročino pa imam od danes zjutraj.
ZDRAVNICA	Slecite srajco, prosim, bom poslušala srce in pljuča. Globoko dihajte. . . . Dobro. Zdaj pa ne dihajte. . . . Pljuča so v redu. Odprite usta in recite aaa . . . Grlo je malo vneto. Tudi nos je zamašen. Najbrž imate gripo. Nekaj dni ostanite v postelji in pijte veliko čaja. Nikar ne hodite bolni okrog.
BEN	A potrebujem kakšna zdravila?
ZDRAVNICA	Zaenkrat vam ne bom predpisala nobenih zdravil. Jemljite tablete proti vročini in bolečinam po potrebi, lahko štirikrat na dan po dve tableti. Dobite jih v lekarni brez recepta. Če čez štiri dni ne bo izboljšanja, pridite nazaj.

Vocabulary

globoko	deeply	**predpi|sati** -šem pf.	to prescribe
izboljšanje	improvement		
jemati jemljem ipf.	to take	**proti** (+D)	against
		recept	prescription
lekarna	pharmacy	**tableta**	pill
noben	not any	**vnet**	inflamed
po potrebi	as needed	**zaenkrat**	for now
		zamašen	stuffed

Vocabulary note

štírikrat na dan po dvẹ tablẹti 'two tablets four times a day'

Language point

Prohibitions

Prohibitions are formed by negating the imperative. For example:

Ne dihajte.	Don't breathe.
Ne hodite bolni okrọg.	Don't walk around sick.

Notice how the doctor uses **nikar** with the negated imperative to strengthen the prohibition:

Nikar ne hodite bolni okrọg.   Do not walk around sick.

Particularly on public signs you will find prohibitions formed with **prepovẹdano (je)** 'is forbidden' or **ni dovọljeno** 'is not allowed' + the infinitive. For example:

Kaditi prepovẹdano.	Smoking prohibited.
Prepovẹdano hoditi po travi.	Walking on the grass is prohibited.

Prepovẹdano naslanjati kolẹsa na zid.
Leaning bikes against the wall is prohibited.

A noun derived from a verb can be used instead of the infinitive:

Kajenje ni dovọljeno.	Smoking is not allowed.
Prehod prepovedan.	Crossing prohibited.
Prepovẹdano parkiranje.	Parking prohibited.

In spoken language, you will often hear **ne** + the infinitive (without the final **-i**) for prohibitions, e.g., **ne kadit** 'don't smoke', **ne hodit po trav(i)** 'don't walk on the grass', **ne jọkat** 'don't cry'.

Prepoved

Exercise 6

Translate the following doctor's instructions to the patient.

1 Stay in bed for a few days.
2 Drink a lot of water or tea.
3 Eat fruit and vegetables.
4 Take medication for the pain.
5 Go to the pharmacy.
6 Don't drink alcohol.
7 Don't walk around sick.
8 Don't eat overly salty (**slan**) food.
9 Don't take antibiotics.
10 Don't smoke.

Dialogue 3

Težave pred izpíti   Trouble before exams **(Audio 2:48)**

Nejc is surprised that Lara came to the party without Jan. He finds out why.

NEJC   Zakaj pa Jana nísi pripeljala na žur?
LARA   Jan je ostal doma, ker je bolan. Kíha, kašlja in sploh se ne
       počúti dobro.

NEJC A ima grípo?

LARA Míslim, da je samọ prehlajen, ker níma vročíne. On vẹdno zbolí pred izpíti.

NEJC Tọ je čúdno, ker je tak špọrten típ. Teče, igra kọšarko in nogomet in vẹdno izglẹda v dobri fọrmi.

LARA Rẹs se ukvarja s špọrtom, ampak drugače ne živí zdravo. Vẹdno jẹ píce in hamburgerje, premalo spí in pred izpíti je pod velíkim pritískom, ker prej ne študíra.

NEJC Izpíti se začnejo šelẹ drúgi tẹden. Upam, da se bo do takrat že pozdravil.

Vocabulary

fọrma	(physical) shape	**pritísk**	pressure
izglẹdati ipf.	to look (a certain way)	**špọrten**	athletic
		típ	type
izpít	exam	**ukvarjati se z** (+l) ipf.	to occupy oneself with
kọšarka	basketball		
osta|ti -nem pf.	to stay	**žur**	party (coll.)
pozdraviti se pf.	to get well		

Language point

Expressing causality

Causal clauses, answering the question **Zakaj?** 'why?', are introduced with the conjunction **ker** 'because'. The word-order rules are the same as you learned with the conditional clauses. Some examples:

Jan je doma, ker je bolan. Jan is home because he is sick.

Zakaj je Jan pred izpíti pod velíkim pritískom? Ker prej ne študíra.

Why is Jan under great pressure before the exams? Because he didn't study earlier.

Ker igra košarko, je v dobri formi.
Because he plays basketball, he is in good shape.

Exercise 7

Answer the questions with causal clauses.

1 Zakaj ne bomo šli na piknik? (The weather will be bad tomorrow.)
2 Zakaj je Jan velikokrat bolan? (He doesn't live healthily.)
3 Zakaj ti zdravnica ni predpisala antibiotika? (I have the flu.)
4 Zakaj je Ben kupil nov suknjič? (He lost the old one.)
5 Zakaj Jan ni prišel na izpit? (He is sick.)
6 Zakaj je Alenka peljala Bena k svoji zdravnici? (Andrej's doctor is on vacation.)

Reading

 Iz domače lekarne* (Audio 2:50)

Šipek

Plodovi šipka imajo zelo veliko vitamina C. Šipkov čaj izboljša odpornost, zato je še posebno koristen v zimskih mesecih, ker nas varuje pred gripo in prehladi. Če pa smo že zboleli, nam šipkov čaj pomaga hitreje okrevati.

Priprava čaja

Naberite zrele plodove šipka, jih razrežite, posušite, zdrobite in shranite v temnih steklenih kozarcih. Za čaj vzemite eno žlico posušenih šipkovih plodov, jih prelijte z 2 dcl mrzle vode in pustite vreti 10 minut. Precedite, lahko dodate sladkor in limonin sok. Pijte večkrat na dan ne le ob prehladih, ampak vse leto. Čaj je dober tudi hladen.

Šipek

Vocabulary

izbǫljšati pf.	to improve		**priprava**	preparation
nab|rati **-erem** pf.	to pick		**razrę|zati** **-žem** pf.	to cut up
odpǫrnost f.	immunity		**shraniti** pf.	to save
okrẹvati ipf.	to recover		**šipẹk**	rose hip
plǫd	fruit (e.g., berry)		**varovati pred** (+I)	to protect from
posuš/ti pf.	to dry		**vrẹti vre** ipf.	to boil
preced/ti pf.	to strain		**zdrob/ti** pf.	to crush
prel/i|ti -jem pf.	to pour over			

* **Domača lekarna** 'home pharmacy' refers to home remedies, which are quite popular with Slovenes, particularly remedies derived from plants. Herbal teas are widely consumed and sold in supermarkets, but also in specialized stores and pharmacies. These also carry herbal remedies for common ailments in other forms (pills, ointments, drops). In a regular **lekarna** they will be available as **zdravila brez recepta** 'over-the-counter medicines'. Particularly with colds and flu, it is believed and even doctors recommend that one should drink a lot of tea—not just any liquid will do.

Unit Sixteen

Na Gorenjsko ali proti morju?

To Upper Carniola or towards the coast?

In this unit you will learn about:

- Landscape, geography
- Slovene regions
- Speaking hypothetically
- The comparative and superlative
- Feminine nouns ending in a consonant
- Pronouns with prepositions

Dialogue 1

Kam na izlet? Where to go on a day trip?
(Audio 2:51)

Once Ben is well again, his hosts offer to take him on a day trip. They are discussing different options. What region do they decide to see? Why would a cave be a good choice?

ALENKA Vaš obísk v Slovęniji se bo žę skoraj iztękel. Ostal je samǫ še en tęden. Z Andrejem bi vas pred odhǫdom rada peljala na daljši izlet.

ANDREJ Lahko bi šli na Gorenjsko, proti Blędu in Bohinju, ali pa na Primorsko. Kaj bi raje videli?

BEN Obožujem Gorenjsko in Alpe, ampak na Blędu in v Bohinju sem bil že dvakrat. Primorsko slabše poznam. Bil sem samo v Postojnski jami in Lipici.

ANDREJ Potęm gremo lahko v Škocjanske jame in naprej proti obali, v Piran in Portorož.

ALENKA Se strinjam, jame bodo v tej vročini dobra osvežitev, ker je v njih temperatura vedno okrog deset stopinj. Od Škocjanskih jam tudi ni daleč do Pirana.

ANDREJ Res ni, park Škocjanske jame je na poti proti morju. Z avtoceste se zavije pri Divači in potęm je do parka samo še par kilometrov po regionalni cęsti.

ALENKA Če gremo dovolj zgodaj, bo tudi gnęča manjša kot kasneje. Jame si lahko ogledamo dopoldne in smo do kosila že v Piranu. Poględala bom, kdaj se začnejo oględi.

Vocabulary

avtocęsta	highway	**par**	a couple
gnęča	crowd	**pred** (+l)	before
izlet	day trip	**Primorska**	Littoral
izte|či -čem se pf.	to come to an end	**regionalna cęsta**	local road
jama	cave	**strinjati se** pf.	to agree
obala	coast	**vročina**	heat
osta|ti -nem pf.	to remain	**zač|eti -ne se** pf.	to start
osvežitev f.	something refreshing		

Vocabulary notes

Blęd, Bohinj: Slovene lake resorts beneath the Alps;
Postǫjnska jama: 'the Postojna cave' is the largest cave in Slovenia;
Lípica: village in the Littoral region known for its stud farm (**kobilarna**);
Škocjanske jame: 'the Škocjan caves' are a UNESCO World Heritage site;
Piran, Portorǫž: coastal cities.

Language points

The comparative

Notice the comparative degree of the adjectives in these sentences:

> **Z Andrejem bi vas rada peljala na *daljši* izlet.**
> Andrej and I would like to take you on a longer day trip.

> **Gnęča bo zgǫdaj dopoldne *manjša* kot kasneje.**
> It will be less crowded early in the morning than later [in the day].

The comparative is formed from adjectives denoting quality in these two ways:

1 Most of the time it is derived with suffixes **-ji**, **-ši**, or **-ejši** (the ending will change depending on the gender, number, and case).
  The following changes occur before **-ji** or **-ši** is added:

  (a) the suffixes **-ek** and **-ok** are dropped;
  (b) the consonants before **-ji** and **-ši** change as follows:

$$k \to č \quad\quad h \to š \quad\quad z \to ž$$
$$g \to ž \quad\quad s \to š \quad\quad d \to j$$

Examples:

sladẹk	sweet	**slajši**
visok	high, tall	**višji**
drạg	dear, expensive	**dražji**
nízẹk	low; (vertically) short	**nížji**
tíh	quiet	**tíšji**

The chart shows which adjectives use each suffix to form the comparative:

Indefinite adjectives		Suffix	Examples
Monosyllabic adj. Adjectives in **-ek, -ok**	-č, -š, or -ž before the suffix	-ji	drag – dražji tíh – tíšji nízek – nížji
	consonant other than -č, -š, or -ž before the suffix preceded by a vowel	-ši	lep – lepši mlad – mlajši
Polysyllabic adj. Monosyllabic adj. ending in two consonants		-ejši	hladen* – hladnejši udoben – udobnejši čist clean – čistejši

* Remember to drop the fleeting vowel before attaching the suffix.

There are quite a few exceptions to these rules. Here are exceptional comparatives of some of the most common adjectives:

dober – boljši	majhen – manjši	star – starejši
kratek – krajši	velik – večji	nov – novejši
dolg – daljši	lahek – lažji	poceni – cenejši

2 Some adjectives form the comparative with the adverb **bolj** 'more' preceding the adjective. Among those are colors (**zelen – bolj zelen**), adjectives that are originally participles (**znan** 'known' – **bolj znan, vroč – bolj vroč**), or adjectives that do not have both definite and indefinite forms (**bratov, slovenski**). In colloquial language this type is often used even when derivation with the suffix is standard. You will, for example, hear people say **bolj čist, bolj drag, bolj nízek** instead of **čistejši, dražji, nížji.**

Comparing

The conjunction **kot** 'than' is used to make a comparison. If it is between two nouns, both are in the nominative case. For example:

Ben je starejši kot Špela.	Ben is older than Špela.
Ljubljana je manjša kot London.	Ljubljana is smaller than London.

Danes je vreme lępše, kot je bilǫ včęraj.
Today the weather is nicer than it was yesterday.

When comparing two nouns (nominal phrases), like in the first two sentences above, the preposition **od** with the genitive can be used instead of **kot** with the nominative, i.e., **Bęn je starejši od Špęle**, or **Ljubljana je manjša od Lǫndona.**

However, comparatives are not always used for comparison, but rather to express a large degree of certain quality. For example:

Dajte mi nęko močnejše zdravilo proti bolečinam.
Give me some strong(er) medication for [against] pain.

The collocation **vse** (or **zmeraj**) + comparative means an increasingly higher degree. For example:

Bencin je vse dražji.   Gas/petrol keeps getting more expensive.
Ljubljana je vse lępša.   Ljubljana keeps getting prettier.

Exercise 1

Fill in the appropriate comparative forms of the adjectives in parentheses.

1 Moja kava je veliko _____ od tvoje. (sladek)
2 Zdravnik mi je predpisal neko _____ zdravilo. (nov)
3 Če bo temperatura jutri _____, pridite nazaj. (visok)
4 Jutri bo vreme _____ kot je bilo danes. (lep)
5 Naš novi avto je veliko _____ od starega. (udoben)
6 Punčke so danes _____, kot so bile včeraj. (miren)
7 Letošnji julij je precej _____ od lanskega. (vroč)
8 Potrebujem _____ krilo, to je prekratko. (dolg)

Exercise 2

Compare the two items in parentheses. Say which one is:

1 older (**Robbov vodnjak, Tromostovje**)
2 larger (Germany, Austria)
3 shorter (February, March)
4 more expensive (house, studio apartment)
5 lighter (oil, water)
6 younger (Andrej, his sister)

Language points

The superlative

The superlative (highest grade) is formed with the prefix **naj-** added to the comparative. Both parts are accented. Here are some examples that might appear in advertisements or headlines:

> **20 najlepših razgledov na svetu**
> 20 of the most beautiful views in the world

> Odprli **največji** nakupovalni center v državi.
> The largest shopping mall in the country opened.

> **Najhitrejši** nakup na spletu
> The fastest shopping on line

> **Najboljši** in **najmodernejši** slovenski stadion spet v Ljubljani.
> The best and most modern Slovene stadium again in Ljubljana.

Adjectives that form the comparative with **bolj**, use **najbolj** for the superlative, e.g., **najbolj vroč**.

Gradation of adverbs

Adverbs derived from adjectives, like **hitro, tiho, nizko, vroče** have the same comparative and superlative as the same-sounding adjectives, except that in standard language the suffix usually drops **š** after **j** and **j** after **č, ž, š**, e.g., **hitrejše** → **hitreje, tišje** → **tiše, nižje** → **niže, bolj vroče**. Spoken language prefers the variant without dropping **š** and **j** or gradation with **bolj**, e.g., **bolj tiho**.

Pokrajine 'regions' (Audio 2:53)

Except for **Prekmurje** and **Bela krajina**, the names of Slovene **pokrajine** are adjectives in **-ska/-sko, -ška/-ško** used as nouns. When not used with prepositions for origin, destination, or location (in G, A, L), they all have neuter and feminine variants.

Pokrajina	Center
Gorenjska/Gorenjsko Upper Carniola	Kranj
Dolenjska/Dolenjsko Lower Carniola	Novo mesto
Štajerska/Štajersko Styria	Maribor
Primorska/Primorsko Littoral	Koper
Notranjska/Notranjsko Inner Carniola	Postojna
Goriška/Goriško Gorizia Region	Nova Gorica
Koroška/Koroško Carinthia	Slovenj Gradec

The feminine variant is preferred. Examples:

Obožujem Gorenjsko.	I adore Upper Carniola.
Primorske ne poznam dobro.	I don't know Littoral well.

Only neuter forms are used with the preposition **na** in the accusative and locative to express destination and location, respectively. Examples:

Prijatelje bomo peljali na Štajersko.	We will take our friends to Styria.
Najboljše češnje rastejo na Primorskem.	The best cherries grow in Littoral.

To express origin, either form can be used in the genitive case with the preposition **z/s**. The feminine form, which is more common here as well, can also be used with **iz**. Examples:

Anitin fant je iz/z Gorenjske.	Anita's boyfriend is from Upper Carniola.
Vlak je pripeljal s Štajerskega.	The train arrived from Styria.

To simplify: be aware of dual gender in certain cases, but you can practically get by with feminine everywhere, except with the preposition **na**, where you need to use the neuter. The same rule works for country names in **-ska/-ška**, e.g., **Norveška**, **Poljska**, **Madžarska**, **Češka**.

Poljska leži vzhodno od Češke.	Poland lies east of the Czech Republic.
Svojega moža sem spoznala na Češkem.	I met my husband in the Czech Republic.
Včeraj so se vrnili iz Madžarske.	They returned from Hungary yesterday.

Exercise 3

Complete each response with the name of the region to which the city from the first sentence belongs. Use the name with the appropriate preposition and in the correct case.

1 Novakovi so šli včeraj v Koper. – Pogosto hodijo _____.
2 Ben je predaval v Mariboru. – Že večkrat je bil _____.
3 Nada je rojena v Postojni. – Nisem vedela, da je _____.
4 Tine in Irena zdaj živita blizu Kranja. – Kdaj pa sta se preselila _____?
5 A ste že bili v Novem mestu? – Ne, ampak moj oče je rojen _____.
6 A veš, od kod je Marko? – Mislim, da je _____, iz Slovenj Gradca.

Dialogue 2

Popoldne na obali An afternoon on the coast
(Audio 2:55)

Once Alenka finds out the hours of the Škocjan caves, they plan out the rest of their trip. What do they plan to do on the Slovene coast?

ALENKA Oględi Škocjanskih jam so vsako uro. Začnejo se ob desetih in trajajo približno uro in pol.

ANDREJ Ravno prav, lahko bomo kosili v Piranu, morda na Tartinijevem trgu ali v kakšni restavraciji na obrežju, čisto ob morju. Od tam se lepo vidi cel Piranski zaliv.

ALENKA Po kosilu se bomo peljali še malo naprej proti jugu, do Sečoveljskih solin. Soline so zaščiten krajinski park z edinstveno floro in favno ter solinarsko arhitekturo. Tu še danes po starih metodah pridelujejo sol.

ANDREJ Nekje blizu solin je tudi ena imenitna gostilna, kjer sva lani na terasi s pogledom na soline jedla najokusnejše ribe. Tam se bomo morali ustaviti za večerjo in to bo lep zaključek našega izleta.

Piran – Tartinijev trg. Photograph by Lea H. Greenberg.

Vocabulary

edínstven	unique	sol f.	salt
favna	fauna	terasa	patio
krajínski park	landscape park	zakljúček	conclusion
obrežje	(sea) shore	zalív	bay
po (+L)	after	zaščíten	protected
približno	approximately		

Vocabulary notes

Tartínijev trg: main square in Piran with the statue of the composer and violinist Giuseppe Tartini, born in Piran;
Sečoveljske solíne 'the Sečovlje salt pans';

sol*i***narski** (adj.) 'pertaining to salt harvesting';
po st*a***rih met***ọ***dah** 'using old methods';
pridel|ovati -*u***jem** ipf. 'to cultivate', here referring to salt-harvesting;
v*i***di se c***ẹ***l Piranski zal***i***v**: **se** is used for passivization here, to say
'the entire Bay of Piran is [can be] seen'.

Language point

Feminine nouns ending in a consonant

A sizable group of feminine nouns end in a consonant in the nominative singular, like the nouns **stvar** 'thing', **p***ọ***t** 'path, way, journey', or **sol** 'salt', **j***ẹ***d** 'dish'. Since in their 'dictionary' form they look like masculine nouns, their gender needs to be individually learned; the glossaries in this book mark the gender when it is not predictable from the ending. You will be able to recognize some of these nouns by these suffixes or desinences:

-***ẹ***v: **c***ẹ***rk***ẹ***v** church, **b***u***k***ẹ***v** beech, **mol***i***t***ẹ***v** prayer
-ost: **mlad***ọ***st** youth, **hitr***ọ***st** speed, **slab***ọ***st** weakness
-***ẹz***en: **bol***ẹ***zen** disease, **ljub***ẹ***zen** love

The nouns in -***ẹ***v decline the same as the regular feminine nouns except for N/A sg. (e.g., **c***ẹ***rk***ẹ***v**) and I sg., which has the ending -**ijo** (e.g., **c***ẹ***rkvijo**).
    The rest follow the two patterns below.

1 Nouns with more than one syllable (and very few one-syllable ones):

Singular		Dual	Plural
N=A	**slab***ọ***st**	N=G=A **slab***ọ***sti**	
G=D=L	**slab***ọ***sti**	D=I **slab***ọ***st(i)ma**	D **slab***ọ***stim**
I	**slab***ọ***stjo***	L **slab***ọ***stih**	
			I **slab***ọ***stmi**

* Nouns ending in a cluster of consonants separated by schwa in N sg. have endings -**ijo**, -**ima**, -**imi** instead of -**jo**, -**ma**, -**mi**, e.g. **bol***ẹ***znijo**, **bol***ẹ***znima**, **bol***ẹ***znimi**.

2 Most one-syllable nouns:

Singular	Dual	Plural
N=A **stvar**	N=G=A **stvarí**	
G **stvarí**	D=I **stvaréma**	D **stvarém**
D=L **stvarí**	L **stvaréh**	
I **stvarjó**		I **stvarmí**

Besides the difference in the dual and plural endings, notice the difference in stress: this group has stress alternating between the stem and the ending in the singular and stressed endings in the dual and plural.

Adjectives used with these nouns will have feminine endings, i.e., the same as with feminine nouns in -**a**. For example:

Odšel je na dolgo pot. He set off on a long journey.
Ustavili smo se pred baročno We stopped in front of a
cerkvijo. baroque church.

Note: The masculine noun **ljudje** 'people' has the same declension as **stvari** (pl.).

Exercise 4

Fill in the correct forms of the nouns **jed**, **sol**, or **bolezen**, as appropriate.

1 A ti je zdravnik povedal, katero _____ imaš?
2 Juha brez _____ mi ni všeč.
3 Katere slovenske _____ imaš najraje?
4 Za veliko _____ še ni zdravil.
5 Ponekod imajo navado, da goste sprejmejo s kruhom in

_____.

6 Zdravilo vzemite trikrat na dan pred _____.
7 V gostilni blizu solin sva jedla ribo, pečeno* v _____.

* **pečen** 'baked'

Exercise 5

Answer these questions about the two dialogues.

Soline. Photograph by Lea H. Greenberg.

1 Kam želita Andrej in Alenka peljati Bena?
2 Katero pokrajino Ben bolje pozna kot Primorsko?
3 Katere kraje za ogled predlaga Andrej?
4 Zakaj Alenka misli, da bi bilo dobro obiskati jame?
5 Kje bodo imeli kosilo?
6 Kje se nahajajo Sečoveljske soline?
7 Kaj bodo videli v solinah?
8 Kje bodo zaključili izlet?

Dialogue 3

Če bi bil*a* tu Špẹla in S*i*mon ... If Špela and Simon were here ... (Audio 2:58)

On their trip to the coast, Ben is trying to imagine how it would be if Špela and Simon were with him.

ALENKA　Takọ lepọ je tu, škọda, da Špẹla in Simon nista z nami.
BEN　　　Rẹs bi bilọ lepọ, če bi prišla z mano. Ampak Špẹla ima sorọdnike na Štajerskem in najbrž bi bila onadva pri njih, medtẹm ko bi jaz dẹlal na inštitutu.
ANDREJ　Ob vikendih bi pa lahkọ hodili na izlẹte po Slovẹniji.
BEN　　　Če bi bili vsi trije tu, bi gotovo najẹli avto in bi ostali v Slovẹniji še v prvi polovici julija. Šli bi vsaj za en tẹden na počitnice – na mọrje, v hribe ali v toplice.
ALENKA　A bi Simon imẹl kaj družbe pri Špẹlinih sorọdnikih?
BEN　　　Simon bi šel verjẹtno v kakšno polẹtno šọlo slovẹnščine. Dobro bi bilọ, če bi se naučil pisati in bọlje govoriti slovẹnsko. Mogọče drugo lẹto . . .
ALENKA　Upam, da boste lahkọ vsi prišli. Z Andrejem bi zelọ rada spoznala Špẹlo in Simona in vas vse pripeljala v Piran in soline.
BEN　　　O, hvala. Gotovo bi jima bile všẹč, kot so bile meni.

Vocabulary

medtem ko	while	**polẹtna šọla**	summer school
naučiti se pf.	to learn	**toplice** pl.	spa

Language points

Personal pronouns: the locative and instrumental cases

Notice the locative and instrumental forms of pronouns in the dialogue. For example:

Onadva bi bila pri njih.　The two of them would stay at their house.

Škọda, da Špẹla in Simon nista z nami.
It's a shame that Špela and Simon are not with us.

Since these are both prepositional cases, there are only full forms, and no clitic forms.

	N (kdọ?)	L ([pri] kọm?)	I ([s] kọm?)
sg.	jaz	meni	mano
	ti	tebi	tabo
	on, ono	njem	njim
	ona	njej	njọ
du.	midva, mẹdve	nama	nama
	vidva, vẹdve	vama	vama
	onadva, onidve	njima	njima
pl.	mi, mẹ	nas	nami
	vi, vẹ	vas	vami
	oni, one, ona	njih	njimi

The shaded forms are new, the rest are familiar either from the dative or accusative.

Personal pronouns with prepositions in other cases

In the genitive and dative, only full forms (refer to the charts in the corresponding sections) can be used with prepositions. For example:

Špẹla ima sorọdnike na Štajerskem. Drugo lẹto bo prišla k njim.

Špela has relatives in Styria. She will come to their house next year.

Lẹtos je Bẹn prišẹl brez njẹ v Slovẹnijo.

This year, Ben came to Slovenia without her.

Remember that to say 'at one's place' you use the preposition **pri** + L of the noun (phrase) or pronoun denoting the owner, as in the example **Onadva bi bila pri njih.** Similarly, to say 'to/from one's place' the prepositions **k** and **od** are used with the appropriate cases of the noun (phrase) or pronoun, as in the example **Drugo lẹto bo prišla k** *njim.*

In the accusative, there are special forms in the third person for use with prepositions:

sg.	(m./n.)	-nj
	(f.)	-njo
du.		-nju
pl.		-nje

They are spelled together with the prepositions, which also carry the stress (e.g., **zanj, zanjo, zanju, zanje**). In the first- and second-persons singular, clitic forms are used the same way with the prepositions (**zame, zate**), while in the dual and plural stressed forms are used with the prepositions as in other cases (e.g., **za naju, za vaju, za nas, za vas**). When the preposition ends in a consonant, a schwa comes between it and -nj, e.g., **prędenj, pǫdenj, nadenj**; **v** gets an **a** when spelled together with any of these forms (**vanj, vanjo, . . .**).

The reflexive pronoun **se/sebe, si/sebi** 'oneself' follows the declension pattern of **ti**. It does not distinguish gender, number, or person, nor does it have a nominative form, since it refers to the subject. Examples:

Poględal se je v ogledalo.　He looked at himself in the mirror.
Nimam denarja s sabo.　I don't have money with me.
Kupi nękaj zase.　Buy something for yourself.

Exercise 6

Say it in Slovene. Use the locative and instrumental of personal pronouns.

1　Have you been at his house?
2　Ben can ride with the two of them.
3　Tomorrow we will go to their house.
4　Marko was sitting behind her.
5　What did you buy for them?
6　I would like to talk with her.
7　Lara is living with us.
8　This present is for her.

Language point

Hypothetical conditions

The same conjunction (**če**) is used and the same word-order rules apply as with the real conditional clauses. However, in expressing hypothetical conditions, conditional forms of verbs are used in both clauses. Notice how Ben speaks of the possibility of having his family with him:

Rẹs bi bilọ lepọ, če bi Špẹla in Simon prišla z mano.
It would really have been nice if Špela and Simon had come with me.

Če bi bili vsi trije tu, bi gotovo najẹli avto.
If all three of us were here, we would most likely have rented a car.

Notice that in the auxiliary clause, the subject (and sometimes other constituents) comes between **bi** and the participle, except for the participle of **biti**, e.g., **če bi Špẹla lẹtos prišla** vs. **če bi bila Špẹla lẹtos** . . . .

Reading

Škocjanske jame (Audio 2:60)

Škocjanske jame so edini slovenski spomenik na Unescovem seznamu svetovne dediščine. Ustvarila jih je reka Reka. Reka izvira pod goro Snežnik in teče po površju okoli 55 kilometrov. Ko priteče na Kras, to je kamnito ozemlje iz apnenca, nekaj kilometrov še teče po površju, nato pa pri vasi Škocjan izgine v podzemlje in teče pod površjem 34 kilometrov.

Del Škocjanskih jam, po katerem teče Reka, se imenuje Šumeča jama. To je podzemna soteska, dolga okoli 3,5 kilometra, široka 10 do 60 metrov in visoka več kot 100 metrov. Ta soteska se na nekaj mestih razširi v ogromne podzemne dvorane. Največja je Martelova dvorana, ki je s prostornino 2,2 milijona kubičnih metrov največja doslej odkrita podzemna dvorana v Sloveniji in ena največjih na svetu.

(Podatki z uradne spletne strani Parka Škocjanske jame)

Vocabulary

apnenec	limestone	**podatki** pl.	information
dediščina	heritage	**podzemlje**	underground
dvorana	hall, chamber	**površje**	surface
edini	the only	**prostornina**	volume
gora	mountain	**razširiti se** pf.	to widen
izgin|iti -em pf.	to disappear	**seznam**	list
izvirati ipf.	to originate	**soteska**	gorge
Kras	Karst	**svet**	world
odkrit	discovered	**svetoven** adj.	
ogromen	enormous	**šumeč**	rustling
okoli	about	**uraden**	official
ozemlje	territory		

Exercise 7

Based on the text, pair the names on the left with the information on the right. Two phrases are extra.

1 **Reka**
2 **Škocjanske jame**
3 **Kras**
4 **Snežnik**
5 **Šumeča jama**
6 **Martelova dvorana**

A the Reka river runs through it
B its base consists of limestone
C largest chamber in the caves
D entrance to the caves
E source of the Reka river
F waterfall in the caves
G created the Škocjan caves
H on Unesco's World Heritage list

Grammar summary

This summary consolidates the grammar material introduced in this book for quick review and reference. For a complete grammar overview refer to one of the grammars listed in the Introduction.

Noun declension

Masculine

	Sg.	Du.	Pl.
N	hotel	hotela	hoteli
G	hotela	hotelov	hotelov
D	hotelu	hoteloma	hotelom
A	hotel*	hotela	hotele
L	hotelu	hotelih	hotelih
I	hotelom	hoteloma	hoteli

* For animate nouns (**potnik**) in sg. A=G (**potnika**).

Some exceptions to the basic pattern:

1 Nouns in **c, č, j, š,** or **ž** (**prijatelj**) replace **o** with **e** in the endings (**prijateljem, prijateljema, prijateljev**).
2 Most nouns with a schwa in the final syllable (**listek**) drop it when adding the endings (**listka**).

3 Personal names and loan words ending in unstressed -o (**Marko**, **ẹvro**) in N/A sg. otherwise follow the basic pattern.
4 The noun **oče** and Slovene male personal names (**Jure**) ending in -e, add -t- before adding the endings (**očeta**, **Jureta**).
5 Most nouns with more than one syllable ending in a vowel (except schwa) + r (**krompír**) add **j** to the stem before adding the endings (**krompírja**).
6 Some monosyllabic nouns (**mọst**) have -*u* in G sg. (**mostu**) and extend the stem with -**ov**- in the non-singular before adding regular endings (**mostovi**), except in G pl. (**mostov**).

Neuter

	Sg.	Du.	Pl.
N	mẹsto*	mẹsti	mẹsta
G	mẹsta	mẹst	mẹst
D	mẹstu	mẹstoma	mẹstom
A	mẹsto	mẹsti	mẹsta
L	mẹstu	mẹstih	mẹstih
I	mẹstom	mẹstoma	mẹsti

* Nouns with **c, č, j, š,** or **ž** before the ending, end in -e (**parkiríšče**) and replace **o** with **e** in other endings as well (**parkiríščem, parkiríščema**).

Some exceptions to the basic pattern:

1 In G du/pl. the end cluster of a consonant + **m, n, r, v,** or **l** is broken by -**e**- (**písmo** – **písem**); a consonant (not **l** or **n**) + **j** – the cluster is broken by -**i**- (**mọrje** – **mọrij**).
2 Nouns extending the stem in oblique cases: **telọ** – **telẹsa, okọ** – **očẹsa, uhọ** – **ušẹsa; vreme** – **vremẹna**.

Feminine

	Sg.	Du.	Pl.
N	h*i*ša	h*i*ši	h*i*še
G	h*i*še	h*i*š	h*i*š
D	h*i*ši	h*i*šama	h*i*šam
A	h*i*šo	h*i*ši	h*i*še
L	h*i*ši	h*i*šah	h*i*šah
I	h*i*šo	h*i*šama	h*i*šami

An exception to the basic pattern:

> In G du/pl. certain combinations of consonants at the end are broken by -e- (**sestra – sester**) or -i- if the second consonant is **j** (**ladja – ladij**).

Feminine nouns ending in a consonant

(a) Nouns with more than one syllable (and a few one-syllable ones):

Sg.	Du.	Pl.
N=A slabǫst	N=G=A **slabosti**	
G=D=L **slabǫsti**	D=I **slabǫst(i)ma**	D **slabǫstim**
I **slabǫstjo***	L **slabǫstih**	
		I **slabǫstmi**

* Nouns ending in a cluster of consonants separated by schwa in N sg., have endings -**ijo**, -**ima**, -**imi** instead of -**jo**, -**ma**, -**mi**, e.g. **bolęznijo, bolęznima, bolęznimi**.

(b) Most one-syllable nouns:

Sg.		Du.		Pl.
N=A	stvar		N=G=A **stvar*i***	
G	stvar*i*	D=I **stvar*ẹ*ma**		D **stvar*ẹ*m**
D=L	stvar*i*		L **stvar*ẹ*h**	
I	stvar*jọ*			I **stvar*mi***

Adjective declension

Singular

	m.	n.	f.
N	lẹp (1)	lẹpo (3)	lẹpa
G	lẹpega		lẹpe
D	lẹpemu		lẹpi
A	lẹp (2)	lẹpo	lẹpo
L	lẹpem		lẹpi
I	lẹpim		lẹpo

1 For the definite form -**i** is added in N/A m. (**lẹpi**).
2 With animate nouns, A=G (**lẹpega**).
3 Adjectives with **c**, **č**, **j**, **š**, or **ž** before the ending, end in -**e** (**vrọče**) in N/A n.
4 Adjectives with a schwa in the final syllable (**dọbẹr** – **dobrega**) drop it when adding the endings.

Plural

	m.	n.	f.
N	lępi	lępa	lępe
G	lępih		
D	lępim		
A	lępe	lępa	lępe
L	lępih		
I	lępimi		

Dual

	m.	n.	f.
N=A	lępa	lępi	
G=L	lępih		
D=I	lępima		

Pronouns

Declension of personal pronouns

1 The nominative of personal pronouns used as a subject is normally omitted; it is used for emphasis or to avoid confusion.
2 In G, D, A short forms (clitics) are normally used, unless they are emphasized or used with a preposition.

Singular

	1	2	3		
			m.	n.	f.
N	jaz	ti	on	ono	ona
G	mene/me	tebe/te (1)	njega/ga		nję/je
D	meni/mi	tebi/ti	njemu/mu		njej/ji
A	mene/me	tebe/te	njega/ga/-nj (2)		njǫ/jo/-njo
L	meni	tebi	njem		njej
I	mano	tabo	njịm		njǫ

1 The same declension for **sebe/se** 'oneself'.
2 The third A form is for use with prepositions (e.g., **zanj, pǫnjo**).

Dual

	1		2		3	
	m.	f.	m.	f.	m.	n./f.
N	m*i*dva	m**ẹ**dve	v*i*dva	vẹdve	onadva	onidve
G	na*j*u (1)		vaju		nj*i*ju/ju	
D	nama		vama		nj*i*ma/jima	
A	naju		vaju		nj*i*ju/ju/-nju	
L	naju		vaju		nj*i*ju	
I	nama		vama		nj*i*ma	

1 In first and second persons, G, D, A clitic forms are the same as full forms minus the stress.

Plural

	1		2		3		
	m.	f.	m.	f.	m.	n.	f.
N	m*i*	m**ẹ**	v*i*	vẹ	oni	ona	one
G	na*s* (1)		vas		nj*i*h/jih		
D	nam		vam		nj*i*m/jim		
A	nas		vas		nj*i*h/jih/-nje		
L	nas		vas		nj*i*h		
I	nami		vami		nj*i*mi		

1 In first and second persons, G, D, A clitic forms are the same as full forms minus the stress.

Possessive pronouns

They behave like adjectives (agree with nouns) and follow adjectival declension.

1 owner	2 owners	>2 owners
moj	najin	naš
tvoj	vajin	vaš
njegov njen	njun	njihov

The reflexive possessive pronoun is **svoj**.

Interrogative pronouns

Kdo and **kaj** have their own declension, **kakšen**, **kateri**, **čigav** decline like adjectives.

N	kdo	kaj
G	koga	česa
D	komu	čemu
A	koga	kaj
L	kom	čem
I	kom	čim

The same for **nekdo** and **nekaj**.

The pronoun ves*

Singular

	m.	n.	f.
N	ves	vse	vsa
G	vsega		vse
D	vsemu		vsej
A	ves/vsega	vse	vso
L	vsem		vsej
I	vsem		vso

Plural

	m.	n.	f.
N	vs*i*	vs*a*	vse
G	vseh		
D	vsem		
A	vse	vs*a*	vse
L	vseh		
I	vsemi		

Dual

	m.	n.	f.
N=A	vs*a*	vs*i*	
G=L	vseh		
D=I	vsema		

* Similar declension for **ta/ta/tǫ** 'this', except that the vowels in the oblique case endings are long and closed, e.g., **tęga, tęmu, tǫ**.

Verbs

Present-tense conjugation

The auxiliary biti

	Sg.	Du.	Pl.
1	sem	sva	smo
2	si	sta	ste
3	je	sta	so

Other verbs

The infinitive (dictionary form) ends in **-ti** or **-či**. To form the present tense, sometimes you just remove **-ti** and add one of the present-tense endings, but often the vowel (or even a larger part) preceding **-ti** changes in the present tense. Learn the first-person singular with the infinitive.

Present-tense endings

	Sg.	Du.	Pl.
1	*-m	-va	-mo
2	-š	-ta	-te
3	—	-ta	-jo

* The vowel before the ending is **a**, **e**, or **i** and remains the same throughout the conjugation. Below are examples of the conjugation for all three types.

	Sg.			Du.			Pl.		
	-am	-em	-im	-am	-em	-im	-am	-em	-im
1	delam	pišem	vidim	delava	piševa	vidiva	delamo	pišemo	vidimo
2	delaš	pišeš	vidiš	delata	pišeta	vidita	delate	pišete	vidite
3	dela	piše	vidi	delata	pišeta	vidita	delajo	pišejo	vidijo

Exceptions: *iti* – **grem**, *jesti* – **jem**, *vedeti* – **vem**, **dati** – **dam** (all conjugating like **vem**).

	Sg.	Du.	Pl.
1	**vem**	**veva**	**vemo**
2	**veš**	**vesta**	**veste**
3	**ve**	**vesta**	**vejo**

Past and future tenses

Both past and future tenses are constructed of two parts: the auxiliary verb and the -l-participle of the verb you want to use in that tense. The participles have endings for number and gender.

Formation of the -l-participle

The -l-participle is formed from the infinitive by replacing the -ti with -l, e.g., **predavati** → **predaval**, **čakati** → **čakal**, **videti** → **videl** (m. sg.; for other genders and numbers add the endings as in the chart).

	m.	f.	n.
Sg.	delal	delala	delalo
Du.	delala	delali	delali
Pl.	delali	delale	delala

Exceptions:

1 Verbs in -sti: **nesti** – **nesel nesla**, **jesti** – **jedel jedla**, **lesti** – **lezel lezla**.
2 Verbs in -či: **peči** – **pekel pekla**, **streči** – **stregel stregla**.
3 Verb **iti** (**šel šla**) and prefixed verbs from **iti** (**priti** – **prišel**, **oditi** – **odšel**).

The past tense is constructed from the present tense of the auxiliary **biti** + -l-participle, e.g., **delal(a) sem**, **delal(a) si**, **delal(a) je**, . . .

The future tense is constructed from the future tense of the auxiliary **biti** (see the chart) + -l-participle, e.g., **delal(a) bom**, **delal(a) boš**, **delal(a) bo**, . . .

Future-tense conjugation of biti

	Sg.	Du.	Pl.
1	bom	bova	bomo
2	boš	bosta	boste
3	bo	bosta	bojo

Note: The conditional is constructed similarly to these two tenses: **bi** (does not change) + -l-participle (with the appropriate ending for number and gender), e.g., **delal(a) bi**, **delali bi**, **delale bi**.

The imperative

It is formed from the present tense.

Present tense		Imperative (2 sg.)	
-am	ča~~kam~~	-aj	čakaj
-em	p*i*~~šem~~	-i	p*i*ši
-im	k*u*~~pim~~		k*u*pi
-(V)j-em*	p*i*~~jem~~	—	p*i*j

* verbs having a vowel + **j** before **-em**.

For 2 du./pl. **-ta/-te** and for 1 du./pl. **-va/-te** is added to the 2 sg. form.

Verbs in **-či** ending in **-čem** and **-žem** in the present: **-č-** → **-c-**, **-ž-** → **-z-**, e.g., **peci, str*i*zi**.

Some irregular imperatives:

*i*ti (gr*e*m)	p*o*jdi	pov*e*dati (pov*e*m)	povej
b*i*ti (sem)	b*o*di	im*e*ti (im*a*m)	imej
v*e*deti (v*e*m)	v*e*di	gl*e*dati (gl*e*dam)	glej
j*e*sti (j*e*m)	jej		

Prepositions

Organized by the cases they require, the commonest prepositions are listed with their meanings and examples of use.

Case	Preposition	Meaning	Example
G	**blizu**	near	**Blizu šole je nova restavracija.** There is a new restaurant near the school.
	brez	without	**Kava brez sladkorja je grenka.** Coffee without sugar is bitter.
	do	up to	**Peljite do križišča.** Drive up to the intersection.
		till	**Čakal sem te do petih.** I waited for you till five.

Case	Preposition	Meaning	Example
	iz	out of	**Stopila je iz sobe.** She stepped out of the room.
		from	**Marjeta je iz Slovenije.** Marjeta is from Slovenia.
	mimo	past	**Pojdite mimo ambasade.** Go past the embassy.
	nasproti	across from	**Avtobus ustavi nasproti tržnice.** The bus stops across from the marketplace.
	od	(away) from a source	**Od postaje vozi devetka.** Bus number nine runs from the station.
	okrog/ okoli	around	**Plečnik je uredil prostor okrog knjižnice.** Plečnik designed the space around the library.
	z/s	down from	**Prišli so s Triglava.** They came down from mount Triglav.
		from	**Potujejo z morja.** They are traveling from the coast.
	zaradi	because of	**Priporočam grad zaradi razgleda.** I recommend the castle because of the view.
D	**k (h)**	towards, to (a person)	**Preselil se je k staršem.** He moved to his parents' house.
	proti	towards, in the direction of	**Veter piha proti morju.** The wind is blowing towards the sea.
A	**čez**	across	**Šla sta peš čez most.** They went across the bridge on foot.
		past	**Ura je petnajst čez osem.** It is eight fifteen.
	skozi	through	**Peljali smo se skozi dolg predor.** We drove through a long tunnel.
	za	for	**Alenka je kupila srajco za Andreja.** Alenka bought a shirt for Andrej.

Case	Preposition	Meaning	Example
L	**na***	on	**Bili so na Triglavu.**
			They were on mount Triglav.
		at	**Marko je na morju.**
			Marko is at the coast.
	o	about	**Pogovarjamo se o filmu.**
			We are talking about the film.
	ob*	next to, along	**Sprehajava se ob reki.**
			We are strolling along the river.
	po	along the trajectory	**Pojdite naravnost po Cankarjevi.**
			Go straight along Cankarjeva Street.
		all over the surface of	**Včeraj smo hodili po Ljubljani.**
			Yesterday we walked around Ljubljana.
		after	**Po kosilu Andrej razreže torto.**
			After lunch, Andrej cuts the cake.
	pri	at, near	**Oče ima sorodnike nekje pri Ribnici.**
			My father has relatives somewhere near Ribnica.
	v*	inside of	**Koncert bo v veliki dvorani.**
			The concert will be in the large hall.
		in, at	**A ste že v Mariboru?**
			Are you in Maribor yet?
	med*	between, among	**Tržnica je med reko in katedralo.**
			The marketplace is between the river and the cathedral.
I		during	**Med predstavo je začelo deževati.**
			It started raining during the show.
	nad*	above	**Nad trgovinami so stanovanja.**
			There are apartments above the stores.
	pod*	under, below	**Reka izvira pod goro Snežnik.**
			The Reka river originates under Snežnik mountain.

Case	Preposition	Meaning	Example
	pred*	in front	**Čakal te bom pred spomenikom.** I will wait for you in front of the monument.
		before	**Pred kosilom smo si ogledali jamo.** We visited the cave before lunch.
	z/s	with	**Anita je prišla na piknik z novim fantom.** Anita came to the picnic with a new boyfriend.
		by	**V službo se vozim z vlakom.** I go to work by train.
	za*	behind, after	**Za hišo imajo velik vrt.** They have a large garden behind the house.

* These prepositions are used with the accusative when they express the goal or destination of verbal action denoting motion. Example: **Pridi pred spomenik.** 'Come to the front of the monument.'

Conjunctions

Meanings and uses introduced in this book:

in and
Žena prevaja in piše.
My wife translates and writes.

ali or
Lahko greš z vlakom ali se pelješ z mano.
You can go by train or you can ride with me.

pa while/on the other hand
Oče je Slovenec, mama pa Američanka.
My father is Slovene, while my mother is American.

a but
Sin dobro razume slovensko, a slabo govori.
My son understands Slovene, but he speaks poorly.

ampak but
Zelo je okusno, ampak jaz nisem več lačna.
It is very tasty, but I am not hungry any more.

zato therefore
Danes je nedelja, zato ne grem v službo.
Today is Sunday, therefore I don't go to work.

da that	**Upam, da niste bolni.**
	I hope that you are not sick.
ker because	**Sladkarij ne jem, ker niso zdrave za zobe.**
	I don't eat sweets because they are not good for the teeth.
če if	**Če bo lepo vreme, greste na Grad lahko peš.**
	If the weather is good, you can go to the castle on foot.
ko when	**Ko boš velik, boš zdravnik.**
	When you grow up, you will be a doctor.
kadar whenever	**Kadar imam čas, rada kolesarim.**
	When I have time, I like to bike.
kot than	**Danes je topleje, kot je bilo včeraj.**
	It is warmer today than it was yesterday.
ki (that) which	**Tu je kavarna, ki je zelo priljubljena med študenti.**
	Here is a café which is very popular among students.

Clitic order

With the exception of yes/no questions, clitics occupy the second position in a clause, i.e., they follow a fully stressed independent word,* a phrasal unit, or a subordinating conjunction. If there are more than one, they appear in the order shown in the table.

* Unless this word appears inside of a phrasal unit, like the words **moj**, **samo**, and **jutri** in the phrases **moj sin**, **samo otroci**, **jutri zjutraj**, as clitics do not break phrasal units.

	1	2	3	4	5	6	
	Present tense auxiliary starting with s- or **bi**	Reflexive pronoun **se/si**	Personal pronoun D	Personal pronoun A	Personal pronoun G	Auxiliary **je** or future tense of **biti**	
(a) **Marko**			mi	ga		je	dal.
(b) **Dal**	sem		ti	jo.			
(c) **Otroci**	so	se			je		bali.
(d) **Zakaj**	ste	se	mu				smejali?
(e) **Če**	bi	se	nam				smejali, bi nam bilo nerodno.
(f) **Smejal**		se	ji			je.	
(g) **Peter**		si		vas		bo	zapomnil.
(h) **Zapomnili**	smo	si		jo.			

(a) Marko gave it/him to me.
(b) I gave it/her to you.
(c) Children were afraid of her.
(d) Why did you laugh at him?
(e) If they laughed at us, we would be embarrassed.
(f) He laughed at her.
(g) Peter will remember you [pl.].
(h) We remembered her.

Key to exercises

Unit 1

Exercise 1

1 dobro jutro/na svidenje 2 dober dan/na svidenje 3 dober dan/na svidenje 4 dober večer/lahko noč 5 dober večer/lahko noč

Exercise 2

1 si 2 ste 3 smo 4 sem 5 sta 6 je 7 sva

Exercise 3

1 nisi 2 niste 3 nismo 4 nisem 5 nista 6 ni 7 nisva

Exercise 4

1 To sta Marko in Mojca. 2 To je Miran. 3 To je oče. 4 To sta gospod in gospa Kranjec. 5 To so Janez, Miha in Andrej. 6 To je Marinka Zupan.

Exercise 5

1 A si ti Marko? 2 Je to gospa Kos? 3 A ste vi gospodična Peterka? 4 A sta vidva Borut in Mitja? 5 A ste vi gospod Dolinar?

Exercise 6

1 Ja, sem. 2 Ja, je. 3 Ja, sem. 4 Ne, nisva. 5 Ne, nisem.

Exercise 7

1 (d) 2 (e) 3 (a) 4 (i) 5 (b) 6 (c) 7 (g)

Exercise 8

Dober, ste, redu, kako, ti, hvala, Je, to, sem, Me

Unit 2

Exercise 1

1 Samantha je Angležinja. 2 Marco je Italijan. 3 Sandra je Nemka. 4 Anna je Madžarka. 5 Josip je Hrvat. 6 Tim je Američan. 7 Alice je Francozinja.

Exercise 2

(a) 1 slabo govoriš 2 slabo govorim 3 slabo govori 4 slabo govorite (b) 1 dobro razumeš 2 dobro razumem 3 dobro razume 4 dobro razumete

Exercise 3

1 Marko razume nemško. 2 Slabo govorim angleško. 3 Ana ne razume italijansko. 4 Dobro razumemo hrvaško. 5 Ne znam madžarsko. 6 A govori kitajsko? 7 A govoriš slovensko? 8 A govorite doma francosko?

Exercise 4

(a) 6 Ja, govori 7 Ja, govorim 8 Ja, govorimo (b) 6 Ne, ne govori 7 Ne, ne govorim 8 Ne, ne govorimo

Exercise 5

1 Angležinja 2 nemško 3 Italijanščina 4 slovensko 5 madžarsko

Exercise 6

1 tvoja žena 2 njen dedek 3 njegova hiša 4 njihovo mesto 5 naš sin 6 moj prijatelj 7 vaša mama 8 naš vrt

Exercise 7

1 prijatelj 2 tvoja 3 Francoz 4 tvoj 5 babica

Exercise 8

1 (d) 2 (c) 3 Kdo je to? (a) 4 A Peter razume nemško? (b) 5 Je to vaš vrt? (e)

Unit 3

Exercise 1

1 kolesariš 2 prevaja 3 smučam 4 delate 5 govorim 6 študiraš 7 pišete 8 igra

Exercise 2

1 Ti poleti nikoli ne kolesariš. 2 Luka nikoli ne prevaja. 3 Jaz nikoli ne smučam. 4 Vi nikoli ne delate doma. 5 Jaz nikoli ne govorim počasi.

Exercise 3

1 prevajalka 2 učiteljica 3 biolog 4 profesorica 5 kuhar 6 prodajalka 7 knjižničar 8 podjetnica

Exercise 4

1 (e) 2 (f) 3 (b) 4 (c) 5 (a)

Exercise 5

1 Andrej je arhitekt. 2 Riše. 3 Benova žena prevaja in piše. 4 Pozimi smuča. 5 Ne, Ben ne smuča. 6 Hodi v srednjo šolo. 7 Ne, ni zaposlena. Študentka je. 8 Anita hoče biti sodnica.

Exercise 6

1 živijo 2 govorimo 3 študirajo 4 razumeta 5 stanujeta 6 žurirate

Exercise 7

1 (5) 2 (20) 3 (14) 4 (17) 5 (9) 6 (8) 7 (13) 8 (0) 9 (11)

Exercise 8

1 In Ljubljana 2 In Domžale 3 Translation agency 4 Translation of technical texts (economics, technology, law)

Unit 4

Exercise 1

1 To so pošte. 2 To so mesta. 3 To so kioski. 4 Tu so znamke. 5 Tu so sporočila. 6 A so to šole? 7 Kje so jezera? 8 Tu so kavarne.

Exercise 2

Sg.: 1 Hiša je velika. 2 Parkirišče je veliko. 3 Mesto je veliko. 4 Stavba je velika. 5 Banka je velika. 6 Hotel je velik.
Pl.: 1 Hiše so velike. 2 Parkirišča so velika. 3 Mesta so velika. 4 Stavbe so velike. 5 Banke so velike. 6 Hoteli so veliki.

Exercise 3

1 dober 2 dobri 3 dobra 4 težki 5 težka 6 Težke

Exercise 4

1 Knjižnica je zaprta. 2 Galerije so dobre. 3 Bazen je nov. 4 Internetna kavarna je nova. 5 Pošta je zaprta. 6 Banke so zaprte. 7 Restavracija Jelen je dobra. 8. Muzeji so zaprti.

Exercise 5

1 Kje lahko kupijo (kupita) znamke? 2 Tamle lahko zamenjamo (zamenjata) denar. 3 Kje lahko pogledajo (pogledata) elektronsko pošto? 4 Tu lahko pošljete (pošljeta) sporočilo domov.

Exercise 6

2 Kakšni so kioski? 3 Kakšna je Sonjina hiša? 4 Kašen je ta profesor? 5 Kakšne so slovenske hiše? 6 Kakšen je njegov priimek?

Exercise 7

1 rdeča + rumena = oranžna 2 bela + črna = siva 3 rumena + modra = zelena 4 modra + rdeča = vijolična

Exercise 8

1 čez cesto 2 na desni 3 spodaj, zgoraj 4 blizu 5 daleč 6 na levi

Unit 5

Exercise 1

1 Kavo, prosim. 2 Sok, prosim. 3 Mineralno vodo, prosim. 4 Belo vino, prosim. 5 Pivo, prosim. 6 Kapučino, prosim.

Exercise 2

1 Ana bi rada kavo. 2 Miran bi rad sok. 3 Peter in Sonja bi rada mineralno vodo. 4 Metka, Marko in Matjaž bi radi belo vino. 5 Mama in oče bi rada pivo. 6 Andreja in Tjaša bi radi kapučino.

Exercise 3

1 torto, Alenko 2 pivo, Andreja 3 Bena, kavo 4 prijatelja, Mirana 5 kozarec, gospoda

Exercise 4

1 Alenka je utrujena. 2 Ben in Alenka sta žejna. 3 A je pivo hladno? 4 Tu imajo zelo dobro kavo. 5 Lahko naročimo mineralno vodo in sok. 6 Rad bi kavo s smetano in čokoladno torto. 7 A lahko prinesete led? 8 Natakarica prinese torto za Alenko in Bena. 9 Za vino je še prezgodaj.

Exercise 5

(a) 35 (b) 68 (c) 24 (d) 57 (e) 99 (f) 46 (g) 73 (h) 82

Exercise 6

1 Koliko stane veliko pivo? 2 A lahko plačam? 3 Izvolite. 4 Je že v redu. 5 Želite, prosim? 6 Lahko prinesem led. 7 Štiri evre trideset, prosim. 8 Drobiž, prosim.

Exercise 7

1 Dva evra sedemdeset, prosim. 2 Tri evre šestdeset, prosim. 3 Pet evrov sedemdeset, prosim. 4 Tri evre, prosim. 5 Štiri evre petdeset, prosim. 6 Osem evrov, prosim.

Unit 6

Exercise 1

1 do 2— 3 čez 4 čez 5 do 6 čez 7 do 8—

Exercise 2

1 pol šestih 2 petnajst/četrt čez deset 3 ena 4 dvajset čez tri 5 deset čez sedem 6 petindvajset do desetih 7 petnajst/četrt do petih 8 dvajset do dvanajstih

Exercise 3

1 Jana gre v knjižnico. 2 Peter in Marko gresta v park. 3 Vi greste v šolo. 4 Jaz grem v mesto. 5 Prijatelji grejo v kino. 6 Midva greva na koncert. 7 Vidva gresta na fakulteto. 8 Ti greš na sestanek.

Exercise 4

1 Lara teče na faks. 2 Predavanje ima opoldne. 3 Pred predavanjem gre v knjižnico. 4 Ta semester je njen urnik natrpan. 5 Vsak dan ima predavanje in dvakrat na teden ima prakso. 6 Ja, čas za kosilo ima jutri ali v petek. 7 Nejc gre lahko na kosilo v petek.

Exercise 5

2 V torek leti v Moskvo. 3 V sredo leti v Pariz. 4 V četrtek leti v Prago. 5 V petek leti v Berlin. 5 V soboto leti na Kreto.

Exercise 6

1 Ob ponedeljkih ob dvanajstih in ob sredah ob deset čez enajst. 2 Ob torkih ob dvajset do devetih, ob sredah ob deset do osmih in ob petkih ob deset do osmih. 3 Ob torkih ob deset čez enajst, ob sredah ob dvanajstih in ob petkih ob pol desetih. 4 Ob ponedeljkih ob dvajset do devetih, ob torkih ob dvajset čez deset in ob petkih ob dvanajstih. 5 Ob ponedeljkih ob deset do osmih, ob četrtkih ob pol desetih in ob petkih ob deset čez enajst. 6 Ob torkih ob dvanajstih in ob četrtkih ob dvajset do devetih.

Exercise 7

1 Ambulanta je ob sredah odprta od enih do sedmih, ob četrtkih od enih do dveh in ob petkih od sedmih do dvanajstih. 2 Sistematski

pregledi so ob torkih od sedmih do pol enajstih in ob četrtkih od sedmih do enih.

Unit 7

Exercise 1

2 Mleko, prosim. – Žal nimam mleka. 3 Palačinke, prosim. – Žal nimam palačink. 4 Jajca, prosim. – Žal nimam jajc. 5 Marmelado, prosim. – Žal nimam marmelade. 6 Jabolka, prosim. – Žal nimam jabolk. 7 Kruh, prosim. – Žal nimam kruha. 8 Skuto, prosim. – Žal nimam skute.

Exercise 2

1 jem, pije 2 jejo 3 pijeva 4 pije 5 jesta 6 ješ

Exercise 3

1 Prijatelj ima rad pomarančni sok. 2 A imaš rad palačinke? 3 Ne, raje imam kruh in marmelado. 4 Mojca in Luka imata rada žitarice za zajtrk. 5 Kaj imaš najraje za kosilo? 6 Peter ima rad Majo.

Exercise 4

1 Andrej, Sonja in Marko radi hodijo v hribe. 2 Tina rada plava. 3 Marko rad kolesari. 4 Tina in Sonja radi igrata tenis. 5 Andrej, Tina, Marko in Sonja radi smičajo. 6 Andrej in Marko rada igrata golf.

Exercise 5

1 A imaš rada čaj brez sladkorja? – Ne, ne maram čaja brez sladkorja. 2 A imaš rada kavo brez kofeina? – Ne, ne maram kave brez kofeina. 3 A imaš rada kosilo brez mesa? – Ne, ne maram kosila brez mesa. 4 A imaš rada pivo brez alkohola? – Ne, ne maram piva brez alkohola. 5 A imaš rada žitarice brez mleka? – Ne, ne maram žitaric brez mleka.

Exercise 6

juhe: zelenjavna juha, goveja juha; solate: mešana solata, zelena solata; priloge: testenine, krompir, riž, kuhana zelenjava; mesne jedi: puranji zrezek, ocvrt piščanec, svinjska pečenka, golaž; sladice: torta, palačinke, sladoled, potica

Exercise 7

1 A bi še solato? 2 Ne, hvala, nisem več lačen. 3 Juha je zelo okusna. 4 A bi sladico? 5 A si vegetarijanec? 6 A imate radi začinjeno hrano?

Exercise 8

a Favorite/least favorite foods: Sara – sweets/vegetables Blaž – Wiener schnitzel and French fries/— Eva – ice cream/— Polona – vegetables, salads/spinach Žiga – sea food/— b Sara, Blaž, Eva, Polona

Unit 8

Exercise 1

1 Sestra živi v univerzitetnem mestu. 2 Starši živijo v stari hiši. 3 Profesor živi v lepi soseski. 4 Teta živi v majhnem kraju. 5 Bratranec živi v velikem bloku. 6 Prijatelj živi v novem stanovanju.

Exercise 2

1 Sestre živijo v univerzitetnih mestih. 2 Starši živijo v starih hišah. 3 Profesorji živijo v lepih soseskah. 4 Tete živijo v majhnih krajih. 5 Bratranci živijo v velikih blokih. 6 Prijatelji živijo v novih stanovanjih.

Exercise 3

1 Parizu, Pariz 2 šolo, šoli 3 fakulteti, srednjo šolo 4 službo, službi 5 Rim, Rimu 6 restavracije, restavracijah

Exercise 4

1 (b) 2 (a) 3 (a) 4 (c)

Exercise 5

1 Benov mlajši brat je še študent. 2 Chris še ni poročen. 3 Andrejevi starši imajo sina in hčerko. 4 Andrejeva družina je majhna. 5 Andrejeva sestra ima enega otroka in jeseni pričakuje drugega. 6 Andrejeva mama je že upokojena. 7 Dedek in babica varujeta vnučko.

Exercise 6

1 gresta 2 sedijo, klepetajo 3 skuha, pripravi 4 Pridejo 5 zajtrkujejo 6 imajo 7 prinese 8 pozajtrkuje, prebere 9 kuhata 10 razreže 11 vstane The order of sentences: 11, 3, 5, 8, 1, 9, 4, 6, 10, 7, 2.

Exercise 7

1 se piše 2 se (najprej) stuširam, se oblečem 3 se (nameravata) poročiti 4 se (vsak dan) pogovarjata 5 se (zelo dobro) počuti

Exercise 8

1 Danes je nedelja. 2 Alenka. 3 Prebere e-pošto, stušira in obleče se, gre na sprehod. 4 Ne gresta. 5 Andrej danes praznuje rojstni dan. 6 Torto in potico. 7 Ne, sedijo, pojejo in klepetajo skoraj do večera.

Unit 9

Exercise 1

1 potoval(i) 2 mislil(i) 3 imel(i) 4 videl(i) 5 šel, šli 6 peljal(i) 7 jedel jedli 8 pil(i) 9 prinesel prinesli

Exercise 2

Prišli so Andrejevi starši, sestra, svak in nečakinja. Tu so bili tudi Alenkini starši in Anitin fant. Kosilo smo imeli ob enih, ogromno je bilo, kosili smo skoraj do treh. Po kosilu je Andrej razrezal torto, mi pa smo zapeli Kol'kor kapljic tol'ko let . . . Alenka je prinesla tudi potico in kavo. Ob potici in odličnem primorskem vinu smo potem sedeli na vrtu, peli in klepetali skoraj do večera.

Exercise 3

2 A je Alenka peljala Bena na železniško postajo? – Ja, je. 3 A je Anita imela izpit iz ekonomije? – Ne, ni. 4 A je Andrej praznoval rojstni dan v službi? – Ja, je. 5 A sta Anita in Alenka povabili Bena na kosilo? – Ja, sta. 6 A je Benov vlak pripeljal v Ljubljano ob 7h? – Ne, ni. 7 A sta Alenka in Andrej čakala Bena na ljubljanski postaji? – Ja, sta.

Exercise 4

1 z letalom 2 z ladjo 3 z avtom 4 z vlakom 5 z gotovino 6 s sladkorjem 7 z avtobusom 8 z motorjem

Exercise 5

1 zna 2 veste 3 pozna 4 zna 5 vesta 6 poznam 7 zna 8 veste

Exercise 6

1 T 2 F 3 F 4 NI 5 T 6 T 7 F 8 T

Exercise 7

1 (c) 2 (d) 3 (a) 4 (b) 5 (c) 6 (a)

Unit 10

Exercise 1

1 me 2 je 3 nas 4 vas 5 naju 6 te

Exercise 2

2 Ja, prodala sta ga. 3 Ja, ustavila sta jih. 4 Ja, poklical ga je. 5 Ja, vidi jih. 6 Ja, zgradili so jo. 7 Ja, naredil ga je.

Exercise 3

1 zajtrkujem, sem zajtrkoval(a) 2 stanuje, stanuje, je stanoval 3 pričakujejo, Pričakovali so 4 potrebujeta, potrebovala sva 5 potuje, je potovala

Exercise 4

1 Andrej je telefoniral Ireni. 2 Lara je poslala Janu SMS. 3 Vi ste dali študentom nalogo. 4 Alenka je kupila prijateljema darilo. 5 Ti si prinesel Andreju vino za rojstni dan. 6 Ben je pisal Špeli.

Exercise 5

1 K staršem v Maribor. 2 K prijateljem v Ljubljano. 3 K babici v mesto. 4 K sorodnikom na morje. 5 K bratu na Gorenjsko. 6 H gospodu Kovaču v bolnico.

Exercise 6

1 B 2 E 3 D 4 C 5 A

Exercise 7

1 kopalna kad, umivalnik 2 kuhinjske omare, pomivalno korito, štedilnik 3 kavč, regal, klubska miza 4 postelja, garderobna omara 5 pisalna miza, police 6 posteljnina, odeje, preproga

Exercise 8

1 Nejc stanuje v študentskem domu, Jan v dvosobnem stanovanju. 2 Ker se je njegov preselil nazaj k staršem. 3 Udobno, svetlo in mirno je. 4 Ima spalnico, dnevno sobo, kuhinjo, kopalnico in WC. 5 Pohištvo je še precej novo. 6 Stanovanje je na Viču, blizu faksa in postaje mestnega avtobusa.

Unit 11

Exercise 1

1 bo 2 bodo imeli 3 Sedeli bodo, pekli 4 bo, spekla 5 boš, povabila 6 bomo prenočili 7 bo, pospravila, bo šel 8 bomo krenili

Exercise 2

1 Maja bom prodal hišo. 2 Junija se bom preselil v Chicago. 3 Julija se bo Chris poročil. 4 Avgusta bom z družino potoval v Slovenijo. 5 Septembra bom začel novo službo.

Exercise 3

1 Marko ima rad suha in vroča poletja. 2 Sestra bo diplomirala spomladi. 3 Kakšna je jesen v Sloveniji? 4 A ima knjižnica zdaj poletni urnik? 5 Letos smo imeli jesensko vreme že julija. 6 Peter kolesari poleti in smuča pozimi.

Exercise 4

2 P: Koliko jajc želite? V: Deset jajc, prosim. 3 P: Koliko zrezkov želite? V: Dva zrezka, prosim. 4 P: Koliko piščancev želite? V: Enega piščanca,

prosim. 5 P: Koliko kotletov želite? V: Štiri kotlete, prosim. 6 P: Koliko klobas želite? V: Sedem klobas, prosim. 7 P: Koliko jabolk želite? V: Tri jabolka, prosim.

Exercise 5

1 šestdeset dek govedine 2 štiri steklenice piva 3 petindvajset dek sira 4 dve kili paradižnika 5 pol kile salame 6 pet kil krompirja.

Exercise 6

hlebec črnega kruha, 2 kg paradižnika, 1 kg solate, 4 kumare, ½ kg mlade čebule, 10 steklenic piva, 4 plastenke ledenega čaja, ½ kg mlete svinjine, 70 dkg mlete govedine, 1 kg puranjega mesa, 6 svinjskih zrezkov, 3 klobase.

Exercise 7

1 puranje meso, puranjega mesa 2 temno pivo, temnega piva 3 svinjski kotleti, svinjskih kotletov 4 mrzlo limonado, mrzle limonade 5 svežih rib, sveže ribe 6 jabolčni zavitek, jabolčnega zavitka

Exercise 8

1 June 2 March, summer 3 February 4 beginning of fall 5 fall 6 July 7 spring

Unit 12

Exercise 1

1 iz Amerike 2 iz Nemčije 3 v Ljubljani 4 v Staro Ljubljano 5 blizu Prešernovega trga 6 na Ljubljanski grad 7 Od hotela do Tromostovja 8 Na tržnici

Exercise 2

1 Dobiva se pred gledališčem. 2 Parkirišče je pod tržnico. 3 Vodič govori turistom pred vodnjakom. 4 Nad trgovinami so stanovanja. 5 Galerija se nahaja med parkom in opero. 6 Čakal(a) bom pred postajo.

Exercise 3

1 narodnim 2 glavno 3 baročnim 4 zanimivimi 5 mestnim, državno 6 železniško

Exercise 4

1 Mestna knjižnica je v Kersnikovi. 2 Univerza je na Kongresnem trgu. 3 Narodni muzej je na Prešernovi. 4 Pošta je v Čopovi. 5 Blagovnica Maxi je na Trgu republike.

Exercise 5

1 Zahodna 2 Južno, vzhodno 3 severu 4 jug 5 zahodni

Exercise 6

1 Oprostite, kje je Stari trg? 2 Oprostite, kje je tržnica? 3 Oprostite, kako se pride do Tromostovja? 4 Oprostite, kako se pride do železniške postaje? 5 Greste naravnost po Čopovi do Slovenske, potem pa zavijete desno. 6 Greste do semaforja in tam prečkate ulico. 7 Tromostovje je blizu Prešernovega trga. 8 Zavijete za galerijo in greste skozi podhod.

Exercise 7

1 Ker bo peljal Davida in Monico po Ljubljani. 2 V hotelu Union. 3 Grad in Staro Ljubljano. 4 Na Mestni trg. 5 Ne, samo kopija vodnjaka. 6 Na tržnico. 7 Plečnikove arkade. 8 Ker je razgled čudovit. 9 Peš s Starega trga ali z mestno vzpenjačo.

Exercise 8

1 Potrebujem dvoposteljno sobo. 2 Vaša soba je v drugem nadstropju. 3 Kje lahko parkiram? 4 Vhod v garažo je za hotelom. 5 Kdaj strežete zajtrk? 6 A bomo šli v drugo nadstropje z dvigalom ali po stopnicah?

Unit 13

Exercise 1

1 tretji 2 sedemnajsta 3 petintrideseti 4 deseto 5 četrta 6 enajsto 7 drugo 8 deveta 9 šestindvajset

Exercise 2

1 tretji razred 2 sedemnajsto vrsto 3 petintrideseti rojstni dan 4 desetem nadstropju 5 četrte knjige

Exercise 3

1 Kvartet Bartók bo nastopil četrtega junija ob osmih. 2 Moški komorni zbor Bolgarija bo nastopil petnajstega julija ob devetih. 3 Kvartet Orfeo bo nastopil petindvajsetega julija ob devetih. 4 Ljubljanski trio violončel bo nastopil drugega avgusta ob pol devetih. 5 Nikola Matošič trio bo nastopil šestega avgusta ob devetih.

Exercise 4

1 Andrej bi rad kupil vstopnice za *Carmen*. 2 Marko in Mira bi rada slišala Boba Dylana. 3 Moji prijatelji bi radi videli balet *Ana Karenina*. 4 Mi bi radi gledati slovensko dramo. 5 Ben bi rad peljal prijatelje v Staro Ljubljano.

Exercise 5

1 Rada bi videla opero in balet. 2 *Carmen* je prej na sporedu. 3 Ker bo takrat na morju. 4 Balet z njegovo glasbo. 5 Ne bo, ker takrat ne bo več v Ljubljani. 6 Zanima ga Paco de Lucia. 7 Zelo bogata. 8 Vsak dan so tam brezplačne predstave z znanimi slovenskimi umetniki.

Exercise 6

1 Irenino 2 Andrejevem 3 Čajkovskega 4 prijateljevim 5 Ivane Kobilice 6 slavnega arhitekta

Exercise 7

1 središču mesta 2 naredil načrt 3 rdeče opeke, sivega kamna 4 uredil prostor 5 poletnem gledališču

Exercise 8

1 Rad bi dve vstopnici za koncert Boba Dylana. 2 Kje bi radi sedeli? 3 V parterju, v peti ali šesti vrsti. 4 Na žalost sta peta in šesta vrsta že razprodani. 5 Kje imate proste sedeže? 6 Imam dva prosta sedeža v deseti vrsti. 7 A imajo študenti popust?

Exercise 9

1 He opened an architectural studio in Vienna. 2 He started lecturing in Prague. 3 He returned to Ljubljana and became professor of architecture. 4 He finished the renovation of Prague castle.

Unit 14

Exercise 1

(a) 2 Sivi suknjič mi je prekratek. 3 Rdeče krilo je Anki preozko. 4 Črni plašč ti je preozek. 5 Modra obleka je Bredi in Vesni preširoka. 6 Rjavi klobuk vam je premajhen. (b) 1 Rdeči pulover mu je prevelik. 3 Rdeče krilo ji je preozko. 5 Modra obleka jima je preširoka.

Exercise 2

(a) 1 Žal nam je. 2 Bilo nama je nerodno. 3 A vam je vroče? 4 Bilo jim je slabo. 5 Bilo jima je vroče. (b) 1 Ni nam žal. 2 Ni nama bilo nerodno. 3 A vama ni vroče? 4 Ni jim bilo slabo. 5 Ni jima bilo vroče.

Exercise 3

1 svoj, njegov 2 njihovo, svojo 3 s svojim avtom, vaš 4 svojo, njena naše, svoje

Exercise 4

1 Bil je svetlosiv. 2 Nazadnje sem ga nosil včeraj zvečer na večerji v gostilni Pri dveh lipah. 3 Ne spomnim se, če sem ga imel. 4 Alenka je telefonirala. 5 V gostilni niso našli mojega suknjiča. 6 Če ga ne najdem, bom moral kupiti novega. 7 Ne, vaš suknjič mi bo premajhen.

Exercise 5

1 A vam je všeč Ljubljana? Ja, Ljubljana mi je všeč. 2 A je Simonu všeč Slovenija? Ja, Slovenija mu je všeč. 3 A je bil Davidu in Monici všeč hotel Union? Ja, hotel Union jima je bil všeč. 4 A jima je bila všeč Plečnikova arhitektura? Ja, Plečnikova arhitektura jima je bila všeč. 5 A so Špeli všeč velika mesta? Ja, velika mesta so ji všeč. 6 A vam je všeč slovenska hrana? Ja, slovenska hrana mi je všeč.

Exercise 6

Peter mora spakirati nogavice, suknjič, srajco, spodnje perilo, pižamo, hlače, kravato

Exercise 7

P: A vam lahko kaj pomagam? V: Iščem plašč. P: Katera barva vam je všeč in katero številko nosite običajno? V: Všeč so mi svetle barve. Nosim številko 40. P: Lahko pomerite tega svetlorjavega. V: Ta mi je malo prevelik. P: Najbrž potrebujete številko 38. Lahko pomerite tega svetlomodrega. V: Ta mi je prav. Tudi barva mi je všeč. Dobro, vzela bom svetlomodrega.

Exercise 8

1 F 2 F 3 T 4 T 5 T 6 NI 7 T

Unit 15

Exercise 1

1 Naroči 2 Vprašaj 3 Pojdi 4 Pokliči 5 Počivaj, pij 6 Počakaj 7 Poglej 8 Preseli se 9 Kupi

Exercise 2

Peljite se, parkirajte, pojdite, zavijte, pojdite, poiščite, portrkajte, počakajte, oddajte, počakajte

Exercise 3

1 Andrejevim staršem 2 Benovemu prijatelju 3 angleškim turistom 4 Tvoji hčerki 5 mojemu očetu 6 visokim ženskam

Exercise 4

(a) 1 Bena boli grlo. 2 Bolijo nas oči. 3 Bolijo jo kolena. 4 Bolijo vaju noge. 5 Boli me zob. 6 Ireno bolijo ušesa. 7 Boli ga želodec. 8 Boli te srce.
(b) 1 Bena je bolelo grlo. 2 Bolele so nas oči. 3 Bolela so jo kolena. 4 Bolele so vaju noge. 5 Bolel me je zob. 6 Ireno so bolela ušesa. 7 Bolel ga je želodec. 8 Bolelo te je srce.

Exercise 5

1 Imam vročino. 2 Boli me glava. 3 Boli me grlo. 4 Slabo mi je. 5 Potim se. 6 Kašljam. 7 Zelo sem utrujen. 8 Vedno sem zaspan.

Exercise 6

1 Nekaj dni ostanite v postelji. 2 Pijte veliko vode ali čaja. 3 Jejte sadje in zelenjavo. 4 Jemljite zdravila proti bolečinam. 5 Pojdite v lekarno. 6 Ne pijte alkohola. 7 Ne hodite bolni okrog. 8 Ne jejte preslane hrane. 9 Ne jemljite antibiotikov. 10 Ne kadite.

Exercise 7

1 Ne bomo šli na piknik, ker bo jutri slabo vreme. 2 Jan je velikokrat bolan, ker ne živi zdravo. 3 Ni mi predpisala antibiotika, ker imam gripo. 4 Kupil je nov suknjič, ker je izgubil starega. 5 Ni prišel na izpit, ker je bolan. 6 Peljala ga je k svoji zdravnici, ker je Andrejev zdravnik na dopustu.

Unit 16

Exercise 1

1 slajša 2 novejše 3 višja 4 lepše 5 udobnejši 6 mirnejše 7 bolj vroč 8 daljše

Exercise 2

Robbov vodnjak je starejši od Tromostovja. 2 Nemčija je večja od Avstrije. 3 Februar je krajši od marca. 4 Hiša je dražja od garsonjere. 5 Olje je lažje kot voda. 6 Andrejeva sestra je mlajša kot Andrej.

Exercise 3

1 na Primorsko 2 na Štajerskem 3 iz Notranjske 4 na Gorenjsko 5 na Dolenjskem 6 iz Koroške

Exercise 4

1 bolezen 2 soli 3 jedi 4 bolezni 5 soljo 6 jedjo 7 soli

Exercise 5

1 Želita ga peljati na daljši izlet. 2 Bolje pozna Gorenjsko. 3 Andrej predlaga Škocjanske jame, Piran in Portorož. 4 Ker bodo dobra osvežitev v vročini. 5 V Piranu. 6 Malo naprej od Pirana proti jugu. 7 Posebno floro in favno, solinarsko arhitekturo in kako po starih metodah pridelujejo sol. 8 V eni dobri gostilni blizu solin.

Exercise 6

1 A si že bil pri njem? 2 Ben se lahko pelje z njima. 3 Jutri bomo šli k njim. 4 Marko je sedel za njo. 5 Kaj ste kupili zanje? 6 Rad bi govoril z njo. 7 Lara živi pri nas. 8 To darilo je zanjo.

Exercise 7

1 G 2 H 3 B 4 E 5 A 6 C

Slovene–English glossary

The glossary provides the meanings in which the words appear in this book. For a wider range of meanings the learner should consult a dictionary. To use the glossary effectively, note the following:

1 Gender is marked in nouns when not predictable from the ending.
2 Number is marked when the noun is given in the plural or is plural-only.
3 Verbs always have the aspect marked and the first-person present-tense form is given if it is not predictable from the infinitive.
4 Offset entries are adjectives sharing the English translation with the preceding noun, and verbs differing from the previous verb only in aspect (in both cases the English translation is only given once); set phrases are also given offset under the main entry.

A		**ameriški**	American *adj.*
a	particle starting yes/no question; but	**ampak**	but
		angleščina	English language
adijo	(good)bye	**angleški**	English *adj.*
advokat	lawyer	**angleško**	in English
aha	oh (I see)	**Anglež, -inja**	English person *m./f.*
akademija	academy		
alergija	allergy	**Anglija**	England
ali	or; particle starting yes/ no question	**apnenec**	limestone
		april	April
		arhitekt, -ka	architect *m./f.*
alkohol	alcohol	**arhitektura**	architecture
ambasada	embassy	**atelje** m.	studio
ambulanta	clinic	**ati**	daddy
Američan, -ka	American person *m./f.*	**avgust**	August
		avto m.	car

avtobus	bus	bratranec	male cousin
avtocesta	highway	breskev f.	peach
avtomat	vending	breskov adj.	
	machine	brez	without
		brezalkoholen	non-alcoholic
B		brezkofeinski	decaffeinated
babica	grandmother	brezplačen	gratis
balet	ballet	brisača	towel
banana	banana	bruhati ipf.	to vomit
banka	bank	bukev f.	beech
bankomat	ATM		
bazen	swimming pool	C	
bel	white	cel	whole
besedilo	text	Celzij	Celsius
bi	would	cena	price
biografija	biography	cenejši	cheaper
biolog, -inja	biologist m./f.	cenik	price list
biologija	biology	cerkev f.	church
biti	to be	cesta	road, street
blagajna	ticket counter;	regionalna	local road
	cash register	cesta	
blazina	pillow	cimer	roommate
bled	pale adj.	copat(a)	slipper
blizu	close by, near		
bližnji	close adj.	Č	
blok	apartment	čaj	tea
	building	čakalnica	waiting room
bluza	blouse	čakati ipf.	to wait (for)
bogat	rich	počakati pf.	
bolan bolna	sick	čas	time
bolečina	pain	delovni čas	hours of
boleti boli ipf.	to hurt		operation
bolezen f.	illness	če	if
bolj	more (higher	čebula	onion(s)
	degree)	čeprav	even if
bolje	better adv.	česati češem (se)	to comb (self)
boljši	better	četrt	quarter
bolnica	hospital	četrtek	Thursday
bolnik, -ica	patient m./f.	četrti	fourth
bos	barefoot	čevelj	shoe
brat	brother	čez	across; past
brati berem ipf.	to read		(hour)

čigav	whose	**dežnik**	umbrella
čist	clean	**dihati** ipf.	to breathe
čisto v centru	right in the center	**dijak, -inja**	high-school student
čisto	entirely	**diplomirati** pf.	to graduate
čitalnica	reading room	**dnevna soba**	living room
član	member	**do**	up to; till
človek	person	**dober**	good
čokolada	chocolate	**dober tek**	bon appétit
čokoladen adj.		**dobiti** pf.	to get
črn	black	**dobiti se** pf.	to meet up
črni kruh	wholewheat bread	**dobro**	well
		dobrodošel	welcome
čuden	strange	**dodan**	added
čudovit	wonderful	**dodati** pf.	to add
		dograditi pf.	to finish building
D			
da	that *conj.*; yes (formal)	**dokončno**	ultimately
		Dolenjska	Lower Carniola
daleč	far (away)	**dolg**	long
daljši	longer	**dom**	home
dan	day	**domač** adj.	
danes	today	**doma**	at home
dati dam pf.	to give	**domov**	(to) home
december	December	**dopoldne**	before noon
dedek	grandfather	**dosęči -žem** pf.	to reach
dediščina	heritage	**dovolj**	enough
deka	decagram	**dovoljenje**	licence
del	part	**voznaško d.**	driver's licence
delati ipf.	to do; to work	**drag**	expensive; dear
delavlec, -ka	worker *m./f.*	**drobiž**	change (coins)
delo	work	**drugače**	otherwise
denar	money	**drugačen**	different
deset	ten	**drugi**	second; another
desni	right *adj.*		
desno	on/to the right	**drugič**	another time
devet	nine	**drugo leto**	next year
devetka	(bus) number 9	**družba**	company
dež	rain	**družina**	family
dež|evati -uje ipf.	to rain	**družinski** adj.	
		država	country
deževen	rainy	**državljan, -ka**	citizen, national

Dunaj | Vienna
dunajski adj. |
dunajski zrezek | Wiener schnitzel
dva, dve | two
dvajset | twenty
dvigalo | elevator
dvorana | hall, chamber
dvorišče | courtyard

E
edini | the only
edinstven | unique
en, eden, ena | one
enak | the same
energetsko varčen | energy efficient
evro m. | euro

F
fakulteta | college
faks (coll.) |
fant | boy(friend)
favna | fauna
februar | February
fizika | physics
fižol | bean(s)
forma | (physical) shape
fotelj | armchair
Francija | France
francosko | in French
francoščina | French language
Francoz, -inja | French person m./f.
frizer | hairdresser

G
galerija | art museum, gallery
garsonjera | studio
glasba | music
glasben adj. |
glava | head

glavni | main
glavno mesto | capital (city)
glavobol | headache
gledališče | theater
gledališki adj. |
gledati ipf. | to watch
glede | regarding
globok | deep
gneča | crowd
goba | mushroom
golaž | goulash
golf | golf
gora | mountain
Gorenjska | Upper Carniola
gospa | Mrs., lady
gospod | Mr., gentleman
gospodična | Miss
gost | thick, pulpy
gost | guest
gostilna | restaurant
gostitelj | host
gotovina | cash
gotovo | most likely
govedina | beef
goveji adj. |
govoriti ipf. | to speak
grad | castle
gripa | flu
grlo | throat
grozno | terribly

H
hčerka, hči | daughter
hiša | house
enonadstropna h. | two-story h.
pritlična h. | one-story h.
hiter | fast, quick
hit|eti -im ipf. | to hurry
hitrost f. | speed
hlače pl. | pants, slacks, trousers

hlad<u>e</u>n	cool, chilly	izb<u>o</u>ljšati pf.	to improve
hlad/lnik	refrigerator	izd<u>e</u>lati pf.	to create
hl<u>e</u>b<u>e</u>c	(round) loaf	iz*g/n*|iti -em pf.	to disappear
hod/ti h<u>o</u>dim ipf.	to go (multi-direct.)	izgl<u>e</u>dati ipf.	to look (a certain way)
hod/ti v hr/be	to hike	izhod	exit
hodn/k	corridor	izkaznica	ID
hot<u>e</u>l	hotel	izlet	day trip
hot<u>e</u>lski adj.		izm<u>e</u>riti pf.	to measure
hot<u>e</u>ti h<u>o</u>čem ipf.	to want	izp/t	exam
hrana	food	izst|op/ti -<u>o</u>pim pf.	to exit
hrb<u>e</u>t	back		
hr/b	hill	izte|či -čem se pf.	to come to an end
hruška	pear	izv<u>e</u>dba	rendition
hrvaščina	Croatian language	izv/rati ipf.	to originate
Hrvaška	Croatia	izv<u>o</u>li(te)	here you go
hrvaško	in Croatian		
Hrvat, -/ca	Croatian person *m./f.*	**J**	
		ja	yes
hvala	thank you	jabolko	apple
		jabolč<u>e</u>n adj.	
I		jagoda	strawberry
ideja	idea	jajce	egg
igrati	to play	jakna	jacket
im<u>e</u> -na n.	name	jama	cave
imen|ovati -*u*jem se ipf.	to be called	januar	January
		jas<u>e</u>n	clear
imen/t<u>e</u>n	excellent	jav<u>e</u>n	public
im|<u>e</u>ti -*a*m ipf.	to have	jaz	I
in	and	j<u>e</u>d f.	dish (food)
informacija	information	jed/lnica	dining hall
inštitut	institute	jed/lnik	menu
iskati /ščem ipf.	to look for	jemati jemljem ipf.	to take
/sti	the same		
Italijan, -ka	Italian person *m.f.*	jes<u>e</u>n	fall
		jes<u>e</u>nski adj.	
italijanščina	Italian language	jes<u>e</u>ni	in the fall
/ti gr<u>e</u>m ipf.	to go (one-direct.)	j<u>e</u>sti jem ipf.	to eat
		j<u>e</u>tra pl.	liver
iz	from, out of	j<u>e</u>z<u>e</u>n	angry
izb<u>o</u>ljšanje	improvement	j<u>e</u>zero	lake

jezik	language, tongue	**kem*i*ja**	chemistry
j*o*gurt	yogurt	**ker**	because
j*o*kati ipf.	to cry	**ki**	which *conj.*
j*o*pica	cardigan	**k*i*hati** ipf.	to sneeze
ju*g*	south	**k*i*la**	kilogram
juž*e*n adj.		**k*i*no** m.	movie theater, cinema
ju*h*a	soup	**kip*a*r**	sculptor
ju*l*ij	July	**kit*a*jski**	Chinese
ju*n*ij	June	**kit*a*jščina**	Chinese language
ju*t*ri	tomorrow		
ju*t*ro	morning	**kj*e***	where
		klav*i*r	piano
K		**klepet*a*ti** ipf.	to chat
k	to, towards	**kl*i*|cati -čem** ipf.	to call
k*a*dar	when(ever) *conj.*	**pokl*i*cati** pf.	
kad*i*ti ipf.	to smoke	**klju*č***	key
k*a*j	what; any	**klob*a*sa**	sausage
kajenje	smoking	**klobu*k***	hat
kak*o*	how	**knj*i*žnica**	library
kakš*e*n	what kind; some	**knj*i*žničar, -ka**	librarian *m./f.*
ka*m*	where to	**ko**	when *conj.*
kam*e*n	stone	**k*o*ča**	cottage
kamniški	adj. from Kamnik	**kol*e*gica**	colleague *f.*
kan*a*l	channel	**kol*e*no**	knee
k*a*pa	cap	**koles*a*riti** ipf.	to bike
kap*e*la	chapel	**k*o*liko**	how much/many
kapu*č*ino	cappuccino	**kol*o*, G kol*e*sa**	bicycle
k*a*rta	ticket	**koncert**	concert
k*a*rtica	card, pass	**konč*a*n**	finished
kasneje	later	**konč*a*ti (se)** pf.	to end
ka*š*ljati ipf.	to cough	**konč*e*n**	final
kat*e*ri	which	**končno**	finally
k*a*va	coffee	**kon*e*c**	end
kavarna	café	**konf*e*kcija**	apparel
i*n*ternetna k.	cyber café	**kop*a*lke** pl.	swimsuit
kav*č*	sofa	**kop*a*lnica**	bathroom
kd*a*j	when; sometime, ever	**k*o*pati (se)** ipf.	to bathe (self)
		k*o*pija	copy
		kos*i*lo	lunch
kd*o*	who	**k*o*siti** ipf.	to have lunch
		kost*i*m	suit (women's)

košara	basket	**lesen**	wooden
košarka	basketball	**lesti lezem** ipf.	to crawl
kot	as, like; than	**letalo**	airplane
kovček	suitcase	**letati** ipf.	to fly (multi-
kozarec	glass (drinking)		direct.)
kraj	town	**let|eti** -*im* ipf.	to fly (one-
krajinski	landscape *adj.*		direct.)
kranjski	Carniolan	**letni**	yearly
Kras	Karst	**letni čas**	season
kratek	short	**leto**	year
kratke hlače.	shorts	**letos**	this year
kravata	tie	**letošnji**	this year's
kreniti krenem pf.	to set out	**levi**	left
krilo	skirt	**levo**	on/to the left
krompir	potato(es)	**likati** ipf.	to iron
kruh	bread	**linija**	(bus) line
kuhan	boiled, cooked	**lipa**	linden
mehko kuhan	soft-boiled	**listek**	(shopping) list
kuhar, -ica	cook *m./f.*	**liter**	liter
kuhati ipf.	to cook	**ljubezen** f.	love
skuhati pf.		**ljubezenski** adj.	
kuhinja	kitchen	**ljubitelj**	admirer
kultura	culture	**ljubiti ljubim** ipf.	to love
kulturen adj.		**ljubljanski**	adj. from
kumara	cucumber		Ljubljana
kup|ovati	to shop	**ljudje**	people
-ujem ipf.		**lokal**	bar or
kupiti kupim pf.	to buy		restaurant
		lokalen	local
L			
lačen	hungry	**M**	
ladja	ship	**mačeha**	stepmother
lahek	light; easy	**Madžar, -ka**	Hungarian
lahko	can, may		person *m./f.*
lani	last year	**Madžarska**	Hungary
las, pl. **lasje**	hair	**madžarsko**	in Hungarian
lažji	lighter	**maj**	May
led	ice	**majhen**	small
leden adj.		**majica**	T-shirt
ledvice pl.	kidneys	**maketa**	diorama
lekarna	pharmacy	**malica**	snack
lep	beautiful	**malo**	a little, few

mama	mother	miza	table
mami(ca)	mommy	klubska miza	coffee table
manjši	smaller	pisalna miza	desk
mansarda	loft	mizar	carpenter
marati	to like, care for	mladost f.	youth
marec	March	mleko	milk
marelica	apricot	močen	strong
mareličen adj.		moči morem ipf.	to be able to
marmelada	jam	moder	blue
marmor	marble	mogoče	perhaps
maščoba	fat	mogočen	impressive
matematika	math	moj	my
med	between	moka	flour
medicina	medicine	moker	wet
	(field)	molitev	prayer
medkrajeven	inter-city	morati ipf.	must
mednaroden	international	morje	sea
medtem	meanwhile	moški	man; male adj.
medtem ko	while	motor	motorcycle
medve	we (two, f.)	mož	husband
megla	fog	mraz	cold
meglen	foggy	mrzel adj.	
mehiški	Mexican	muzej	museum
melodičen	melodic		
mesec	month	**N**	
meso	meat	na svidenje	'bye
mesen adj.		nab|rati -erem pf.	to pick
mleto meso	ground meat,	nabirati ipf.	
	mince	načrt	plan
mesto	city/town	nad	above
mesten adj.		nahajati se ipf.	to be located
mestna hiša	city/town hall	nahod	sniffles
mešan	mixed	najbolj	most (highest
metoda	method		degree)
mi, me	we m./f.	najbrž	probably
midva	we (two, m.)	najemnina	rent
milijarda	billion	naj|eti -amem pf.	to rent
milijon	million	najin	our (2 owners)
mimo	past prep.	najljubši	favorite
mineralen	mineral adj.	naj|ti -dem pf.	to find
miren	peaceful	nakupovalni	shopping mall
misliti ipf.	to think	center	

nakupovanje	shopping	**nekje**	somewhere
naložiti pf.	to load		(location)
nameravati ipf.	to intend	**Nemčija**	Germany
namreč	namely	**Nemlec, -ka**	German person
napitek	beverage		*m./f.*
napitnina	tip	**nemščina**	German
napoved	forecast		language
naprej	forward	**nemško**	in German
narava	nature	**nerad**	reluctantly
naravnost	straight	**neroden**	awkward
narediti pf.	to make	**neslti -em** ipf.	to carry (one-
narobe	wrong		direct.)
naročiti pf.	to order	**nestrpen**	impatient
naročiti se	to make an	**nevihta**	thunderstorm
	appointment	**nič**	zero, no; nothing
naroden	national	**nihče**	nobody
naslanjati ipf.	to lean	**nikjer**	nowhere
naslov	address	**nikoli**	never
nasproti	across from	**nizek**	low; short
nastlopiti	to appear (in a		(vertically)
-**opim** pf.	show)	**njegov**	his
naš	our (>2 owners)	**njen**	her
natakar, -ica	waiter, waitress	**njihov**	their (>2 owners)
natančno	precisely	**njun**	their (2 owners)
natikač	flip-flops	**noben**	not any
natrpan	crowded	**nocoj**	tonight
naučiti se pf.	to learn	**noč** f.	night
navada	habit, custom	**nočna omarica**	night stand
nazadnje	last *adv.*	**noga**	leg, foot
nazaj	back to	**nogavica**	sock
ne	no, not	**nogomet**	soccer
nečak, -inja	nephew, niece	**nos**	nose
nedelja	Sunday	**nositi nosim** ipf.	to carry (multi-
neizbrisen	indelible		direct.); to
nekaj	a few, some;		wear
	something	**notranjost** f.	interior
nekako	somehow	**nov**	new
nekakšen	some kind	**november**	November
nekam	somewhere		
	(destination)	**O**	
nekateri	some (of)	**o**	oh
nekdo	someone	**ob**	at; by, near

oba, obe	both	ogledalo	mirror
obala	coast	oglẹdati si pf.	to view
občina	county office	ogrẹ|ti -jem se pf.	to get warm
običajno	usually	ogromen	enormous
obisk	visit	oklẹvanje	hesitation
obiskovalec	visitor	oko, pl. oči	eye
oblačen	cloudy	okoli	about
oblačiti ipf.	to put clothes on	okrẹvati ipf.	to recover
oblẹ|či -čem pf.		okrog	around
oblẹka	clothing; dress;	oktober	October
	suit (men's)	okusen	tasty
obljubiti pf.	to promise	olje	oil
obož|evati -ujem	to adore	omara	closet, cabinet
ipf.		on, ona, ono	he, she, it
obraz	face	onadva, onidve	they (two) m./f.
obrẹžje	(sea) shore	oni, one, ona	they m./f./n.
obrten	trade adj.	opeka	brick
obutev f.	footwear	opoldne	at noon
obuvati ipf.	to put shoes on	opolnoči	at midnight
obu|ti -jem pf.		opravek	errand
ocvrt	fried	opremljen	furnished
očaran	fascinated	oprostiti	to excuse
oče	father	oranžen	orange
oči	daddy	oseba	person
očim	stepfather	oseben	personal
od	from (a source)	osem	eight
oddajati ipf.	to rent out	osnovnošol|ec,	elementary
oddati pf.	to hand in	-ka	student
oddelek	department	osta|ti -nem pf.	to stay, to
odeja	blanket		remain
odgovoriti pf.	to answer	osvežitev f.	something
odhod	departure		refreshing
odkrit	discovered	otrok, pl. otroci	child
odličen	excellent	ozek	narrow
odp|eljati -eljem	to depart, drive	ozemlje	territory
pf.	away		
odpornost f.	immunity	**P**	
odpr|eti -em pf.	to open	pa	and; but; while;
odprt	open		on the other
odvaditi	to break a habit		hand conj.
oglas	advertisement	pakirati ipf.	to pack
ogled	viewing	palačinka	crêpe

p**a**r	a couple	pla**š**č	coat
parad**i**žnik	tomato(es)	pl**a**vati	to swim
parad**i**žnikov		pl**a**ža	beach
adj.		pl**ę**s	dance
p**a**rk	park	pl**ęs**en adj.	
park**i**ranje	parking	plj**u**ča pl.	lungs
parkir**i**šče	parking lot	pl**ọ**d	fruit (e.g., berry)
p**a**rter	orchestra	pl**o**ha	shower (rain)
	seating	po	on surface of;
pe**č**at	seal, imprint		after
pe**č**enka	roast	poc**ę**ni	cheap
pe|**č**i -**č**em ipf.	to bake	po**č**asi	slowly
spe|**č**i pf.		po**č**itnice pl.	vacation
pelj**a**ti p**ę**ljem ipf.	to drive (one-	po**č**ivati ipf.	to rest
	direct.); to	po**č**|ut**i**ti -**ču**tim	to feel
	take, lead	se ipf.	
pelj**a**ti se	to go by vehicle	podar**i**ti pf.	to give as a gift
per**ọ**n	platform	pod**a**tki pl.	information
p**ę**š	on foot	podhod	underpass
p**ęs**ec	pedestrian	podj**ę**tje	enterprise
p**ę**t	five	podj**ę**tn|ik, -ica	entrepreneur
p**e**ta	heel		m./f.
p**ęt**ek	Friday	podp**i**s	signature
p**ę**ti p**o**jem ipf.	to sing	podz**ę**mlje	underground
p**i**ca	pizza	pogl**ę**dati pf.	to look at
p**i**hati ipf.	to blow	pog**o**sto	frequently
pij**a**ča	drink	pogov**a**rjati se ipf.	to converse
p**i**knik	picnic	poh**i**štvo	furniture
p**i**san	colorful	po|isk**a**ti -**i**ščem	to find (by
pis**a**rna	office	pf.	active search)
pis**a**telj, -ica	writer m./f.	poj**u**trišnjem	the day after
pis**a**ti p**i**šem ipf.	to write		tomorrow
p**i**smo	letter	poka|zati -žem pf.	to show
piš**č**an**e**c	chicken	pokl**i**c	occupation
pišk**ọ**t	cookie	pokopal**i**šče	cemetery
p**i**|ti -jem ipf.	to drink	pokr**a**jina	region
p**i**vo	beer	pol	half of
piž**a**ma	pajamas	pol**ę**ti	in summer
pla**č**ati pf.	to pay	pol**ę**tje	summer
plan**i**na	mountain	pol**ęt**en adj.	
plan**i**n**e**c	mountaineer	pol**i**ca	shelf
plast**e**nka	plastic bottle	polic**i**ja	police (station)

poljub kiss
poln full
polovica half
pomagati pf./ipf. to help
pomaranča orange
  pomarančen adj.
pomeriti pf. to try on
pomivalno korito kitchen sink
pomlad spring
  pomladen adj.
pomoč f. help
pon|uditi -udim pf. to offer
ponavadi usually
ponedeljek Monday
ponoči at night
ponudba offerings
  ponujen offered
popoldne (in the) afternoon
  popoldanski adj.
popust discount
porcija portion
poročen married
poročiti se to get married
posebej separately
posebno especially
poslati pošljem pf. to send
  pošiljati ipf.
poslušati ipf. to listen to
posoda dishes
pospraviti pf. to clean up
postaja station
  avtobusna p. bus s.
  železniška p. train s.
posta|ti -nem pf. to become
postava figure (body)
postelja bed
posteljnina linens
posušiti pf. to dry

pošta post office
pot f. path, way
potekati ipf. to run (event, show)
potem after that, then
potica nut roll
potiti se ipf. to sweat
potni list passport
potnik passenger
potovalna agencija travel agency
potovanje travel, trip
pot|ovati -ujem ipf. to travel
potreba need
potreb|ovati -ujem ipf. to need
potrkati pf. to knock
pov|abiti -abim pf. to invite
povabljen invited
pove|dati -m pf. to tell
povraten round-trip
površje surface
pozabiti pf. to forget
pozdrav greeting
pozimi in the winter
poznati to know, be familiar with
pozno late
praksa internship
pralni stroj washing machine
prati perem ipf. to wash (clothes)
prav right
  biti prav komu to fit well
pravi real, true
pravo law (field)
prazen empty
prazn|ovati -ujem ipf. to celebrate

pre- (+ adj.)	too	prevajal|ec, -ka	translator *m./f.*
prebrati pf.	to read	prevajati ipf.	to translate
precediti pf.	to strain	preveč	too (much)
precej	fair amount, quite	prevoz	transportation
prečkati ipf./pf.	to cross	prezgodaj	too early
pred	in front of;	preživljati ipf.	to spend time
	before	pri	near, by
predaleč	too far	približno	approximately
predavanje	lecture	pričak|ovati	to expect
predavati ipf.	to lecture	-ujem ipf.	
predlagati ipf./pf.	to suggest	pridel|ovati	to cultivate
predlanskim	year before last	-ujem ipf.	
predpi|sati -šem	to prescribe	prihod	arrival
pf.		prihodnji	next, future
predstava	show	priimek	last name
predstaviti pf.	to introduce	prijatelj, -ica	friend *m./f.*
predstavljati ipf.	to represent	prijazen	friendly
predvčerajšnjim	day before	prijeten	pleasant
	yesterday	priključek	hook-up
pregled	exam	prile|či -že se	to do (feel)
prehlad	cold (illness)	ipf./pf.	good
prehlajen	having a cold	priloga	side dish
prehod	crossing	priložnost f.	opportunity
preiskati pf.	to search	Primorska	Littoral
	through	primorski adj.	
prej	earlier;	prine|sti -sem pf.	to bring by
	beforehand		carrying
prejšnji	previous	prip|eljati	to bring by
prejšnji mesec	last month	-eljem pf.	vehicle, to
prekrasen	gorgeous		bring along
preli|ti -jem pf.	to pour over	prip|eljati -eljem	to arrive by
prenočiti pf.	to overnight	se pf.	vehicle
prepoved f.	prohibition	priporočati ipf.	to recommend
prepovedan	prohibited	pripovedovati ipf.	to narrate
prepoznati pf.	to recognize	priprava	preparation
preproga	rug	pripraviti pf.	to prepare
pres|eliti -elim	to move	pripravljati ipf.	
se pf.		pristajati ipf.	to look good on
presenetiti pf.	to surprise		someone
prestolnica	capital (city)	pri|ti -dem pf.	to come, arrive
preurejati ipf.	to redesign	pritisk	pressure
preurediti pf.		prizorišče	scene, stage

problem	problem	razstava	exhibit
prodajal|ec, -ka	sales clerk *m./f.*	razstavljen	displayed
prodajati ipf.	to sell	razširiti se pf.	to widen
prodati pf.		razumeti -em	to understand
profesor, -ica	professor *m./f.*	pf./ipf.	
proga	(bus) line	razumeti se ipf.	to get along
promet	traffic	rdeč, rdeča	red
prositi prosim ipf.	to ask for	recept	prescription
prosim	please	receptor	receptionist
prost	available, free	re|či -čem pf.	to say
prostor	space, room	reden	regular
prostoren	spacious	redko	rarely
prostornina	volume	reka	river
proti	towards,	restavracija	restaurant
	against	reševalen	rescue *adj.*
prst	finger, toe	rešiti pf.	to solve
pršut	prosciutto	rezanci pl.	noodles
prvi	first	rezati ipf.	to cut
prvič	first time	rezervacija	reservation
pulover	sweater	rezervirati ipf./pf.	to reserve
punca	girl(friend)	riba	fish
punčka	little girl	ri|sati -šem ipf.	to draw
puranji	turkey *adj.*	riž	rice
		rjav	brown
R		rojen -ena	born
račun	bill	rojsten	birth *adj.*
računalničar, -ka	computer	rojstni dan	birthday
	expert *m./f.*	roka	arm, hand
računalnik	computer	rokav	sleeve
rad	gladly, like to	rumen	yellow
rad bi	would like	Rus, -inja	Russian
rad imeti	to like		person *m./f.*
ravno	just, exactly	rusko	in Russian
razgled	view		
razglednica	postcard	**S**	
različen	various;	s	with, by; from
	dissimilar	sadje	fruit
razni pl.	various	saden adj.	
razprodaja	sale	salama	salami
razprodan	sold out	samo	only
razred	class	samopostrežen	self-serve
razre|zati -žem pf.	to cut up	samski	single

sandal(a)	sandal	slišati -im ipf./pf.	to hear
se(be)	oneself	Sloven|ec, -ka	Slovene
sedem	seven		person m./f.
sedeti -im ipf.	to sit	Slovenija	Slovenia
sedež	seat	slovenski	Slovene adj.
semafor	traffic light	slovensko	in Slovene
semester	semester	slovenščina	Slovene
september	September		language
sestra	sister; nurse	slovnica	grammar
sestrična	female cousin	služba	job
seveda	of course	smerokaz	signpost
sever	north	smetana	cream
severen adj.		SMS [es-em-es]	text message
seznam	list	smučati ipf.	to ski
sezuvati ipf.	to take shoes	snaha	daughter-in-law
	off	sneg	snow
sezu|ti -jem pf.		snežen	snowy
shraniti pf.	to save	snežiti ipf.	to snow
sij|ati -e(m) ipf.	to shine	soba	room
sin	son	enoposteljna s.	single room
sinoči	last night	sobota	Saturday
sir	cheese	sodelavec	co-worker
sistematski	physical exam	sodni|k, -ca	judge m./f.
pregled		sok	juice
sit	satiated	sol f.	salt
siv	gray	solata	salad
skodelica	cup	solina	salt pan
skoraj	almost	solinarski adj.	
skozi	through	sonce	sun
skupaj	together	sončen	sunny
skuta	cottage cheese	soparen	humid
slab	bad	sorodnik	relative
slabo	poorly, bad	soseska	neighborhood
slabost	weakness	soteska	gorge
slačiti ipf.	to undress	souporaba	joint use
sle|či -čem pf.		spalnica	bedroom
sladica	dessert	spati spim ipf.	to sleep
sladkarije pl.	sweets	splačati se	to be
sladkor	sugar		worthwhile
sladoled	ice cream	sploh	at all
slaven	famous	spodaj	beneath,
slikovit	picturesque		downstairs

spodnje perilo	underwear	stol	chair
spodnji	lower	stolp	tower
spominek	souvenir	stopinja	degree
spominjati se ipf.	to remember	stopiti stopim pf.	to step
spomniti se pf.		stopnice pl.	stairs
spomladi	in the spring	stopnišče	stairway
spored	program	stran f.	side
sporočilo	message	stranišče	restroom,
spoznati pf.	to meet (for the		toilet
	first time)	strasten	passionate
spredaj	in front	stre|či -žem ipf.	to serve
sprehod	stroll	streha	roof
spreh|oditi	to take a walk	strinjati se pf.	to agree
-odim se pf.		strm	steep
spremeniti pf.	to change	stuširati se pf.	to shower
srajca	shirt	stvar f.	thing
srce	heart	suh	dry
sreča	good fortune,	suknjič	blazer
	happiness	svak, -inja	brother/sister-
na srečo	fortunately		in-law
srečen	(profoundly)	svet	world
	happy	svetoven adj.	
srečno	good luck	svetel	bright, light
sreda	Wednesday	svetilka	lamp
srednješol|ec, -ka	high-school	svet|ovati -ujem	to advise
	student m./f.	ipf.	
srednji	middle	svila	silk
stadion	stadium	svinčnik	pencil
stanovanje	apartment	svinjina	pork
stan|ovati -ujem	to reside	svinjski adj.	
ipf.		svoj	one's own
star	old		
stara mama	grandmother	Š	
stari oče	grandfather	šal	scarf
starinarnica	antique shop	še	still
starši pl.	parents	šest	six
stati stane ipf.	to cost	šipek	rose hip
stati stojim ipf.	to stand	širok	wide
stavba	building	škatla	box
steklenica	bottle	škoda	pity
sto	hundred	školjka	toilet
stojnica	stand, stall	škorenj	boot

šǫla	school
osnovna š.	elementary s.
srędnja š.	high s.
špinača	spinach
špǫrten	athletic
Štajerska	Styria
štedi/lnik	stove
šti/rje, šti/ri	four
študent, -ka	college student *m./f.*
študentski adj.	
študentski dǫm	student dorm, hall of residence
študi/rati	to study
šumeč	rustling
šunka	ham
T	
ta, tǫ	this
tabla	(display) board
tablęta	pill
takǫ	so
tako da	therefore *conj.*
takǫj	right away
takrat	at that time
tam(le)	(over) there
tast	father-in-law
tašča	mother-in-law
te|či -čem ipf.	to run
tęden	week
na tęden	per week
tehtati ipf.	to weigh
tęk	appetite; run
tękati ipf.	to run (multi-direct.)
telęčji	veal *adj.*
telefǫn	telephone
telefoni/rati ipf./pf.	to call on the phone
televi/zor	TV set
tęmęn	dark

temperatu/ra	temperature
tęnis	tennis
terasa	patio
testeni/ne pl.	pasta
teta	aunt
tęža	weight
težęk	difficult; heavy
ti/	you (sg.)
ti/h	quiet
ti/p	type
ti/soč	thousand
ti/sti	that
tla pl.	floor
topęl	warm
topli/ce pl.	spa
toplomęr	thermometer
toręk	Tuesday
tǫrta	layer cake
trajati ipf.	to last
trami/nec	variety of white wine
trava	grass
trd	hard
trdno pravilo	strict rule
trenu/tęk	moment
trenu/tno	currently
tretji	third
trg	square
trgovi/na	store
tri/indvajsetka	(bus) number 23
tri/je, tri/	three
tri/lętęn	three-year-old
trta	grapevine
tržnica	marketplace
tu/(kaj)	here
tu/di	also
tu/jęc	foreigner
turi/st	tourist
tu/š	shower
tuši/rati se ipf.	to shower
stuši/rati se pf.	
tvǫj	your

U

učen|ec, -ka	pupil *m./f.*
uč*i*telj, -ica	teacher *m./f.*
udob*e*n	comfortable
ug*o*dna c*e*na	good price
uh*o*, pl. uš*e*sa	ear
ukv*a*rjati se (z) ipf.	to occupy oneself (with)
*u*lica	street
um*e*tnost*e*n	art *adj.*
umiv*a*lnik	sink
um*i*vati (se) ipf.	to wash (self)
univerza	university
*u*pati ipf.	to hope
upok*o*jen	retired
*u*ra	hour; clock, watch
urban*i*st	urban planner
ured*i*ti pf.	to arrange
*u*rnik	schedule
*u*sta pl.	mouth
ust*a*viti (se) pf.	to stop
ustv*a*riti pf.	to create
utruj*e*n	tired
už*i*t*e*k	pleasure

V

v	into; in
v*a*jin	your (2 owners)
var|ov*a*ti -*u*jem ipf.	to take care; to protect
v*a*š	your (>2 owners; 1 owner— formal)
vč*a*sih	sometimes
vč*e*raj	yesterday
več	more; any more (with negated verb)
več*e*r	evening
več*e*rja	dinner

več*i*na	majority
v*e*čji	bigger
v*e*deti v*e*m ipf.	to know (a fact)
v*e*dno	always
vegetarijan|*e*c, -ka	vegetarian *m./f.*
vegetarij*a*nski adj.	
veleblagovnica	department store
vel|ik -*i*ka	large
vel*i*ko	a lot, many
velik*o*st f.	size
verj*e*tno	probably
v*e*s vsa vse	all
ves*e*l	merry, happy
veselje	pleasure
v*e*t*e*r	wind
vetrov*e*n	windy
vhod	entrance
vi, v*e*	we *m./f.*
v*i*d|eti -im ipf./pf.	to see
v*i*dva, v*e*dve	you (two)
vijol*i*č*e*n	purple
v*i*kend	weekend; weekend house
v*i*no	wine
vinot*e*ka	wine cellar
visok	tall
viš*i*na	height
v*i*t*e*k	slim
viz*i*tka	business card
vklj*u*čen	included
vključ|ev*a*ti -*u*jem ipf.	to include
vl*a*k	train
vn*e*t	inflamed
vn*u*k, -inja	grandson/ granddaughter
voda	water
vodni adj.	

vod*i*č	guide	**Z**	
vodnjak	fountain	**z**	with, by; from
vojna	war	**za**	for; behind
volna	wool	**zabava**	entertainment,
voz*i*č<u>e</u>k	cart		party
voz*i*lo	vehicle	**zač|<u>e</u>ti -ne se** pf.	to start
voz*i*ti v<u>o</u>zim ipf.	to drive (multi-	**zač*u*d<u>e</u>n**	surprised
	direct.)	**zadnji**	last, recent;
voz*i*ti se	to ride		back
vozni r<u>e</u>d	timetable	**zadnje č*a*se**	recently
vozovnica	transportation	**zadnjič**	the other day
	ticket	**zadr<u>e</u>ga**	embarrassment
vožnja	drive, ride	**zaenkrat**	for now
vpra*š*ati pf.	to ask (a	**zahod**	west
	question)	**zah<u>o</u>d<u>e</u>n** adj.	
vr<u>e</u>d<u>e</u>n	worthwhile	**zajtrk**	breakfast
vreme	weather	**zajtrk|ov*a*ti**	to have
vrem<u>e</u>nski adj.		**-*u*jem** ipf.	breakfast
vr<u>e</u>ti vre ipf.	to boil	**pozajtrkov*a*ti**	
vrn*i*ti v*r*nem se pf.	to return	pf.	
vr<u>o</u>č	hot	**zakaj**	why
vroč*i*na	fever; heat	**zaključ<u>e</u>k**	conclusion
v*r*sta	row	**zal*i*v**	bay
v*r*t	garden	**zamašen**	stuffed
vsaj	at least	**zam<u>e</u>njati** pf.	to exchange
vsak	every	**zamud*i*ti** pf.	to be late; to
vse	everything		miss
vseeno	nevertheless	**zan*i*č**	lousy
vsekakor	by all means	**zan*i*mati** ipf.	to interest
vselj*i*v	ready to move	**zanim*i*v**	interesting
	in	**zap<u>e</u>ti** pf.	to start singing
vs*i* pl.	all, everybody	**zaposlen**	employed
vstajati ipf.	to get up	**zap*r*t**	closed
vsta|ti -nem pf.		**zaradi**	because of
vstop|*i*ti -im pf.	to enter	**zas<u>e</u>den**	taken, occupied
vst<u>o</u>pnica	ticket	**zaspan**	sleepy
vš<u>e</u>č (b*i*ti)	to appeal	**zast<u>o</u>nj**	to no avail; for
vt*i*s|niti -nem pf.	to imprint		free
vz<u>e</u>ti vz*a*mem pf.	to take	**zašč*i*ten**	protected
vzhod	east	**zat<u>o</u>**	therefore
vzh<u>o</u>d<u>e</u>n adj.		**zavarovanje**	insurance
vzpenja*č*a	funicular	**zav<u>e</u>sa**	curtain

zav*i*t*e*k	strudel; package	znamen*i*t	renowned
zav*i*|ti -jem pf.	to turn	znamen*i*tost f.	landmark
zav|rn*i*ti -*r*nem pf.	to refuse	znamka	stamp
zbol|*e*ti -*i*m pf.	to get sick	zn*a*n	well-known
zbor	choir	zn*a*ti	to know
ZDA [z*e*-de-*a*]	USA	zn*o*traj	inside
zdaj	now	z*o*b, pl. zobj*e*	tooth
zdrav	healthy	zobozdravn|*i*k,	dentist m./f.
zdravil*i*šče	health resort	-*i*ca	
zdrav*i*lo	medication	zr*a*ven	alongside
zdraviti ipf.	to cure	zr*e*z*e*k	cutlet
zdraviti se ipf.	to recuperate	z*u*naj	outside
zdravje	health	zv*e*č*e*r	in the evening
zdr*a*vstven adj.			
zdr*a*vstveni	health center	**Ž**	
d*o*m		ž*a*l	unfortunately
zdravn|*i*k, -*i*ca	physician m./f.	biti ž*a*l	to be sorry
zdr*a*vo	hello/'bye	ž*a*lost*e*n	sad
zdrob*i*ti pf.	to crush	ž*e*	already
zelen	green	žej*e*n	thirsty
zelenj*a*va	vegetable	žel|*e*ti -*i*m ipf.	to wish, want
zelenjav*e*n adj.		žel*e*znica	railway
zel*o*	very	žel*o*d*e*c	stomach
zet	son-in-law	ž*e*na	wife
zg*o*daj	early	ž*e*nska	woman
zgodov*i*na	history	ž*e*nski	female adj.
zgoraj	upstairs, above	ž*i*tarice pl.	cereal
zgrad*i*ti pf.	to build	ž*i*valski vrt	zoo
zgrajen	built	živ|*e*ti -*i*m ipf.	to live
z*i*d	wall	ž*i*vjo	hello/'bye
z*i*ma	winter	življenje	life
z*i*mski adj.		ž*u*r	party (coll.)
zj*u*traj	in the morning	žur*i*rati ipf.	to party

English–Slovene glossary

The qualifiers in *italics* next to English words disambiguate meanings and should be read as follows: *n.* = noun, *adj.* = adjective, *v.* = verb, *adv.* = adverb. The abbreviations on the Slovene side are used as in the rest of the book.

When two Slovene verbs are separated by a slash, the first one is imperfective, the other perfective. When the verb is given with a prefix in parentheses, the prefixed verb is perfective, the non-prefixed one imperfective.

A

above	**nad**
across	**čez** (+A)
across from	**nasproti**
add	**dodati**
address	**naslov**
advertisement	**oglas**
advise	**svet|ovati -ujem**
after	**po** (+L)
afternoon *n.*	**popoldne**
against	**proti**
agree	**str\i njati se** pf.
airplane	**letalo**
alcohol	**alkohol**
all	**ves vsa vse**
almost	**skoraj**
already	**že**
also	**tudi**
always	**vedno**
American *adj.*	**ameriški**
American person	**Američan, -ka**
and	**in, pa**

answer *v.*	**odgovarjati/ odgovoriti**
antibiotic	**antibiotik**
apartment	**stanovanje**
appeal *v.*	**biti všeč**
appear (in a show)	**nast|opiti -opim** pf.
appetite	**tek**
apple *adj.*	**jabolčen**
apple *n.*	**jabolko**
approximately	**približno, okrog**
apricot *adj.*	**mareličen**
apricot *n.*	**marelica**
April	**april**
architect	**arhitekt, -ka**
arm	**roka**
armchair	**fotelj**
around	**okrog**
arrive	**pri|ti -dem** pf.
arrive (by vehicle)	**prip|eljati -eljem se** pf.
as	**kot**

ask (a question)	**vprašati** pf.	better *adj.*	**boljši**
ask (for	**prositi** ipf.	better *adv.*	**bolje**
something)		between	**med**
at (a person)	**pri** (+L)	bicycle	**kolo**, G **kolesa**
at (a place)	**v, na** (+L)	bigger	**večji**
at (near)	**pri, ob** (+L)	bike *v.*	**kolesariti** ipf.
at all	**sploh**	bill *n.*	**račun**
at least	**vsaj**	billion	**milijarda**
athletic	**športen**	birth *adj.*	**rojsten**
ATM	**bankomat**	birthday	**rojstni dan**
August	**avgust**	black	**črn**
aunt	**teta**	blanket	**odeja**
available	**prost**	blazer	**suknjič**
awkward	**neroden**	blouse	**bluza**
		blow	**pihati** ipf.
B		blue	**moder**
back *adj.*	**zadnji**	board	**tabla**
back *adv.*	**nazaj**	boiled	**kuhan**
bad	**slab**	boot	**škorenj**
bake	**(s)pe|či -čem**	born	**rojen -ena**
banana	**banana**	both	**oba, obe**
bank	**banka**	bottle	**steklenica**
bathe	**kopati (se)** ipf.	box	**škatla**
bathroom	**kopalnica**	boy(friend)	**fant**
bay	**zaliv**	bread	**kruh**
be	**biti**	breakfast	**zajtrk**
be able to	**moči morem** ipf.	breathe	**dihati** ipf.
be late	**zamuditi**	bright	**svetel**
beautiful	**lep**	bring (by	**prine|sti**
because	**ker**	carrying)	**-sem** pf.
because of	**zaradi**	bring along	**prip|eljati**
become	**posta|ti -nem** pf.		**-eljem** pf.
become sick	**zbol|eti -im** pf.	brother	**brat**
bed	**postelja**	brother-in-law	**svak**
bedroom	**spalnica**	brown	**rjav**
beef *adj.*	**goveji**	build	**(z)graditi**
beef *n.*	**govedina**	building	**stavba**
beer	**pivo**	built	**zgrajen**
before	**pred** (+I)	bus *adj.*	**avtobusen**
beforehand	**prej**	bus *n.*	**avtobus**
behind	**za; zadaj**	but	**ampak, a, pa**
beneath	**pod; spodaj**	buy	**kupiti kupim** pf.

by	pri, ob; z/s	choir	zbor
'bye	na svidenje,	church	cerkev f.
	adijo, živjo	cinema	kino m.
		city adj.	mesten
C		city n.	mesto
cabinet	omara	class	razred
café	kavarna	clear	jasen
cake	torta	clinic	ambulanta
call	(po)kli|cati -čem	clock	ura
call (by phone)	telefonirati	close adv.	blizu
	ipf./pf.	closed	zaprt
can	lahko	clothing	obleka
capital (city)	glavno mesto	cloudy	oblačen
cappuccino	kapučino	coast n.	obala
car	avto m.	coat	plašč
cardigan	jopica	coffee	kava
carry (multi-	nositi nosim ipf.	cold (illness)	prehlad
direct.)		cold adj.	mrzel
carry (one-direct.)	nes|ti -em ipf.	cold n.	mraz
cart	voziček	college	fakulteta, faks
cash	gotovina	colorful	pisan
cash register	blagajna	comfortable	udoben
castle	grad	computer	računalnik
cave	jama	converse v.	pogovarjati se
celebrate	prazn|ovati		ipf.
	-ujem	cook v.	(s)kuhati
Celsius	Celzij	cooked	kuhan
cereal	žitarice pl.	cool	hladen
chair	stol	copy	kopija
change (coins)	drobiž	corridor	hodnik
change v.	spremeniti pf.	cost v.	stati stane ipf.
chat	klepetati ipf.	cottage cheese	skuta
cheap	poceni	cough v.	kašljati ipf.
cheaper	cenejši	country	država
cheese	sir	couple	par
chemistry	kemija	courtyard	dvorišče
chicken	piščanec	cousin f.	sestrična
child	otrok, pl. otroci	cousin m.	bratranec
Chinese adj.	kitajski	cream	smetana
Chinese language	kitajščina	create	ustvarjati/
chocolate adj.	čokolade		ustvariti
chocolate n.	čokolada	crêpe	palačinka

cross *v.*	prečkati ipf./pf.	drive (one-direct.)	peljati peljem ipf.
crowded	natrpan	drive *n.*	vožnja
cry	jokati ipf.	dry	suh
culture *adj.*	kulturen		
culture *n.*	kultura		
cup	skodelica	**E**	
custom	navada	ear	uho, pl. ušesa
cut *v.*	(raz)rezati	earlier	prej
cutlet	zrezek	early	zgodaj
		east *adj.*	vzhoden
D		east *n.*	vzhod
daddy	oči	easy	lahek
dance *adj.*	plesen	eat	(po)jesti (po)jem
dance *n.*	ples	egg	jajce
dark	temen	eight	osem
daughter	hčerka, hči	elevator	dvigalo
day	dan	employed	zaposlen
dear	drag	empty	prazen
decagram	deka	end *n.*	konec
deep	globok	end *v.*	končati (se) pf.
degree (heat)	stopinja	English (language)	angleščina
dentist	zobozdravn|ik, -ica	English *adj.*	angleški
depart (by vehicle)	odp|eljati -eljem (se) pf.	English person	Anglež, -inja
		enter	vstop|iti -im pf.
department	oddelek	entirely	čisto
departure	odhod	entrance	vhod
desk	pisalna miza	errand	opravek
dessert	sladica	especially	posebno
different	drugačen	euro	evro m.
dinner	večerja	even if	čeprav
dish	jed f.; posoda	evening, in the evening	večer, zvečer
do	delati		
downstairs	spodaj	ever	kdaj
draw (picture)	(na)ri|sati -šem	every	vsak
dress *n.*	obleka	everybody	vsi pl.
dress *v.*	oble|či -čem /oblačiti	everything	vse
		exam (medical)	pregled
drink *n.*	pijača	exam (school)	izpit
drink *v.*	pi|ti -jem ipf.	excellent	odličen
drive (multi-direct.)	voziti vozim (se) ipf.	exchange	(za)menjati
		excuse *v.*	oprostiti

exhibit	razstava	foot	noga
exit *n.*	izhod	footwear	obut*e*v f.
exit *v.*	izst|op*i*ti	for	za
	-*o*pim pf.	forecast	napoved
expensive	drag	foreigner	tuj*e*c
eye	ok*o*, pl. oč*i*	forget	poz*a*biti pf.
		forward	naprej
F		fountain	vodnjak
face	obraz	four	št*i*rje, št*i*ri
fall, in fall	jes*e*n, jes*e*ni	fourth	čet*r*ti
fall *adj.*	jes*e*nski	France	Francija
family *n.*	druž*i*na	free	prost;
famous	slav*e*n		brezplač*e*n
far	daleč	French *adj.*	franc*o*ski
fascinated	očaran	French language	franc*o*ščina
father	oče	French person	Franc*o*z, -inja
father-in-law	tast	frequently	pog*o*sto
favorite	najljubši	Friday	p*e*tek
February	f*e*bruar	friend	prij*a*telj, -ica
feel	poč|ut*i*ti -č*u*tim	friendly	prijaz*e*n
	se ipf.	from	iz, od (+G)
female *adj.*	ž*e*nski	fruit *adj.*	sad*e*n
fever	vroč*i*na	fruit *n.*	sadje
few	malo	full	poln
final	konč*e*n	full (satiated)	s*i*t
find (by	poisk*a*ti -*i*ščem	funicular	vzpenjača
searching)	pf.	furnished	opr*e*mlj*e*n
find *v.*	naj|ti -dem pf.		
finger	p*r*st	**G**	
finished	konč*a*n	garden	vrt
first	p*r*vi	gentleman	gosp*o*d
first time	p*r*vič	German *adj.*	n*e*mški
fish	r*i*ba	German	n*e*mščina
five	p*e*t	language	
floor	nadstr*o*pje;	German person	N*e*m|ec, -ka
	tla pl.	Germany	N*e*mčija
flour	m*o*ka	get (acquire)	dob*i*ti pf.
flu	gr*i*pa	get along	razum*e*ti se ipf.
fly (multi-direct.)	l*e*tati ipf.	get up	vstajati/vsta|ti
fly (one-direct.)	let|*e*ti -*i*m ipf.		-nem
fog	m*e*gla	girl(friend)	punca
food	hrana	give	d*a*ti pf.

gladly	**rad**	heat	**vročina**
glass (drinking)	**kozarec**	height	**višina**
go (multi-direct.)	**hoditi hodim** ipf.	hello (greeting)	**dober dan, živjo**
go (one-direct.)	**iti grem** ipf.	hello (phone)	**halo**
golf	**golf**	help n.	**pomoč** f.
good	**dober**	help v.	**pomagati**
gorgeous	**prekrasen**	her(s)	**njen**
graduate	**diplomirati**	here	**tu(kaj)**
grammar	**slovnica**	high school	**srednja šola**
granddaughter	**vnukinja**	high-school	**srednješollec,**
grandfather	**dedek, stari oče**	student	**-ka**
grandmother	**babica, stara**	hill	**hrib**
	mama	his	**njegov**
grandson	**vnuk**	history	**zgodovina**
grass	**trava**	home (at)	**doma**
gray	**siv**	home (to)	**domov**
green	**zelen**	home n.	**dom**
greeting	**pozdrav**	hope v.	**upati** ipf.
guest	**gost**	hospital	**bolnica**
guide	**vodič**	hot	**vroč**
goulash	**golaž**	hotel adj.	**hotelski**
		hotel n.	**hotel**
H		hour	**ura**
habit	**navada**	house	**hiša**
hair	**las**, pl. **lasje**	how	**kako**
half	**pol, polovica**	how much/many	**koliko**
hall of residence	**študentski dom**	humid	**soparen**
ham	**šunka**	hundred	**sto**
hand	**roka**	hungry	**lačen**
happiness	**sreča**	hurry	**hitleti -im**
happy	**srečen, vesel**	hurt v.	**boleti boli** ipf.
hard	**trd**	husband	**mož**
hat	**klobuk**		
have	**imleti -am** ipf.	**I**	
he	**on**	I	**jaz**
head	**glava**	ice adj.	**leden**
health adj.	**zdravstven**	ice n.	**led**
health n.	**zdravje**	ice cream	**sladoled**
healthy	**zdrav**	ID	**izkaznica**
hear	**slišlati -im**	if	**če**
	ipf./pf.	ill	**bolan bolna**
heart	**srce**	illness	**bolezen**

immediately	**takoj**	**L**	
impatient	**nestrpen**	lady	**gospa**
in	**v, na** (+L)	lake	**jezero**
in front	**spredaj**	lamp	**svetilka**
in front of	**pred**	landmark	**znamenitost** f.
include	**vključevati**	language	**jezik**
	-ujem ipf.	large	**vellik -ika**
included	**vključen**	last *adj.*	**zadnji, prejšnji**
information	**informacija**	last *adv.*	**nazadnje**
inside	**znotraj**	last *v.*	**trajati** ipf.
institute	**inštitut**	last name	**priimek**
intend	**nameravati** ipf.	last night	**sinoči**
interest *v.*	**zanimati** ipf.	last year	**lani**
interesting	**zanimiv**	late	**pozno**
international	**mednaroden**	later	**kasneje**
introduce	**predstavljati/**	learn	**naučiti se** pf.
	predstaviti	lecture *n.*	**predavanje**
invite	**(po)v|abiti -abim**	lecture *v.*	**predavati** ipf.
it	**ono (ona, on)**	left, on/to the	**levi, levo**
Italian *adj.*	**italijanski**	left	
Italian language	**italijanščina**	leg	**noga**
Italian person	**Italijan, -ka**	letter	**pismo**
		library	**knjižnica**
J		life	**življenje**
jacket	**jakna, suknjič**	light (bright)	**svetel**
jam	**marmelada**	light (not heavy)	**lahek**
January	**januar**	like *conj.*	**kot**
job	**služba, delo**	like *v.*	**rad, imeti rad**
judge	**sodni|k, -ca**	linden	**lipa**
juice	**sok**	line (bus)	**linija, proga**
July	**julij**	list	**seznam;**
June	**junij**		(shopping)
			listek
K		listen to	**poslušati** ipf.
Karst	**Kras**	liter	**liter**
key	**ključ**	little (quantity)	**malo**
kilogram	**kila**	little *adj.*	**majhen, mali**
kitchen	**kuhinja**	live *v.*	**živeti -im** ipf.
knee	**koleno**	living room	**dnevna soba**
knock *v.*	**(po)trkati**	load	**naložiti** pf.
know	**znati, poznati,**	located (to be)	**nahajati se** ipf.
	vedeti	long	**dolg**

longer	daljši	million	milijon
look (at)	(po)gledati	mineral *adj.*	mineralen
look for	iskati iščem ipf.	Miss	gospodična
lots	veliko	mixed	mešan
lousy	zanič	moment	trenutek
love *adj.*	ljubezenski	Monday	ponedeljek
love *n.*	ljubezen f.	money	denar
love *v.*	imeti rad, ljubiti	month	mesec
low	nizek	more	bolj, več
lower	spodnji; nižji	morning (early),	jutro, zjutraj
Lower Carniola	Dolenjska	in the m.	
luck	sreča	morning (late)	dopoldne
lunch, have lunch	kosilo, kositi ipf.	most (highest	najbolj
lungs	pljuča pl.	degree)	
		most likely	gotovo
M		mother	mama
main	glavni	mother-in-law	tašča
majority	večina	motorcycle	motor
make	narediti pf.	mountain	planina, gora
male *adj.*	moški	mouth	usta pl.
man	moški; človek	move *v.*	(pre)s|eliti -elim
many	veliko		se pf.
marble	marmor	Mr.	gospod
March	marec	Mrs.	gospa
marketplace	tržnica	must	morati ipf.
married	poročen	my, mine	moj
math	matematika		
May	maj	**N**	
may	lahko	name *n.*	ime -na n.
meanwhile	medtem	narrow	ozek
meat *adj.*	mesen	national	naroden
meat *n.*	meso	nature	narava
medication	zdravilo	near	blizu; pri, ob
medicine (field)	medicina	need *n.*	potreba
meet	srečati	need *v.*	potreb|ovati
meet (first time)	spoznati		-ujem ipf.
menu	jedilnik	nephew	nečak
message	sporočilo, (text)	never	nikoli
	SMS	nevertheless	vseeno
	[es-em-es]	new	nov
middle	srednji	next	prihodnji,
milk	mleko		naslednji

niece	nečakinja	**P**	
night, at night	nọč f., ponọči	pack *v.*	(s)pakirati
nine	devẹt	package	pakẹt, zavitẹk
no	ne	pain	bolečina
nobody	nihče	pajamas	pižama
noodles	rẹzanci pl.	pale *adj.*	blẹd
noon, at noon	poldne,	pants, trousers	hlače pl.
	opoldne	parents	starši pl.
north *adj.*	sẹverẹn	park	park
north *n.*	sẹver	parking	parkiranje,
nose	nọs		parkirišče
not	ne	part	dẹl
nothing	nič	party	zabava
November	novembẹr	passenger	pọtnik
now	zdaj	past	mimo (+G)
		past (the hour)	čez
O		pasta	testenine pl.
occupation	poklic	path	pọt
occupied	zasẹden	pay	plačati pf.
October	oktọbẹr	peaceful	mirẹn
of course	sevẹda	people	ljudjẹ
office	pisarna	perhaps	mogọče
oil	ọlje	person	osẹba, človẹk
old	star	pharmacy	lekarna
one	en/eden, ena,	physician	zdravn|ik, -ica
	eno	piano	klavir
only	edini; samo	picnic	piknik
open *adj.*	odprt	picturesque	slikovit
open *v.*	odpr|ẹti -em	pill	tablẹta
open market	tržnica	pity	škọda
or	ali	pizza	pica
orange *adj.*	oranžen;	plan	načrt
	pomarančẹn	platform	perọn
orchestra (seating)	parter	play *v.*	igrati (se) ipf.
order *v.*	narọčati/	pleasure	užitẹk, veselje
	naročiti	poorly	slabọ
our (>2 owners)	naš	pork *adj.*	svinjski
our (2 owners)	najin	pork *n.*	svinjina
out of	iz	portion (serving)	pọrcija
outside	zunaj	post office	pọšta
overnight *v.*	prenočiti pf.	postcard	razglẹdnica
own (one's own)	svọj	potato(es)	krompir

prepare	**pripravljati/**	rent out	**oddajati/oddati**
	pripraviti	reservation	**rezervacija**
prescription	**recept**	reserve	**rezervirati**
previous	**prejšnji**		ipf./pf.
price	**cena**	reside	**stan|ovati**
probably	**najbrž, verjetno**		**-ujem** ipf.
program	**spored**	rest v.	**počivati** ipf.
prohibition	**prepoved** f.	restaurant	**restavracija,**
promise v.	**obljubiti** pf.		**gostilna**
protect	**var|ovati**	restroom	**stranišče, WC**
	-ujem ipf.	retired	**upokojen**
purple	**vijoličen**	return	**vrniti vrnem**
put shoes on	**obuvati/obu|ti**		**(se)** pf.
	-jem	rice	**riž**
		rich	**bogat**
Q		ride (multi-	**voziti vozim**
quarter	**četrt**	direct.)	**(se)** ipf.
quick	**hiter**	ride n.	**vožnja**
quiet	**tih**	right (correct)	**prav**
quite	**precej**	adv.	
		right (side)	**desni, desno**
R		river	**reka**
rain n.	**dež**	road	**cesta**
rain v.	**deževati**	roast	**pečenka**
rarely	**redko**	roof	**streha**
read	**(pre)brati**	room	**soba, prostor**
real	**pravi, resničen**	rose hip	**šipek**
recently	**zadnje čase**	round-trip	**povraten**
receptionist	**receptor**	row	**vrsta**
recommend	**priporočati/**	run (multi-direct.)	**tekati** ipf.
	priporočiti	v.	
recover	**okrevati** ipf.	run (one-direct.)	**teči -čem** ipf.
red	**rdeč, rdeča**	v.	
refrigerator	**hladilnik**	Russian adj.	**ruski**
regular	**reden**	Russian	**ruščina**
relative n.	**sorodnik**	language	
remain v.	**ostati -nem** pf.	Russian person	**Rus, -inja**
remember	**spominjati/**		
	spomniti se	**S**	
rent n.	**najemnina**	sad	**žalosten**
rent v.	**najleti -amem**	salad	**solata**
	pf.	sale n.	**razprodaja**

sale *v.*	**prodajati/ prodati**	signature	**podpis**
		silk	**svila**
sales clerk	**prodajal|ec, -ka**	sing	**(za)peti**
salt	**sol** f.	single room	**enoposteljna**
salt pan	**solina**		**soba**
salty	**slan**	sink	**umivalnik**
same	**enak, isti**	sister	**sestra**
Saturday	**sobota**	sister-in-law	**svakinja**
sausage	**klobasa**	sit	**sed|eti -im** ipf.
say	**re|či -čem** pf.	six	**šest**
schedule	**urnik**	size	**velikost** f.
school	**šola**	ski *v.*	**smučati** ipf.
sea	**morje**	skirt	**krilo**
search *v.*	**iskati iščem** ipf.	sleep *v.*	**spati spim** ipf.
season	**letni čas**	sleepy	**zaspan**
seat	**sedež**	slim	**vitek**
second *adj.*	**drugi**	slipper	**copat(a)**
see	**vid|eti -im** ipf./pf.	Slovene (adj.)	**slovenski**
self	**se(be)**	Slovene	**slovenščina**
semester	**semester**	language	
send	**pošiljati/poslati pošljem**	Slovene person	**Sloven|ec, -ka**
		slowly	**počasi**
September	**september**	small	**majhen**
serve	**stre|či -žem** ipf.	smaller	**manjši**
seven	**sedem**	smoke	**kaditi** ipf.
she	**ona**	smoking	**kajenje**
shine	**sij|ati -e(m)** ipf.	sneeze *v.*	**kihati/kihniti**
ship	**ladja**	snow *n.*	**sneg**
shirt	**srajca**	snow *v.*	**snežiti** ipf.
shoe	**čevelj**	so	**tako**
shop *v.*	**kup|ovati -ujem**	soccer	**nogomet**
shopping	**nakupovanje**	sock	**nogavica**
short	**kratek**	sold out	**razprodan**
short (vertically)	**nizek**	some (indefinite)	**kakšen**
shorts	**kratke hlače**	some (quantity)	**nekaj**
show *n.*	**predstava**	someone	**nekdo**
show *v.*	**poka|zati -žem** pf.	something	**nekaj**
		sometimes	**včasih**
shower (rain)	**ploha**	somewhere	**nekam**
shower *n.*	**tuš**	(destination)	
shower *v.*	**(s)tuširati se**	somewhere	**nekje**
side	**stran** f.	(location)	

son	**sín**	student dorm	**študentski dọm**
soup	**juha**	study v.	**študirati, učiti**
south adj.	**južen**		**se**
south n.	**jug**	Styria	**Štajerska**
souvenir	**spomínek**	sugar	**sladkor**
spa	**toplíce** pl.	suitcase	**kovček**
space	**prostor**	summer, in	**polẹtje, polẹti**
speak	**govoríti** ipf.	summer	
spring, in spring	**pomlad,**	summer adj.	**polẹten**
	spomladi	sun	**sọnce**
square	**trg**	Sunday	**nedẹlja**
stairs	**stopníce** pl.	sunny	**sọnčen**
stairway	**stopníšče**	sweater	**pulover**
stamp (postage)	**znamka**	swim	**plavati** ipf.
stand v.	**stati stojím** ipf.	swimming pool	**bazẹn**
start v.	**začｌẹti -ne se**	swimsuit	**kopalke** pl.
	pf.		
station	**postaja**	**T**	
stay v.	**ostaｌti -nem** pf.	table	**míza**
steep	**strm**	take	**vzẹti vzamem**
step v.	**stopíti stọpim**		**pf.**
	pf.	take shoes off	**sezuvati/sezuｌti**
still	**še**		**-jem (se)**
stomach	**želọdẹc**	tall	**visok**
stop v.	**ustaviti (se)** pf.	tasty	**okusen**
store	**trgovína**	tea	**čaj**
stove	**štedílnik**	teacher	**učítelj, -ica**
straight	**naravnost**	telephone	**telefọn**
strange	**čuden**	tell	**povｌedati -m** pf.
street	**ulica, cẹsta**	temperature	**temperatura**
stroll n.	**sprehod**	ten	**desẹt**
stroll v.	**sprehajati se/**	tennis	**tẹnis**
	sprehｌodíti	terribly	**grozno**
	-ọdim se	than	**kot**
strong	**močen**	thank you	**hvala**
strudel	**zavítek**	that	**tísti**
student (college)	**študentski**	that conj.	**da**
adj.		theater	**gledalíšče**
student (college)	**študent, -ka**	theater (movie)	**kíno** m.
n.		their (>2 owners)	**njíhov**
student (high-	**srednješọlｌec,**	their (2 owners)	**njun**
school)	**-ka**	then adv.	**takrat**

there	**tam(le)**	train *n.*	**vlak**
therefore	**zato, tako da**	translate	**prevajati/**
thermometer	**toplomer**		**prevesti**
they	**oni, one, ona**	translator	**prevajal|ec, -ka**
they (two)	**onadva, onidve**	travel *v.*	**pot|ovati -ujem**
thing	**stvar** f.	trip, day trip	**potovanje,**
think	**misliti** ipf.		**izlet**
third	**tretji**	trousers	**hlače** pl.
thirsty	**žejen**	try on	**pomeriti** pf.
this	**ta, to**	T-shirt	**majica**
thousand	**tisoč**	Tuesday	**torek**
three	**trije, tri**	turkey *adj.*	**puranji**
throat	**grlo**	turn	**zavi|ti -jem** pf.
through	**skozi**	TV set	**televizor**
thunderstorm	**nevihta**	twenty	**dvajset**
Thursday	**četrtek**	two	**dva, dve**
ticket	**karta**	type	**tip**
ticket (entrance)	**vstopnica**		
ticket	**vozovnica**	**U**	
(transportation)		underpass	**podhod**
tie	**kravata**	understand	**razumeti -em**
till	**do**		**pf./ipf.**
time	**čas**	undress	**slačiti/sleči**
timetable	**vozni red**		**-čem (se)**
tip (money)	**napitnina**	unfortunately	**žal**
tired	**utrujen**	university	**univerza**
to (a person)	**k (+D)**	Upper Carniola	**Gorenjska**
to (a place)	**v/na (+A)**	USA	**ZDA [ze-de-a]**
to (a point)	**do (+G)**	usually	**običajno,**
today	**danes**		**ponavadi**
toe	**prst**		
together	**skupaj**	**V**	
tomato *adj.*	**paradižnikov**	vacation	**počitnice** pl.
tomato(es) *n.*	**paradižnik**	various	**različen, razen**
tomorrow	**jutri**	veal *adj.*	**telečji**
tonight	**nocoj**	vegetable *adj.*	**zelenjaven**
too	**tudi; pre-**	vegetable *n.*	**zelenjava**
tooth	**zob, pl. zobje**	vegetarian *adj.*	**vegetarijanski**
tourist	**turist**	vegetarian *n.*	**vegetarijan|ec,**
towards	**k, proti (+D)**		**-ka**
town	**kraj, mesto**	very	**zelo**
traffic light	**semafor**	view	**razgled**

view v.	oględati si pf.	when conj.	ko
viewing	ogled	when(ever) conj.	kadar
visit n.	obisk	where	kję
visit v.	obiskati	where (to)	kam
	obiščem pf.	which	kateri
visitor	obiskovalec	which conj.	ki
		while	medtem ko
W		while (on the	pa
wait	(po)čakati	other hand)	
waiter, waitress	natakar, -ica	white	bęl
wall	zid	who	kdǫ
want	hotęti hǫčem,	whole	cęl, vęs
	žellęti -im	whose	čigav
war	vojna	why	zakaj
warm	topęl	wide	širok
warm up	ogręti -jem (se)	wife	žena
	pf.	wind	vętęr
wash	umivati/umiti	windy	vetrovęn
	(se)	wine	vino
watch n.	ura	winter adj.	zimski
watch v.	ględati ipf.	winter, in winter	zima, pozimi
water adj.	vodni	wish v.	žellęti -im
water n.	voda	without	brez (+G)
way	pǫt	woman	žęnska
we	mi, mę, vi, vę	wonderful	čudovit
we (two)	midva, mędve	wool	volna
wear	nositi nǫsim	work n.	dęlo
	ipf.	work v.	dęlati
weather adj.	vremęnski	world adj.	svetovęn
weather n.	vreme	world n.	svęt
Wednesday	sręda	worthwhile	splačati se
week	tęden	(to be)	
weekend	vikend	would	bi
weigh	tęhtati ipf.	write	pisati pišem ipf.
weight	tęža	wrong adv.	narǫbe
well	dobro		
well-known	znan	**Y**	
west adj.	zahodęn	year, this year	lęto, lętos
west n.	zahod	year before last	predlanskim
what	kaj	yellow	rumen
what kind	kakšęn	yes	ja, da
when	kdaj	yesterday	včęraj

yogurt **jogurt**

you *sg.* **ti**

you (two) **vidva, vedve**

you (>2 or formal) **vi**

your (1 owner) **tvoj**

your (2 owners) **vajin**

your (>2 owners or formal) **vaš**

youth **mladost** f.

Z

zero **nič**

zoo **živalski vrt**

Index